C000103013

THE PYRAMID TEXTS

Dedicated to the Zion Research Foundation
by whose generosity
the publication of this work has been translated
from dream into reality

PREFACE

The Pyramid Texts of Ancient Egypt are the oldest large body of written material in the world. They are incised on limestone in thousands of lines of hieroglyphics, containing fragments of myths and legends, historical references and astronomical lore, geography and cosmology, religion and rituals, systems of theology, festivals, magic and morals, and with a literary technique capable of expressing the finest religious and ethical thoughts.

The purpose of this work is to furnish in English a translation and commentary of these texts—a translation and commentary which make use of all the texts at present extant and known to the author, and which is designed to be a standard but interim work in this subject until such time in the future as all remaining pyramid texts will have been discovered, which will then, it is hoped, make possible the writing of a complete and definitive work.

The contribution of this publication will be the first translation in English of the ancient Pyramid Texts; the first complete translation and full commentary of the Texts in any language; and an addition to the hieroglyphic text of Sethe of over four hundred lines (in translation) from the pyramids of Neit and Pepi II, in addition to the filling of many lacunae in the body of his text from Neit, Pepi II, and other pyramids, tombs and sarcophagi, discovered since the publication of Sethe's unfinished translation and commentary in German after his death in 1934. Fuller details of these texts, their discovery, nature, extent, and value are given in the introduction.

There still remains the pleasant duty of acknowledging here the immediate help in the preparation of this publication given by the author's colleagues and friends. And first I would mention the kind aid and assistance given me by Dr. Ludlow Bull of the Metropolitan Museum of New York who with the consent of Charles Breasted allowed me to read the late Professor J. H. Breasted's penciled copy of translated portions of the Pyramid Texts, and who with his colleague in the Museum, Dr. William C. Hayes, aided me in many ways. I would also thank Dr. John D. Cooney and Mrs. Elizabeth Riefstahl of the Brooklyn Museum for their many kindnesses, as well as Dr. Drioton of Cairo, Dr. Grapow of Berlin and Professor Garnot of Paris. The memory of the help of others, such as the late Professors Sethe, Gunn, and Breasted, will always remain with me. And the published works of these three scholars, together with those especially of Professor Kees, have been my daily companions. I have an especially deep sense of gratitude to express to the writers of Excursuses, Professors Drioton, Kees, Garnot, Schott, van de Walle, M. Lacau, and Mr. Robert Briggs, in whose essays I have followed as closely as possible the form in which they were submitted to me. The assistance of the Reverend Father Keller, a former pupil of mine, not only in many details in the preparation of this work, but also and especially in the full and complete indexes to the translation which he has contributed, has been a great help and a priceless contribution. Also his map, made especially for the Pyramid Texts, will be found to serve its purpose well. In reading proof, Father Keller and Mr. Briggs have not only avoided many an error in detail, but have also made valuable contributions to the interpretation and illustration of many a difficult passage. Finally, Miss Seville Marshall, who has typed these hundreds of pages, has accomplished, as an expert in her art, a first-class task. But this work could not have been published had it not had the good fortune of receiving a substantial grant from the Zion Research Foundation, who have already on other occasions shown their enlightened interest in the publication of works in the realm of

Biblical and religious research. To this Foundation, and especially to their secretary, Mr. Wilfred B. Wells, and board, the author expresses his most cordial thanks. Nor could the work of printing and publishing have been so efficiently and satisfactorily done without the cordial cooperation of Messrs. Longmans, Green and Company, who have done everything in their power to satisfy us.

SAMUEL A. B. MERCER
Worcester, Massachusetts
August, 1952

CONTENTS

INTRODUCTION

The famous Pyramid Texts herein translated for the first time in English with commentary were found inscribed on the walls of five pyramids at Saḳḳâreh, the ancient necropolis of Memphis in Egypt. These pyramids are those of the kings Unis of the Fifth Dynasty, and Teti, Pepi I, Merenrç' and Pepi II of the Sixth Dynasty. To this translation has been added that of recently discovered additional texts, parallel and complementary, in the pyramids of Oudjebten, Neit, and Apouit, queens of Pepi II, and of Ibi, a king of the Seventh Dynasty, of whom little historically is known. Thus, according to the present generally accepted chronology, these pyramids were constructed, and apparently inscribed, between the years about 2350 to 2175 B.C. It is, however, certain that many of these texts came into existence before the final union of Upper and Lower Egypt, and perhaps long before that date, which is now put at about 3000 B.C. Indeed, some of them possibly existed in oral form before the art of writing was developed. These inscriptions together with others were after that probably written on papyrus and potsherds, many of which in time perished, the rest remaining in various forms until they were collected and incised on the walls of the Saḳḳâreh h pyramids. Evidence of a date previous to about 3000 B.C. is seen in passages which reflect events and conditions previous to the union of the two Lands, for example, the hostility between North and South, before the time of the first king, Menes; in the mode of burying bodies of the dead in the sand; in the pre-civilized era reflected in the so-called Cannibal Hymn; and in the many references to the assembling of the bones of the deceased, passages which indicate a pre-mummification period. And in the historic period various chronological points can be established with fair certainty, such as the time of the Second Dynasty, when both Horus and Set were in favour in royal circles; references to previously written material such as the "Chapter of those who ascend" and the "Chapter of those who raise themselves up," 1245d-e, indicating a time in the historic period in which writing became common; and the formulae for the protection of pyramids, such as, Uts. 600-601, which represent a date after the time of the construction of pyramids. So that the myths and legends, the history and philosophy, the hopes and fears of people (subjects as well as monarchs) of many hundreds of years were finally inscribed in enduring stone, which over four thousand years removed from our time, may now be read with comparative ease and certainty, thanks to the modern discipline of archaeological research and philology. The extent of this written material may be appreciated in saying that it takes well over a thousand pages of two quarto volumes to contain it. In the standard modern edition of the original text, together with parallels and additions from the pyramids of Pepi II, Neit, and others, there are about 7000 lines, most of which are parallels, of more or less completeness of the estimated 2500 lines, which occur in one or other of the pyramids; for most of the utterances occur in more than one pyramid, but very few are repeated in all these pyramids. Thus, the pyramid of Unis has only two hundred and eight utterances out of a total of over seven hundred and thirty; and they with those of the pyramid of Teti are among the oldest in the collection.

A general idea of the contents of this mass of literary material may be seen in the detailed list of Contents preceding this Introduction; but that does not mean that these texts present a coherent whole, for they do not; and while there are clearly three outstanding elements in them, namely, Solar Theology, Religion and Myths of Osiris, and the Political unification of Upper and Lower Egypt, yet the following seven points may be taken to represent the whole collection with fair general accuracy: 1) A funerary ritual of mortuary offerings, connected with the corporeal reconstitution and resurrection of the deceased king, 2) Magical formulae to ward against harm and evil, 3) A ritual of worship, 4) Religious hymns, 5) Mythical formulae, identifying the deceased king with certain deities, 6) Prayers and petitions on behalf of the deceased king, and 7) The greatness and power of the deceased king in heaven.

These pyramid texts were royal texts, and during the Old Kingdom there is no evidence that the people ever took them to themselves and used them in their own tombs. However, at the end of the Sixth Dynasty, Neit, one of the queens of Pepi II, had them applied to herself, though the second person and third person masculine singular were often used and applied to her; but during the Middle Kingdom the use of them spread to the nobles, and in the New Kingdom parts of them were incorporated in the popular Theban Book of the Dead. And doubtless because of their sanctity little attempt was made to put them in accord with changed circumstances.

When these small pyramids were built and inscribed the age of the great pyramids, like those at Giza, had passed, and with it the sense of royal security after this life. The great pyramids had been entered in spite of their thousands of tons of masonry, and kings came to look elsewhere for the assurance of a happy and glorious hereafter. They turned to religion and magic. By mortuary offerings and funerary rites the deceased king was armed for his future life; and by magic he was endowed with physical and spiritual power, becoming a great god and associating with the gods, to avoid whatever in the world to come might otherwise compromise his destiny. The purpose of these royal texts then was to guarantee the deceased king's resurrection and new-birth, his transfiguration and divinity, his successful journey to heaven, and his immortality there with the other gods. There in heaven as a great god, sometimes as the greatest of all the, gods, the deceased king was believed to be able to overcome all difficulties by his own might, or by identifying himself with other gods.

In the earliest of these texts two very ancient doctrines may be discerned: that of the old heaven-god, perhaps Horus the elder, in which the deceased king as a star was prominent, and that of the sun-god where the deceased as the sun-god was contemplated. But the two were harmonized doubtless at a very early period, when the celestial abode of the heaven-and star-gods became identified with that of the solar deities. But what we do see more clearly in the Pyramid Texts are the two opposing systems of theological thought, that of Rç' of Heliopolis and that of Osiris. The Pyramid Texts were largely solar, but long before the texts were inscribed in the pyramids of Saḳḳâreh, there existed Osirian texts as well as Solar ones, though there is reason to believe that the learned men and scribes of Heliopolis were the first to make collections of their texts. And gradually as such collections were being made, there was a tendency to include Osirian texts, as well as, an effort on the part of Osirians to facilitate the entrance of their texts into the great Solar collections (cf. Excursus XXVII), with the result that there was a redaction continually going on, in which not only was the name of Osiris introduced into the collections, especially as an epithet of the king, such as Osiris Teti, but also the name of the solar king was introduced into original Osirian texts. However, the great bulk of the texts remained solar and celestial with comparatively little trace of the underworld character of the Osirian faith. There are also traces in these texts of other systems of theological thought than the Heliopolitan and Osirian, namely, those of Memphis and Hermopolis.

As one reads these ancient texts, there is a primitiveness about them which is not unexpected, though they are never naive. There is much repetition, not much order, contradictions, errors, and sometimes what appear to be ridiculous statements, but in spite of all that, real poetic passages and consistent reasoning are not lacking. There is the art to create images, figures of speech, and metaphores in beautiful and choice language. There are paronomasiae, parallelisms, litanies, and hymns. There are poetic expressions, such as 567a-c; real lyrics, like Ut. 362;

symbolical expressions, such as 681d; and really fine bits, like 307a-c. There are proverbs, such as 396d; and adages, such as 444e. The most symmetrically and mechanically arranged utterance in the whole collection is Ut. 575, which reminds one of Ps. 119. But the overall characteristic of these texts is their religious and funerary, their magical, mythological, and astronomic expressions, interpretations, and predispositions.

Auguste Mariette had the distinction, in the later part of his life, of being the modern discoverer of the inscribed pyramids at Saḳḳâreh, but it was Maspero in 1880 working under Mariette's direction, who discovered the first set of Pyramid Texts. They were those inscribed on the walls of the sarcophagus chamber of the pyramid of Pepi I. Following that, he found texts in the pyramids of Unis of the Fifth Dynasty, as well as in the pyramids of Teti, Merenrç', and Pepi II, in addition to Pepi I, all of the Sixth Dynasty. This work of discovery of pyramid texts did not find a continuation until the years 1920 and 1936, when the Swiss Egyptologist, Jéquier, discovered texts in the pyramids of Oudjebten, Neit, and Apouit, queens of Pepi II, and in that of Ibi, an obscure king of the Seventh Dynasty, besides clearing that of Pepi II, whom Sethe records as N. (Neferkarç').

These texts usually occupy the walls of the sarcophagus chamber except the west side, and are so disposed that the deceased king in his sarcophagus might spiritually see and read them. Texts are also on the walls of the antechamber, on the horizontal passages, and some are on the walls of the vestibule and even on those of the ramp. They are normally in vertical columns, incised on the limestone walls, some excellently done as in the pyramids of Unis and Pepi II, others very crudely done as in that of Ibi.

As Maspero was the discoverer of the Pyramid Texts, so be was the first to make an edition and translation of them. These were all the pyramid texts which were known at the time of their publication in 1894. And in view of what we now know about the difficulties of the Pyramid Texts, this edition and translation were evidence of the genius of the great master. Even today many of his translations accord with the best that is known on those passages, which is an indication of his great learning and insight.

For years before the beginning of this century Kurt Sethe, whose name will be forever associated with the Pyramid Texts, was deeply interested in everything which concerned them. He as well as other trained Egyptologists realized that the earlier copy of the texts was often incorrect, and that a new and scientifically copied edition was a necessity. Accordingly, taking advantage of the work of Dr. Heintze and Ludwig Borchardt, who were in Egypt taking impressions and photographs of the Pyramid Texts for slips in preparation for the making of the great Berlin *Wörterbuch der Aegyptischen Sprache*, Sethe made use of their material in preparing a new edition of the Pyramid Texts. And no Egyptologist was more thoroughly prepared for such an undertaking than Kurt Sethe. And so he began the critical and exacting task of constructing a text principally on the basis of the five versions Unis, Teti, Pepi I, Merenrç', and Pepi II, which was finished and published in 1908-1910 in two great quarto volumes of over a thousand pages of hieroglyphic text, which is now the standard text. To accompany the text, he followed them with a third volume of critical apparatus in 1922 and a fourth of epigraphy in the same year. Thus the great work of giving to the world the text of the oldest collection of mythical, religious, and literary material in existence was finished. However, the text was marred by one blemish, but not due to the science of Sethe. It was due to the fact that a considerable Portion of the texts in the five pyramids was broken, damaged and destroyed—a condition which may never be completely remedied. It is along this line that Egyptologists who were specialists in these texts have been working since the time of Sethe. Already considerable progress has been made in the discovery of texts, anciently copied from the texts in these five pyramids, before they were damaged, and recorded elsewhere; in a further study of the walls of the five pyramids themselves; and in the discovery and publishing of new pyramids and tombs with parallel and additional texts, all which will be used in the future, but not till after many years of archaeological research in Egypt, in the construction of a more complete text. Already between 1920 and 1936 Jéquier discovered at Sakkâreh similar texts in the pyramids of Oudjebten, Neit, and Apouit of the Sixth Dynasty and of Ibi of the Seventh Dynasty; in 1932 the Egyptian Expedition of the Metropolitan Museum of Art discovered in the cemetery surrounding the pyramid of Se'n-Wosret I at Lisht the tomb of an official of the Twelfth Dynasty named Se'n-Wosret-'Ankh, containing a long series of inscriptions drawn from the Pyramid Texts, and published in 1937; and in 1935 William C. Hayes published the "Royal Sarcophagi of the Eighteenth Dynasty," containing parts of the Pyramid Texts, which are useful in filling some lacunae in the Sakkâreh texts. Then older publications are useful, such as that of de Morgan in 1894-1895 of similar texts in a private tomb at Dahshûr; that of Firth and Gunn in 1926 of texts in the Teti Pyramid Cemeteries at Sakkâreh; and that of Borchardt in 1913 of similar texts in the mortuary temple of Sahurç' at Abuṣîr. Then there are the Coffin Texts of the Middle Kingdom and the Theban Book of the Dead of the New Kingdom, which contain Pyramid Texts in modified and further modified form; as well as tombs of kings, such as that of Seti I, and of private individuals, which contain Pyramid Texts sometimes in quite exact quotation. All these and others may be drawn upon in the future construction of a still more perfect version of the famous ancient Pyramid Texts of Sakkâreh. Quite recently T. G. Allen of the University of Chicago has published a most useful guide to all parallel and illustrative Egyptian texts at present known in his valuable book, *Occurrences of Pyramid Texts with cross Indexes of these and other Egyptian Mortuary Texts*, Chicago, 1950.

After the publication of his text, Sethe's next concern was to prepare a translation with a commentary. The central thought in his busy years of research as soon as the text was published was directed towards that purpose, and by 1929 he was ready to begin. He was master of an immense accumulation of philological, historical, and religious facts in the field of

23

ancient Egyptian literature, and with him were associated co-workers and colleagues, such as Lange, Grapow, and Sander-Hansen. He began with Ut. 2 13 and by the time of his death in 1934 had finished up to and including Ut. 506, or less than one half of the text as he had published it. It remained for a commission of his associates to carry on the work. This they began to do immediately after the great master's death.

Sethe's translation and commentary on Uts. 213-506 was not ready for the printer. It needed revising, especially in the later portions, and writing. The Commission received the material left by Sethe and published it much as it was. Before the beginning of the war in 1939 four volumes of translation and commentary were published, which included Uts. 213-506, or between one-third and one-half of the whole. A fifth volume is said to be in preparation.

Not counting the early and tentative translation by Maspero in 1894, Sethe's is the only translation—itself only between one-third and one-half of the whole—in any language of the Pyramid Texts, except one made in French by L. Speleers, a Belgian Egyptologist in 1923-1924, remade in 1934, but without a commentary. No translation in any other language has so far been published. Individual scholars have translated portions here and there for their use in works on various aspects of ancient Egyptian religion and thought, philology and literature, customs and history, such as Kees, Junker, Drioton, Weill, Breasted, Gardiner, Gunn, Sander-Hansen, etc.

The present translation is thus, the only complete one with full commentary in any language. It is not as full as that part of Sethe's which is finished, but it has been planned to be more concise in its comments, leaving longer comments on important points for a series of Excursuses, so as not to interfere with the proportioned flow of comment on the current text. But it has been able to make use of large portions of the pyramids of Pepi II and Neit as well as of publications of other pyramids, tombs, and sarcophagi brought to light since Sethe's day. It has thus added over four hundred lines to the text, besides, filling some smaller lacunae here and there.

It is not claimed to be a definitive translation, because we have not yet a definitive text. Such a text and translation may never be able to be made, because of quite natural causes. But with the further discovery of new texts and a complete comparison with all extant later parallels in texts already published as well as yet unpublished a future text and translation will be called for. For that reason, in this present translation use has been made of material later than the time of the Pyramid Texts themselves only when it was thought to have some light to throw upon a problem difficult of solution, or when it gave a new meaning to a passage. In other words, this is an interim translation and commentary of the Pyramid Texts for the use not only of Egyptologists but likewise of students of religions and comparative religions, of literature and comparative literature, of the history of ideas and customs, and of culture and civilization in general. There is published with it a complete apparatus for general use such as an analysis of each utterance with a discussion of its date, a series of Excursuses on important subjects, a full glossary of useful terms, phrases, and subjects, and a full index to the translation.

In translating and interpreting these texts many things have had to be taken into consideration and many allowances have had to be made. It must he remembered that many of these old utterances or discourses are veritable magic formulae to procure for the deceased king all kinds of material satisfaction, to protect him against any enemies he may meet on his way to the other world, and to procure for him an eternal life; and that very often place names refer to celestial locations and not to ancient places in Egypt. In keeping with their general magical character, most if not all of these utterances begin with the expression *dd mdw*, which is a rubrical direction "to say," that is, the words are to be spoken or recited by someone, often a lector-priest, sometimes the deceased king himself, and sometimes by him in the first person. The rubric sometimes directs that the petition be repeated four times. There is evidence that some of the utterances were written in the first person singular, and were later changed to the third person singular. Ut. 506 is a good example of a text which was surely in the first person singular originally, but in general in translations the third person has been used unless the form of the first person has been reproduced in the hieroglyphic text. It has been useful to notice when the first person is used, for it is one of the signs of an early date for the text in which it is found, for example, Uts. 325 and 563 are late, and one of the indications is that the third person singular is always used. On the whole, the determination of the date of a text is rather uncertain, and sometimes impossible. There can be no systematic ordering of the dates as J. E. D. P. of Old Testament criticism. Nor is n, the sign of the genitive, a sure guide of date, its presence indicating a late and its absence an early date, as the occurrence and the absence of the n in the same sentence or compound sentence proves, Cf. 2056c.

Among the texts of the Saḳḳâreh pyramids there is evidence of redaction of some of them, thus, Ut. 55 is a re-writing for kings of the historic period of an older text, composed for the predynastic kings of Buto; and some long utterances are made up of independent short parts, with some changes added by the redactor, e.g. Ut. 468. Indeed the Pyramid Texts are to a large extent a composition, compiling, and joining of earlier texts. Moreover, there are corruptions in the texts, mistakes in writing, errors in grammar and syntax, contradictions and confusions, expressions which seem ridiculous, and illogical expressions, most of which have been referred to in the Commentary on the text where they occur. There are numerous paronomasiae and words of double meaning; and superstition led to the mutilation of hieroglyphic signs of creatures which were thought, if left whole, may be capable of injuring the deceased king, and the fish for the same reason was used only once (218c, N.) in the inscriptions in his burial chamber.

As there is a minimum of classification and order in the sequence of the texts, a list of Contents of the Pyramid Texts precedes this Introduction. Therein an attempt has been made to find groups of texts without disturbing the sequence of the text in Sethe's edition. Consequently it often happens that we are obliged to group some texts under the heading "Texts of Miscellaneous Contents." However, there are many instances where texts grouped in Sethe's edition form a natural and often perfect group, e.g. the Serpent Charms of Uts. 226-244, or the Ferryman Texts, Uts. 300-337.

In translations an honest effort has been made to express the sense of the original in English, with the result that many translations are literal instead of free, thus in 1004d the original is translated "at the voice of lamentation" instead of "at the sound of lamentation," so that the English will be apt to be stilted instead of elegant. As in all ancient languages, particles, such as adverbs, and conjunctions are rare, with the result that it is often not easy to make the correct sequence or dependence, rendering the sense of the sentence or passage uncertain. Again the same word in different contexts may require varied renderings, such as the word *3gb* which means "flood," "abundance," or "violence," in accordance with the context. To save as much space as possible, very few alternative translations have been introduced, where in many cases the same phrase or sentence could be rendered in different ways. In most lines of the Pyramid Texts the line as it appears in two or more pyramids is given; in other words, in Sethe's edition every line is given in as many pyramids as it occurs; so as a rule the earliest text is the one followed in translating the line unless one of the other pyramids has decidedly the best text. Where important differences occur, they are pointed out in the commentary; but where differences are not helpful in interpretation they are not always noted. Nor are variants in other texts not in the Sethe edition referred to unless they are useful in a better understanding of the meaning of the text. Whenever "to say" occurs if in only one of the parallel pyramids, it is used in the translation. In the Commentary on Uts. 213-506, Sethe's discussions were ever before me, and I felt myself constrained by his logic and learning to follow him, but wherever I felt that another solution to a problem of interpretation was better though different from his I have not hesitated to use it. In other words, in those utterances, Sethe became my standard unless I could improve on it, as I often did, I believe, in the light of additional Nt. or N. texts, or still later texts, or comparative literature or religion. In all my comments, I have felt free to draw upon any sources, especially ancient ones, whenever I felt the need of an illustrative idea or custom. But I have been unable to take advantage of some of the new points made by my colleagues in their Excursuses, due to a difference of date in the completion of the earlier parts of this work and the arrival of their manuscript. At the same time, obvious remarks have been avoided as much as possible, and only important differences and similarities between lines, paragraphs, and utterances have been noted. Minor errors, whether in the original hieroglyphics, or in Sethe's text, are not always noted, neither are the presence or absence of an 'i prosthetic, or a genitival n always mentioned, nor has the analysis of the utterances been too meticulous in unessential matters, for as the German proverb has it:

"Wer auf jede Feder acht,
Nie das Bette fertig macht."

The abbreviations of the pyramids in which texts so far have been found are: W. = Unis, T. = Teti, P. = Pepi I, M. = Merenrç', N. = Pepi II (Neferkarç'), Nt. = Neit, Ip. = Apouit, Wd. = Oudjebten, Ib. = Aba, Se'n = Se'n-Wosret-'Ankh. In the translations of the texts of these pyramids, instead of using the different abbreviations for the different sovereigns, the letter N. (nomen) is used throughout. Other abbreviations may be seen in the "List of Abbreviations" of literature. The square brackets [ ] are used to designate a conjecture made by Sethe, or by me, which has not with satisfaction been textually verified; the round brackets ( ) are used for explanatory words or phrases or for alternative translations. Capitalization is used as sparingly as possible in the translation and commentary, but when common nouns referring to things are personified, or deified, or both, they are written with a capital letter; but punctuation marks are used somewhat excessively, especially where they aid the meaning. I have always made a slight departure from the orthodox method of transliterating hieroglyphics, in the interest of simplicity, in that I have used the accepted '*i* when it is initial, but *i* otherwise; and I use the grammatical word "gentilic" instead of the word "nisbé." In case of the two words usually translated, the first "soul" and the other "double," I use the transliterated forms *b̲ȝ* and *k̲ȝ*, or *ba* and *ka*, to avoid misunderstanding in the supposed English equivalents. In the case of the plural of *ka*, I use the form *ka's* or *kas*, which others also use. Any differences in the transliteration of words, in abbreviations, and in modes of reference, etc., in the Excursuses of authors other than myself are ordinarily retained. In broken passages, the approximate length of the broken line is indicated by—

The Excursuses are meant to treat subjects ordinarily too large for the Commentary, but the discussion is confined to the Pyramid Texts, except for parallel and illustrative matter. The Glossary is meant to give a brief description or definition of important words, names, phrases, and subjects which occur in the Translation and Commentary, with as a rule only one reference, usually the most important one. Other references may be found in the Commentary, in the Index, or in Speleers' excellent Vocabulary. The List of Abbreviations applies to the chief works actually used in this book; and the Index which follows is that to the Translation alone, but which naturally serves the Commentary as well. On account of the lack of hieroglyphic type only a few hieroglyphs, considered essential in the comments, have been used, and are collected together on three plates at the end of the work, but referred to in the Commentary by plate and number. With a few exceptions of names of a general character, only those found in the Translation and Commentary are entered in the map, which appears at the end of the last volume.

As noted above, the only scientific edition of the hieroglyphic texts of the inscribed pyramids was made by Sethe in 1908-1910. The texts form a collection of 714 utterances or chapters, and although most of the utterances occur in more than one pyramid and very few are repeated in all the pyramids in which the texts are found, many of them are damaged and incomplete wherever they are found in the texts published by Sethe. However, since the time of Sethe's publication similar texts have been found in other pyramids at Saḳḳâreh of the Sixth and Seventh Dynasties as well as in private tombs of the Middle Kingdom, and which have been published, and are specified above. A study of these additional texts has made it possible for me to add in translation 386 lines to the approximately 6500 lines in Sethe's hieroglyphic edition, and to make 57 larger restorations, besides many smaller ones, amounting to about 40 additional lines, making in all an addition of about 426 lines, in translation, to Sethe's original edition. The confirmation from texts not available to Sethe of his restorations are not recorded in these lists, but they are given in the Commentary (e.g. that in 130, while emendations and restorations as well as all substantial additions are mentioned in the comments on the lines where they occur. Therefore, for convenience of reference to the published hieroglyphic texts, there follow here two lists, the *first* a list of the *added lines*, and the *second* a list of the *larger restorations*. The additions as well as the restorations, larger and smaller, are also recorded, at their appropriate places in the Commentary:

ADDED LINES

40c-40u,	Nt.	Jéquier,	XII	283-301
41a-43b,	”	”	”	302-308
45a-1 to 49 + 12,	”	”	”	309-328
68i-q,	N.	”	V	392+ I to 392 + 9
1059b + 1 to 1059b + 5,	Nt.	”	XIV	1055 + 47-52, and Jéquier, XXVI 700-XXVII. 706

1060 + 1,	N.	"	XIV	1055 + 49
1061a + f to 1061a + 2,	Nt.	"	XXVII	704, and N. Jéquier, XIV 1055 + 50
1061c + 1 to 1061c + 4,	N.	Jéquier,	XIV	1055 + 5, and Nt. Jéquier, XXVII 705-706
1063c-e,	Teti,	Firth and Gunn,		235
1582a-1586,	Nt.	Jéquier,	VIII	14-17
1675a-b,	N.	"	VII	709 + 40
1676c,	"	"	VII	709 + 41
1676c + 1,	"	"	VII	709 + 42
1757,	Nt.	"	VIII	1
1758b,	"	"	VIII	1
1761c,	"	"	VIII	4
1763a,	"	"	XXXI	806
1764a,	"	"	"	807
1785a,	N.	"	I	171
1792,	"	"	V	474
		"	"	
1793a + 1,	N.	Jéquier,	V	475
1793b,	"	"	"	475-476
1824f-g	Nt.	"	XIII	361-363
1825a-1 and 1825a-2,	"	"	"	358-359
1828a,	"	"	"	363-364
1831a + 1 to 1831a + 5,	"	"	XIII	366-368
1832a + 1,	"	"	"	370
1832b + 1 to 1832b + 14,	"	"	"	371-375

1845a,	N.	”	I	576
1845c,	”	”	”	577
1846b,	”	”	”	577
1854b,	”	”	VII	580
1857a,	”	”	”	582
1859,	”	”	”	583
1859 + 1 to 1859 + 11,	”	”	”	583 to 583 + 3
1882a-1 to 1882d,	”	”	”	709 + 20 to 709 + 21
1883a-d,	”	”	”	709 + 2 1 to 709 + 22
1884-1897,	”	”	”	583 + 4 to 583 + 10
1898a-b,	”	”	IX	719 + 20, and Nt. Jéquier, XXV 658
1899c-f,	N.	Jéquier,	IX	719 + 20 to 719 +21, and Nt. Jéquier, XXV 659-660
1900a-b,	Nt.	Jéquier,	XXV	660
1901a,	N.	”	IX	719 + 21
1901b,	Nt.	”	XXV	661
1902a,	”	”	”	661-662
1902b,	”	”	”	662
1902e,	”	”	”	663
1903b,	”	”	”	663-664
1903c,	”	”	”	664
1904a,	N.	”	IX	719 +23, and Nt. Jéquier, XXV 664
1904b,	N.	Jéquier,	IX	719 + 23
1905a,	”	”	”	219+23
1905b,	Nt.	”	XXV	665
1906a-e,	”	”	”	665-667

1907a-e,	”	”	”	667-668
1908d-e,	”	”	XXVIII	729-730
1909a,	”	”	XVII	480
1909b,	”	”	XXVIII	130
1909c,	Nt.	Jéquier,	XXVIII	731
1910b-c,	”	”	”	731-732
1911-1 to 1911-2,	”	”	”	732
1911,	”	”	”	732-733
1912b, N.	”	”	IX	719 + 27
1912c-d,	Nt.	”	XXVIII	733-734
1913-1,	”	”	”	734
1913a,	”	”	”	734
1914a-c,	N.	”	VI	709 + 2
1914d-f,	Nt.	”	XXVIII	735-736
1916-1,	”	”	”	737
1916-2,	N.	”	VI	709 + 4
1916-3,	Nt.	”	XXVIII	738
1916a-b,	”	”	”	738-739
1917,	”	”	”	739
1818,	”	”	”	739
1919a,	”	”	”	739-740
1919b,	N.	”	VI	709 + 6
1919c,	Nt.	”	XXVIII	740
1920a-b,	”	”	”	740
1921-1,	”	”	”	741
1921-2,	”	”	”	741
1921-3,	”	”	”	741

1921,	"	"	XXVIII	741-742
1921 + 1 to 192 1 + 6,	"	"	"	742-743
1922,	"	"	"	743
1922 + 1 to 1922 + 7,	"	"	"	744-745
1924 + 1 to 1924 + 3,	"	"	"	746
1924+4,	"	"	"	747
1925,	"	"	"	747
1926a +1 to 1926a + 2,	"	"	"	747-748
1926a. + 3,	N.	"	"	709 + 16 and Nt. Jéquier, XXIX 749
1927a-1 to 192 7a-2,	N.	Jéquier,	VI	709 + 16
1927a-3,	Nt.	"	XXIX	750
1927a,	"	"	"	750-751
1927c + 1 to 1927c + 5,	"	"	"	752-754
1927c + 6 to 1927c + 7,	N.	"	VI	709 + 18
1929,	Nt.	"	XXIX	757
1930-1,	"	"	"	758
1930-2,	N.	Jéquier,	VI	709 +19
1930-3 to 1930-5,	Nt.	"	XIX	759-760
1930+ 1,	N.	"	"	709 + 2, Nt. Jéquier, XXIX 761

1931-1 to 1931-3,	Nt.	Jéquier	XXIX	761-762
1932,	”	”	”	763
1932 + 4	”	”	”	763
1933a (differs from Sethe 1933a),	”	”	XXIX	763
1933b (differs from Sethe 1933a),	”	”	”	764
1933b + 1 to 1933b + 4,	”	”	XXIX	764-765
1934a,	”	”	”	765
1934 + 1 to 1934 + 3,	”	”	XXX	766
1935-1 to 1935,”		”	”	766-767
1936b,	”	”	”	XXX 767
1936 + 1 to 1936b + 5,	”	”	”	768-769
1938b,	”	”	”	769
1938b + 1,	”	”	”	769
1939-1 to 1939-4,	”	”	”	769-770
1939+ 1,	”	”	”	771
1940,	”	”	”	771
1940 + 1 to 1940 +6,	”	”	”	771-772
1941b + 1 to 1941b + 3,	”	”	”	773-774
1942b + 1,	”	”	”	774-775

1943a-1 to 1943a-3,	„	„	„	775
1943a,	„	„	„	775-776
1944a + 1 to 1944a-4,	„	„	„	776-778
1945c + 1,	„	„	„	778-779
1946a-1 to 1946a-3,	„	„	„	779
1946a,	„	„	„	779-780
1947b + 1 to 1947b + 6,	„	„	„	780-781
1948c + 1 to 1948c + 3,	„	„	XVII	491
1948c + 4 to 1948c + 7,	„	„	„	491-492
1949-1,	„	„	XXX	783
1950c + 1,	„	„	„	784
1950C + 2,	„	„	„	784
1951-1 to 1951-2,	„	„	„	784
1952 + 1 to 1952 + 6,	„	„	„	785-786
1955a-i,	„	„	„	787
1958b+1,	N.	Jéquier,	X	744
1960a-1 to 1960a-2,	„	„	„	750
1962a + 1 to 1962a + 2,	„	„	„	755
1966c,	„	„	„	756

2120a,	Nt.	”	XXXII	819
2123a,	”	”	”	822-823
2126a-1 to 2126a-6,	”	”	”	822-828
2126a,	”	”	”	828-829
2126b + 1 to 2126b + 2,	”	”	”	829-830
2127a-1 to 2127a-2,	”	”	”	830
2127a,	”	”	”	831
2127b + 1 to 2127b +4,	”	”	”	832-833
2128a-1,	”	”	”	833-834
2128a,	”	”	”	834
2128b + 1 to 2128b +4,	”	”	”	834-835
2130 + 3 to 2130 + 4,	N.	”	XI	1013
2131 + 5,	”	”	”	1014
2133 +4,	”	”	”	1016
2136 + 1 to 2136 + 2,	”	”	”	1016 + 1
2136 + 4 to 2136 + 6,	”	”	”	1016 + 2
2136b + 1,	”	”	XII	1050
2066b,	”	”	”	1051
2168 + 1 to 2168 + 6,	”	”	”	1054-1055 + 4
2176a + 2,	”	”	XX	1309

12b,	N.	Jéquier	II	213, and Ib. Jéquier, III 27
16e,	Nt.	"	IX	68; cf. Hayes Se'n-Wosret-'Ankh, IV 293
1062,	Nt.	Jéquier,	XXVII	706
1739a + 1,	N.	"	XXIV	1350 + 74-75
1745b,	"	"	XX	1315
1757,	Nt.	"	VIII	1
1761a,	Nt.	Jéquier,	VIII	3
1855c,	N.	"	VII	581
1859 + 1 to 1859 + 11,	"	"	VI-VII	583 to 583 + 3
1902c,	N.	Jéquier,	IX	719 + 22, and Nt. Jéquier, XXV 662
1902d,	Nt.	Jéquier,	XXV	662
1923,	"	"	XXIX	745
1924,	"	"	"	745
1927b,	"	"	"	751
1927c,	"	"	"	752
1929c,	"	"	"	757
1930 (Sethe 19390a),	"	"	"	760
1913a-b,	"	"	"	762
1942a,	"	"	XXX	774
1943b,	"	"	"	776
1945c,	"	"	"	778

1947b,	"	"	"	780
1948a,	"	"	"	781
1949,	"	"	"	783
1950c,	"	"	"	783
1951a,	"	"	"	785
1964c,	N.	"	X	756
1966b,	"	"	"	756
1969a,	"	"	"	758
1970b,	"	"	"	759
1970d,	"	"	"	759
1994a,	Nt.	"	XXII	601-602
2083b,	"	"	VII	28
2118c,	"	"	XXII	600-601
2121a,	"	"	XXXII	820
2121b,	"	"	"	820-821
2122b,	"	"	"	821-822
2123b,	"	"	"	823
2124a,	"	"	"	824
2124b,	"	"	"	824
2125b,	"	"	"	825
2126b,	"	"	"	829
2127b,	"	"	"	831
2128b,	"	"	"	834
2134,	N.	"	XI	1016
2136,	"	"	XI	1016 + 1
2156b,	"	"	XII	1039
2163b,	N.	Jéquier,	XII	1047
2163c,	"	"	"	1048

2168,	”	”	”	1053
2176b,	”	”	XX	1309

For reasons given in the Commentary at the points under consideration a few changes in the numbering of lines and utterances have had to be made, a list of which follows:

CHANGES IN NUMBERING OF LINES

1757	=	Sethe	1757a-b
1760a	=	”	1760b
1760b	=	”	1760c
1825a	=	”	1825a-b
1845b	=	”	1845
1857a	=	”	1857
1886a (in part)	=	”	1886
1887b (in part)	=	”	1887
1902c	=	”	1902b
1902d	=	”	1902c
1903a	=	”	1908a
1906f-g	=	”	1906c-d
1909c	=	”	1909b
1909d	=	”	1909c
1928a-b	=	”	1928b
1930	=	”	1930a
1939	=	”	1939b
1943b +1	=	”	1943b (end)
2160b + 1	=	”	2160b
2161b to 2161b + 1	=	”	2161b

CHANGES IN NUMBERING OF UTTERANCES

Ut. 665 (§§ 1898-1907) " 665A (§§ 1908-1918) " 665B (§§ 1919-1930 + 1) " 666 (1931-1 to 1934)	=	Sethe 665A (§§ 1898-1916) Sethe, Ut. 666 (§§1917-1933)
Ut. 667 (§§ 1934 + 1 to 1942b + 1) " 667A (§§ 1943a-1 to 1948c + 3) " 667B (§§ 1948c + 4 to 1948c + 7) " 667C (§§ 1949-1 to 1958b + 1)	=	Sethe, Ut. 667 (§§ 1934-1958)
Ut. 691 (§§ 2120-2125) " 691A (§§ 2126a-1 to 2126b + 2) " 691B (§§ 2127a-1 to 2128b + 4) " 691C (§§ 2129-1 to 2136+6)	=	Sethe, Ut. 691 (§§ 2120-2136)
Ut. 696 (§§ 2163 to 2168 + 6)	=	Sethe, Ut. 696 (§§ 2163-2168)

1.
NUT AND THE DECEASED KING,
UTTERANCES 1-11

Utterance 1.

1a. To say by Nut, the brilliant, the great: This is (my) son, (my) first born, N., opener of (my) womb;
1b. this is (my) beloved, with whom I have been satisfied.

Utterance 2.

1c. To say by Geb: This is (my) son, N., of (my) body————
1d.————

Utterance 3.

2a. To say by Nut, the great, who is within the lower mansion: This is (my) son, N., (my) beloved,
2b. (my) eldest (son), (who is) upon the throne of Geb, with whom he has been satisfied,
2c. to whom he gave his inheritance in the presence of the Great Ennead.
3a. All the gods are in exultation; they say: "How beautiful is N., with whom his father Geb is satisfied!

Utterance 4.

A To say by Nut: N., I have given to thee thy sister Isis,

3c. that she may take hold of thee, that she may give thy heart to thee which belongs to thy body.

Utterance 5.

3d. To say by Nut: N., I have given to thee thy sister Nephthys,

3e. that she may take hold of thee, that she may give thy heart to thee which belongs to thy body.

Utterance 6.

4a. To say by Nut-Nekhbet, the great: This is (my) beloved, N., (my) son;

4b. I have given the horizons to him, that he may be powerful over them like Harachte.

4c. All the gods say: "It is a truth that thy beloved among thy children is N.,

4d. to whom one will do service of courtier for ever."

Utterance 7.

5a. To say by Nut, the great, (who is) within the encircled mansion: This is (my) son N., of (my) heart.

5b. I have given to him the *D₃.t*, that he may be chief therein, like Horus, chief of the *D₃.t.*

5c. All the gods say (to Nut):

5d. "Thy father Shu knows that thou lovest N. more than thy mother Tefnut."

Utterance 8.

6. He lives, king of Upper and Lower Egypt, beloved of Rç', living for ever.

Utterance 9.

7a. Horus [lives], beloved of the two lands, N., king of Upper and Lower Egypt, N., of the two goddesses beloved bodily, N., lords of Ombos, N.

7b. Heir of Geb, whom he loves, N., beloved of all the gods, N., given life, endurance, joy, health, all happiness, like Rç'.

Utterance 10.

8a. Horus lives, living apparition of the king of Upper and Lower Egypt, N.,

8b. (of the land of) the two goddesses, living apparition, N.,

8c. (of the land of) the two lords (of Ombos), N.,

8d. Osiris, lord of the *D3.t*, N.,

8e. the beloved son of Geb, N.,

8f. son of Nut, opener of her body (womb), N.,

8g. endowed with life, endurance, joy, health, like Rç', eternally.

Utterance 11.

8h. To say by Nut: I unite thy beauty with this body (and with) this *ba*, for life, endurance, joy, health

8i. of Horus, divine apparition, king of Upper and Lower Egypt, N. (of the land of) the two goddesses, divine apparition, N.,

8j. powerful lord (of Ombos), N., living eter[nally].

2.
RITUAL OF BODILY RESTORATION OF THE DECEASED, AND OFFERINGS, UTTERANCES 12-203.

Utterances 12-19.

12.

9a.———

13.

9b. To say: I give to thee thy head; I fasten for thee thy head to (thy) bones.

14.

9c. To say: I give to him his eyes, that he may be satisfied. Offering of food and drink.

15.

9d. To say: Geb has given to thee thine eyes, that thou mayest be satisfied—
——

16.

10a. eye of Horus. One *nmś.t*————jar of water.

17.

10b. To say: Thot, he has given his head to him. A pitcher of water.

18.

10c. To say: He has caused it to be brought to him. One drink of water.

19.

10d.————

Utterance 20.

11a. [To say: O] N., I have come in search of thee; I am Horus.
11b. I have pressed for thee thy mouth. I am thy son, thy beloved. I have opened for thee thy mouth.
12a. [He is the defender of his mother when she weeps for him, the defender of her who is united with him].
12b. [How good is the condition (?) of thy mouth after] I have adjusted for thee thy mouth to thy bones!
12c. To say four times: Osiris N., I open for thee thy mouth with the thigh, the eye of Horus. One thigh.

Utterance 21.

13a. [To say: How good is the condition (?) of thy mouth after] . I have adjusted for thee thy mouth to thy bones!
13b. I open for thee thy mouth; I open for thee thine eyes, O N.

13c. I open for thee thy mouth with the *nw3*, the *mšḥtiw*-hook of copper (or, iron), which opens the mouth of the gods.

13d. Horus opens the mouth of this N.; [Horus opens the mouth of this N.].

13e. [Horus has opened] the mouth of this N.; Horus has opened the mouth of this N.

13f. with that wherewith he opened the mouth of his father; with that wherewith he opened the mouth of Osiris;

14a. with the copper, (or, iron) which comes forth from Set, the *mšḥtiw*-hook of copper (or, iron), which opens the mouth of the gods.

14b. He opens the mouth of N. therewith, that he may go,

14c. that he himself may speak before the Great Ennead in the house of the prince, which is in Heliopolis,

14d. that he may carry off the *wrr.t*-crown (which is) with Horus, lord of men.

Utterance 22.

15. To say: Osiris N., I bring to thee thy *ba*, whom thou lovest. I open thy mouth.

Utterance 23.

16a. Osiris, carry off all those who hate N., who speak evilly against his name.

16b. Thot, go, carry off him who has injured Osiris. Bring him who speaks evilly against the name of N.

16c. Get him into thy hand. To say four times: Do not separate thyself from him.

16d. Take care that thou be not separated from him. A libation.

16e. (Nt. Jéquier, IX 68). To say: Thot, hurry, carry off the enemy of this N.

16f.————N. to Osiris.

Utterance 25.

17a. He who goes, goes with his *ka*: Horus goes with his *ka*; Set goes with his *ka*,

17b. Thot goes with his *ka*; the god goes with his *ka*; Osiris goes with his *ka*,

17c. *Mḫnti-'irti* goes with his *ka*; thou also goest with thy *ka*.

18a. O N., the hands of thy *ka* are before thee; O N., the hands of thy *ka* are behind thee;

18b. O N., the feet of thy *ka* are before thee; O N., the feet of thy *ka* are behind thee.

18c. Osiris N., I have given to thee the eye of Horus, so that thy face may be equipped with it.

18d. Let the odour of the eye of Horus adhere to thee. To be said four times: Fire of incense.

Utterances 26-28.

26.

19a. Horus who art in Osiris N., take to thyself the eye of Horus for thou art as the eye of Horus which (lit. who) has extended with its odour.

27.

19b. To say: Osiris N., take the eye of Horus, equip thyself with its odour.

19c. Osiris N., Horus has given to thee his eye that thou mayest equip thy face with it. One pellet of incense (1644a).

Utterance 29.

20a. To say: O N., I have come, I have brought to thee the eye of Horus,
20b. that thou mayest equip thy face with it, that it may purify thee, that its odour may (come) to thee.
20c. The odour of the eye of Horus is for N.; it drives away thy sweat.
20d. It defends thee against the violence (?) of the arm of Set.
21a. O N., the eye of Horus, is pleasing to thee; it is sound for thee. The eye of Horus is sound; thou art sound. Three pellets of incense (1644b).

Utterance 30.

21b. To say: Horus, dweller in Osiris N., equip thee with the eye of Horus; take it to thee.

Utterance 31.

21c. To say: Osiris N., Horus has completely filled thee with his eye.

Utterance 32.

22a. This is thy cool water, Osiris; this is thy cool water, O N., which went forth from thy son, which went forth from Horus.
22b. I have come; I have brought to thee the eye of Horus, that thy heart may be refreshed by it. I have brought it to thee. It is under thy soles.

23a. Take to thyself the efflux (sweat), which goes forth from thee; thy heart shall not be weary thereby.

23b. To say four times, when thou goest forth justified: Libation; two pellets of natron.

Utterance 33.

24a. To say: Osiris N., take to thyself this thy libation, which is offered to thee by Horus,

24b. in thy name of "He who is come from the Cataract"; take to thyself the efflux (sweat) which goes forth from thee.

24c. Horus has made me assemble for thee the gods from every place to which thou goest.

24d. Horus has made me count (for) thee the children of Horus even to the place where thou wast drowned.

25a. Osiris N., take to thyself thy natron, that thou mayest be divine.

25b. Nut has made thee to be as a god to thine enemy (or, in spite of thee) in thy name of "god."

25c. *Ḥrnp.wi* recognizes thee, for thou art made young in thy name of "Fresh water."

Utterance 34.

26a. *Smin, smin* opens thy mouth. One pellet of natron.

26b. O N., thou shalt taste its taste in front of the *sḥ-nṭr*-chapels. One pellet of natron.

26c. That which Horus spits out is *smin*. One pellet of natron.

26d. That which Set spits out is *smin*. One pellet of natron.

26e. That which the two harmonious gods (spit out) is *smin*. One pellet of natron.

26f. To say four times: Thou hast purified thyself with natron, together with Horus (and) the Followers of Horus. Five pellets of natron from Nekheb, Upper Egypt.

Utterance 35.

27a. Thou purifiest (thyself); Horus purifies (himself). One pellet of natron. Thou purifiest (thyself); Set purifies (himself). One pellet of natron.

27b. Thou purifiest (thyself); Thot purifies (himself). One pellet of natron. Thou purifiest (thyself); the god purifies (himself). One pellet of natron.

27c. Thou also purifiest (thyself)————thou who art among them. One pellet of natron.

27d. Thy mouth is the mouth of a sucking calf on the day of his birth.

27e. Five pellets of natron of the North, Wadi Natrûn (*št-p.t*)

Utterance 36.

28a. Thou purifiest (thyself); Horus purifies (himself). Thou purifiest (thyself); Set purifies (himself). Thou purifiest (thyself); Thot purifies (himself).

28b. Thou purifiest (thyself); the god purifies (himself). Thou purifiest (thyself); thy *ka* purifies (himself). Thou purifiest (thyself); thy god purifies (himself).

28c. Thou also purifiest (thyself); it is thou who art among thy brothers, the gods.

29a. Thy natron is on thy mouth; thou purifiest thy bones, (and) all. Equip thyself with that which belongs to thee.

29b. Osiris, I have given to thee the eye of Horus to equip thy face therewith; adhere (to it).

29c. One pellet of natron.

52

Utterance 37.

30a. O N., shut now thy two jaws which were divided. *Pśś-kf*-instrument (or,————bread).

Utterances 38-42.

38.

30b. Osiris N., I open for thee thy mouth. A sacred copper (or, iron) (instrument) of South and North.

39.

31a. N., Take to thyself the eye of Horus, towards which he (Horus) runs; he brings it to thee; put it in thy mouth.

31b. Three pellets of incense of the South; three pellets of incense of the North.

40.

31c. O N., take to thyself the *śik* of Osiris. *śik*-pellets.

41.

32a. Take the tip of the bodily breast of Horus; take it in thy mouth. A jug of milk (or, one jug of fine milk).

42.

32b. Take the breast of thy sister Isis, which is protected(?); take this in thy mouth. An empty *mnṡ₃*-jar.

Utterance 43.

33a. Take the two eyes of Horus, the black and the white; take them to thyself to be in thy face, that they may illuminate thy face.

33b. A white jar, a black jar, for carrying. N. has white *mnw*-stone and black *mnw*-stone *ḥȝtš*-jars (which are) the right eye and the left eye.

Utterance 44.

34a. May the sun in heaven be favourable to thee; may he cause the two lords to be favourable to thee.

34b. May the night be favourable to thee; may the two ladies be favourable to thee.

34c. The offering which is brought to thee is an offering which thou seest, an offering which thou hearest.

34d. An offering is before thee, an offering is behind thee, an offering which is with thee. A *wdȝ.t*-cake.

Utterances 45-48.

45.

35a. Osiris N., take to thyself the white teeth of Horus which equip thy mouth. Five white cakes.

46.

35b. To say four times: A royal offering to the *ka* of N. Osiris N., take to thyself the eye of Horus.

35c. (It is) thy cake; eat thou. A cake of offering, a *wdȝ.t*-cake.

36a. Osiris N., take to thyself the eye of Horus, which is free from Set, and which thou shalt take to thy mouth,

36b. and with which thou shalt open thy mouth. Wine; one white *mnw*-stone *ḥȝtś*-jar.

48.

36c. Osiris N., open thy mouth with that with which thou art full. Wine; one black *mnw*-stone *ḥȝtś*-jar.

Utterances 49-52. 49.

37a. Osiris N., take to thyself the liquid going forth from thee. Beer; one black *mnw*-stone *ḥnw.t*-bowl.

50.

37b. Rç' thou adorest; (he who is) in heaven thou adorest. To N., the lord (belong) all things.

37c. To thy body (belong) all things; to the *ka* of N. (belong) all things; to his body (belong) all things.

37d. To lift up before his face a splendid offering table.

51.

38a. N., take to thyself the eye of Horus, which thou tastest. One *dp.t*-loaf.

52.

38b. Darkness increases (?). One *ȝḥ*-cake.

53.

38c. N., take to thyself the eye of Horus, which thou shalt embrace. One joint of meat.

54.

39a. N., take to thyself the eye of Horus, wrested from Set, which was taken from thee, with which thou openest thy mouth.
39b. One white *mnw*-stone bowl of wine.

55.

39c. N., take to thyself the liquid which went forth from Osiris. One black *mnw*-stone bowl of beer.

56.

40a. N., take to thyself the eye of Horus, which was taken from thee; it is not far from thee. One copper (or, iron) bowl of beer.

57.

40b. N., take to thyself the eye of Horus; equip thyself with it. One *ḥtm*-bowl of beer.

57A.

40c (Nt. Jéquier, XII 2 83). To say: I bring two eyes of Horus. An *'iwn.t*-bow.

57B.

40d (Nt. 284). To say: From (or "in") the place where they fell. Ḥr.t-sea.

57C.

40e (Nt. 285). To say: Take them which I give to thee. A bowstring.

57D.

40f (Nt. 286). To say: He cast them to the ground. A *rwd*-whip.

57E.

40g (Nt. 287). To say: Osiris N., I bring to thee two eyes of Horus. An *'iwn.t*-bow.

57F.

40h (Nt. 288). [To] say: [I gave to thee]————Set. A *pd.t*-bow.

57G.

40i (Nt. 289). To say: I gave [to thee]————heart of Set. A [*d*————].

57H.

40i (Nt. 290). [To say]————n [b].————*rwd.*

57I.

40k (Nt. 291). [To say]————thou (?) hast seized them.————

57J.

401 (Nt. 292). [To say]————[Osir]is N. I bring to thee the two eyes of Horus, [thy] joy (?)————

57K.

40m (Nt. 293). To say: Osiris N., take (?) to thyself the eye of Horus; protect it; let it not cease (to be).

57L.

40n (Nt. 294). To say: Osiris N., take to thyself the eye of Horus, as it was returned to him.

57K-L.

40m-n (Nt. 293-294). Like dry fruit (?) of Horus

57M.

40o (Nt. 295). To say: Osiris N., take to thyself the eye of Horus; protect (it), for it is given (back) to him. The *'idr*-tail.

57N.

40p (Nt. 296). To say: Osiris N., take one eye of Horus. One tail.

57O.

40q (Nt. 297). To say: Osiris N., take to thyself the eye of this Horus, which was taken by him from Set————he had robbed it. One tail.

40r (Nt. 298). To say: Osiris N., take to thyself the eye of Horus, which is guarded by Geb. One *bs*-block.

57Q.

40S (Nt. 299). To say: Osiris N., take to thyself the eye of Horus over which Set enjoyed himself. *Mši* (?) *pn mr.*

57R.

40t (Nt. 300). To say: Osiris N., take to thyself the eye of Horus. which he saw side (by side) with Set. A dagger.

57S.

40u (Nt. 300. To say: Osiris N., take to thyself the eye of this Horus, which was taken by him from Set————[he] had robbed it. One tail.

Utterances 58-71.

58.

41a (Nt. 302). To say: Osiris, N., take to thyself the eye of Horus, and the ointment for him, which [he] put in it. A trimmed garment.

59.

41b (Nt. 303). To say: Osiris N., take to thyself the eye of Horus; be like it (in) its wisdom. A *š3.t*-garment (?).

41c (Nt. 304). To say: Osiris N., take to thyself the eye of this Horus, which was taken by him from Set————he had robbed it. A tail.

42a-b (Nt. 305). To say: Osiris N., I have given him to thee; take him, envelop his heart (to thee). A royal garment of *ntri*-stuff.

42c (Nt. 306). To say: Osiris N., take to thyself the thigh of Set torn out by Horus. A royal garment of *ntri*-stuff.

43a (Nt. 307). To say: Osiris N., take to thyself the water in the eye of Horus. Do not separate thyself from it. A *ḥr-š*-club.

43b (Nt. 308). To say: Osiris N., take to thyself the eye of Horus, whose water Thot saw therein. A trimmed (garment); one *mdw*-club; one sword.

44a. [To say: Osiris N., present thyself to thy son, Horus];

44b. put him in thyself (lit. thy body). A *mhn*-club; an *'isr*-club.

44c.————One *ḥr-š*-club.

45a-i (Nt. 309). To say: Osiris N., make thyself great over him.

45a-b (Nt. 309). To say: Behold, take it to thyself. A *dšr*-club.

45C (Nt. 310). To say: Osiris N., he whom thou lovest is Horus. A *ḥr-ś-*club.

46a (Nt. 311). To say: Osiris N., take to thyself the eye of Horus. One club of *śḥ.t-*wood.

46b (Nt. 312). To say: Osiris N., put *nḥḥw* upon thee, put it in thy hand, *ndśdś wś-*water. An *'iwnw-ḥr-ś-*club.

47a (Nt. 313). To say: Osiris N., take to thyself the water which is in the eye of Horus, O N.

47b (Nt. 314). To say: Fill thy hand with a *ḥr-ś-*club; equip thyself with a *ḥr-ś-*club.

47c (Nt. 3 15). To say: It equips thee like a god; do not separate thyself from it, that it may protect thee; do not separate thyself from it.

47d (Nt. 313-315). One *ḥr-ś-*club.

69.

48a (Nt. 316). To say: Osiris N., take to thyself the finger of Set, which causes the white eye of Horus to see. A *śm₃*-club.

70.

48b (Nt. 317). To say: Osiris N., take to thyself the eye of Horus that it may shine upon the finger of Set. A *d'm*-sceptre.

71.

49 (Nt. 318). To say: Osiris N., take to thyself his hand————the hand of thine enemy. A *d'm*-sceptre.

71A.

49 + 1 (Nt. 3 19). To say: Osiris N., take his *w₃* in thy hand. A *w₃ś-'nḫ*-(sceptre).

71B.

49 + 2 (Nt. 320). To say: Osiris N., thou art mighty, thou art mighty against his two fingers. An *'b.t*-tool.

71C.

49 + 3 (Nt. 32 1). To say: Osiris N., thou livest, thou livest. *R꜂'nḫ*; *An'nḫ*.

71D.

49 + 4 (Nt. 322). To say: Osiris N., take to thyself the eye of Horus, protected by his sons. One *nḫ₃ḫ₃*-whip.

62

71E.

49 + 5 (Nt. 323). To say: Osiris N., take to thyself the hand of *ḥt* (?) that he may give it to them. An *'w.t*-sceptre.

71F.

49 + 6 (Nt. 3 2 4). To say: Slay that *ḥ'* (?). A *pd-ḥ'w*-weapon.

71G.

49 + 7 (Nt. 324). To say: Thot, bring it. A *nw*-weapon

71H.

49 + 8 (Nt. 32 5). To say: Thot, bring it. A sacred decorated (weapon?).

71I.

49 + 9 (Nt. 325). To say: Have I not given it to thee? Take it to thyself (as) thy *nw*. A *rwd-nw*-whip

71J.

49 + 10 (Nt. 3 2 6). To say: Thou belongest to him. To say: Osiris N., seize it for thyself; hasten to Osiris N. A sacred *'ir*-weapon (?).

71K.

49 + 'I (Nt. 327). To say: Said Geb, Thot, bring him that bow. A *pd-'h'w*-weapon.

49 + 12 (Nt. 328)————this *ḥ'*-bow, in the presence of N., the *ḥ'* of N. A *pd-ḥ'w*-weapon.

Heading to Utterances 72-78.

50a. Pouring a libation of oil.

Utterances 72-76.

72.

50b. Osiris N., I fill thine eye for thee with ointment. To say four times. *Śt-ḥb*-oil.

73.

50c. Osiris N., take to thyself that with which a liquid offering is made. *Ḥknw*-oil.

74.

51a. Osiris N., take to thyself the eye of Horus, on account of which he was punished. *Śft*-oil.

75.

51b. Osiris N., take to thyself the eye of Horus, which is united with him. *Nhnm*-oil.

51c. Osiris, N., take to thyself the eye of Horus, with which he brought and carried the gods. *Tw3.t*-oil.

Utterance 77.

52a. Oil, Oil, arise, open thou; (thou) who art on the brow of Horus, arise, open thou.

52b. Thou who art on the brow of Horus, put thyself on the brow of this N.

52c. Make him sweet with thyself; glorify him with thyself.

53a. Make him to have power over his body (himself); put his fear in the eyes of all spirits

53b. who shall look at him, and of everyone who shall hear his name through thee. *H̱3t.t 'š.*

Utterance 78.

54a. Osiris N., I bring to thee the eye of Horus, which he took from thy brow. *H̱3t.t Ṯhnw.*

Heading to Utterances 79-80.

54b. Bring (an offering) before his face.

Utterance 79.

54c. To say four times: Osiris N., join thou the sound eye of Horus to thy face.

54d. Two bags of green cosmetic.

Utterance 80.

55a. To say: Horus, who is in Osiris N., take to thyself the sound eye of Horus.

55b. Horus, who is in Osiris N., join thou it to thy face

55c. (as) Horus joined his sound eye (to his face).

55d. O N., I join for thee thy sound eyes to thy face that thou mayest see with them.

Utterance 81.

56a. Awake thou in peace, (as) *T3i.t* awakes, in peace, (as) *T3it.t* (she of *T3i.t*) awakes in peace,

56b. (as) the eye of Horus in Buto (awakes) in peace, (as) the eye of Horus which is in the houses of the Lower Egyptian crown (awakes) in peace,

56c. (the eye) which the weavers wove (?), (the eye) which the sedan-chairman planned (?).

57a. Cause thou (0 Eye) the two lands to bow to N., as they bow to Horus,.

57b. Cause the two lands to fear N., as they fear Set.

57c. Sit thou before N., as his god; open thou his way before the spirits,

57d. that be may stand before the spirits like Anubis, "First of the Westerners."

57e. To say four times: Forward, forward to Osiris. Two rolls of linen.

Heading to Utterances 82-84.

58a. To say.

58b. To say: It is Thot who brings himself (here) with it. He comes forth with the eye of Horus. One table of offerings. To make a mortuary offering.

83.

58c. To say: The eye of Horus is given to him. He is satisfied with it. O come with the royal offering.

84.

59a. To say: Osiris N., take to thyself the eye of Horus. He was satisfied with it. Royal offering, twice.

Heading to Utterances 85-92.

59b. Place on the ground the table of offerings.

85.

59c. To say: Osiris N., take to thyself the eye of Horus; be satisfied with it. Two offerings of the broad-hall.

86.

59d. To say: Make it return to thee; sit in silence. A royal mortuary offering.

87.

60a. To say: Osiris N., take to thyself the eye of Horus; unite it with thy mouth. Food: One loaf; one beer.

60b. To say: Osiris N., take to thyself the eye of Horus; take care lest he trample it. One *ttw* (?)-bread.

60c. To say: Osiris N., take to thyself the eye of Horus, which intimidates him. One *t3-rtḥ*-loaf.

61a. To say: Osiris N., take to thyself the eye of Horus; what Set has eaten of it is little. One mug of *dśr.t*-beer.

61b. To say: Osiris N., take to thyself the eye of Horus, which they put out for him. One mug of *ḥnmś*-beer.

61c. To say: Osiris N., take to thyself the eye of Horus, put it to thy face. To lift up one bread, one beer.

Utterance 93.

62a. To lift up before his face. To say: Lift up thy face, Osiris; lift up thy face, O N., whose spirit hastens.

62b. Lift up thy face, N., be mighty, be sharp (pre-eminent?),

62c. that thou mayest see that which cometh forth from thee. Praise it (?); partake in it.

63a. Wash thyself, N.; open thy mouth with the eye of Horus.

63b. Summons, thy *ka*, like Osiris, that he may protect thee from all anger of the dead.

63c. N., receive thy bread, even the eye of Horus. To deposit (an offering) on the ground before him.

Heading to Utterances 94-96.

64a. To give food for offering; offering: One loaf, one beer.

94.

64b. To say: O Osiris N., take to thyself the eye of Horus, on which thou mayest live. One *šnš*-cake.

95.

64c. To say: Equip thyself with the liquid which goes forth from thee-four times. One mug of beer.

96. 64d. To say: Osiris N., take to thyself the eye of Horus-a joint of (*šw. t.t*)-meat. One joint of (*šw.t-*) meat.

Utterances 97-99. Heading.

65a. Placed in the left hand.

97.

65b. To say: Osiris N., this eye of Horus is that which he demanded from Set.

98.

65c. To say: Osiris N., Horus has given his eye to thee in thy hand.

66a. To say: Osiris N., O, I give to thee the eye of Horus; give me thy hand, that I may give it to thee.

Postscript.

66b. Go thou there (?).

Utterances 100-102.

Heading.

67a. Placed in his left hand.

100.

67b. To say: Osiris N., he has fought a little; (but) I have loved thee; (I have?) avenged (thee?)————

101.

67c. To say: Osiris N., I who avenge thee am come; seize the eye of Horus————

102.

68a. To say: I am Horus, Osiris, N————
68b. Give (me) thy hand————
68c. Seize————

Postscript.

68d————

Heading to Utterances 103-105.

68e. Placed in his left [hand].

103.

68f. To say: Osiris [N.]————[to] thee

104.

68g. Tosay: Osiris [N.]————thy left————

105.

68h. [To say]:————in it

105A.

68i (N. Jéquier, V 392 + I)————thou

105B.

68j (N. V392 + 2)————thou————thou

105C.

68k (N. V392 + 3). To say: He who lives is living, lived(?)————to them [life]

681 (N. V392 + 4). To say: Father, Osiris N———

68m (N. V392 + 5). To say: He intimidates thee, (but) hinder (take care) lest thou yield; fill thyself, Osiris N.———

68n (N. V392 + 6). [To say]: N., I am come to av[enge]———

68c, (N. V392 + 7). [To say]: N., given (?)———

68p (N. V392 + 8)———to thee, Osiris, I give———to thee.

68q (N. V392 + 9)———thee, to thee, to thee.

Utterance 106.

69a. To say: O N., I am thy son; I am Horus.
69b. I am come; I have brought to thee the two bodily eyes of Horus.
69c. Take them; unite them to thyself.
70a. I have collected them for thee; I have united them for thee———they are whole (?).
70b. Horus [has placed?] them before N.,

70c. that they may lead N. [to ḳbḥ.w, to Horus, to heaven to the] Great [God],

70d. [that they may avenge] N. of a[ll] his enemies.

71a. [O N., I bring to thee the two eyes of] Horus, which make his heart glad.

Utterance 107.

71b. I col[lect them for thee; take them for thyself].

71c.————

Utterances 108-110.

108.

72a. To say: Osiris N., unite to thyself the water which is in it (the eye).

72b. To say four times: For N., a lifting up of the offering, four times. Two cups of water.

109.

72c. To say: Osiris N., take to thyself the eye of Horus, which purifies his mouth.

72d. To say four times: For N., a lifting up of the offering, four times. Two pots of natron.

110.

72e. To say: Osiris N., take to thyself the eye of Horus; unite it to thy mouth.

72f. To say four times: For N., a lifting up of the offering, four times. Food: One loaf, one beer.

111.

73a. To say: Osiris N., take to thyself the eye of Horus, which Set trampled.

73b. To say four times: For N., a lifting up of the offering, four times. One (or two) loaves.

112.

73c. To say: Osiris N., take to thyself the eye of Horus, which intimidates him (Set).

73d. To say four times: For N., a lifting up of the offering, four times. One *tȝ-rtḥ*-loaf.

113.

73e. To say: Osiris N., take (it) upon thee.

73f. To say four times: For N., a lifting up of the offering, four times. Two *ḥt*-loaves.

Utterances 114-116.

114.

74a. To say: Osiris N., I bring to thee that which is befitting to thy f ace.

74b. To say four times: For N., a lifting up of the offering, four times. Two *nḥr*-loaves.

115.

74c. To say: Osiris N., I put in place thine eye.

74d. To say four times: For N., a lifting up of the offering, four times. Four *dp.t*-loaves.

116.

74e. To say: Osiris N., take to thyself the eye of Horus. Prevent him (Horus) from suffering because of it.

74f. To say four times: For N., a lifting up of the offering, four times. Four *psn*-cakes.

Utterances 117-119.

117.

75a. To say: Osiris N., receive thy head.

75b. To say four times: For N., a lifting up of the offering, four times. Four *šnś*-loaves.

118.

75c. To say: Osiris N., take thine eye; seize it (or, take it to thyself).

75d. To say four times: For N., a lifting up of the offering, four times. Four *'im-t₃*-loaves.

119.

76a. To say: Osiris N., take to thyself the eye of Horus, which he swallowed

76b. To say four times: For N., a lifting up of the offering, four times. Four cake-baskets.

120.

76c. To say: Osiris N., take to thyself the eye of Horus,; come, cause it to be respected.

76d. To say four times: For N., a lifting up of the offering, four times. Four *ḥbnn.t*-baskets.

121.

77a. To say: Osiris N., take to thyself the eye of Horus, which intimidates him (Set).

77b. To say four times: For N., a lifting up of the offering, four times. Four *ḳmḥ*-loaves.

122.

77c. To say: Osiris N., take to thyself the eye of Horus, which thou shalt put in thy mouth.

77d. To say four times: For N., a lifting up of the offering, four times. Four *'idȝ.t*-cakes of thy North

123.

78a. To say: Osiris N., take to thyself the eye of Horus; (it is) thy cake; eat thou.

78b. To say four times: For N., a lifting up of the offering, four times. Four *pȝ.t*-cakes.

124.

78c. To say: Osiris N., take to thyself the eye of Horus, which intimidates him.

78d. To say four times: For N., a lifting up of the offering, four times. Four baskets of *t3-3šr*-bread.

125.

79a. To say: Osiris N., take to thyself his teeth, white, sound.

79b. To say four times: For N., a lifting up of the offering, four times. Four bunches of garlic.

Utterances 126-128.

126.

79c. To say: Osiris N., take the joint of meat, the eye of Horus.

79d. To say four times: For N., a lifting up of the offering, four times. One joint of meat.

127.

80a. To say: Osiris N., dance (for joy), Geb is not angry with his legitimate heir.

80b. To say four times: For N., a lifting up of the offering, four times. One joint of meat.

128.

80c. To say: Osiris N., take to thyself the eye of Horus, which thou shalt embrace.

80d. To say four times: For N., a lifting up of the offering, four times. One joint of *ẖnw*-meat.

Utterances 129-131.

129.

81a. To say: Osiris N., take to thyself the *św.t.t*, the eye of Horus.
81b. To say four times: For N., a lifting up of the offering, four times. One joint of *św.t*-meat.

130.

81c. To say: Osiris N., take to thyself those who rebel against thee.
81d. To say four times: For N., a lifting up of the offering, four times. Four ribs of meat.

131.

82a. To say: Osiris N., take to thyself the *'iśś3wk*.
82b. To say four times: For N., a lifting up of the offering, four times. One pot of roast, one liver (?), one spleen, one limb, one breast of meat.

Utterances 132-134.

132.

82c. To say: Osiris N., take to thyself the eye of Horus; mayest thou go to it.
82d. To say four times: For N., a lifting up of the offering, four times. One liver (?).

83a. To say: Osiris N., take to thyself the eye of Horus, to which he goes.

83b. To say four times: For N., a lifting up of the offering, four times. One spleen.

134.

83c. To say: Osiris, N., take to thyself the eye of Horus, which is on his brow.

83d. To say four times: For N., a lifting up of the offering, four times. One limb.

Utterances 135-137.

135.

84a. To say: Osiris N., take the eye of Horus, which is on the brow of Set.

84b. To say four times: For N., a lifting up of the offering, four times. One breast of meat.

136.

84c. To say: Osiris N., take to thyself the severed heads of the Followers of Set.

84d. To say four times: For N., a lifting up of the offering, four times. One goose.

137.

85a. To say: Osiris N., take to thyself as much as the heart desires.

85b. To say four times: For N., a lifting up of the offering, four times. One goose.

Utterances 138-140.

138.

85c. To say: Osiris N., take to thyself the eye of Horus, which he brought.
85d. To say four times: For N., a lifting up of the offering, four times. One goose.

139.

86a. To say: Osiris N., take to thyself those who come when they are faint (?).
86b. To say four times: For N., a lifting up of the offering, four times. One goose.

140.

86c. To say: Osiris N., take to thyself the eye of Horus, prevent him from sickening on it.
86d. To say four times: For N., a lifting up of the offering, four times. One pigeon.

Utterance 141.

86e. To say: Osiris N., take to thyself the eye of Horus, which intimidates him.
86f. To say four times: For N., a lifting up of the offering, four times. One *t3-sif*-bread.

142.

87a. To say: Osiris N., take to thyself the eye of Horus; it shall not be sundered from thee.

87b. To say four times: For N., a lifting up of the offering, four times. Two *š'.t*-loaves.

143.

87c. To say: Osiris, N., the eye of Horus is assigned to thee.

Utterances 143-145.

End of 143.

87d. To say four times: For N., a lifting up of the offering, four times. Two baskets of *np3.t.*

144.

88a. To say: Osiris N., take the eye of Horus, out of which he poured (?) the water.

88b. To say four times: For N., a lifting up of the offering, four times. Two pots of liver.

145.

88c. To say: Osiris N., take to thyself the eye of Horus; what Set has eaten of it is little.

88d. To say four times: For N., a lifting up of the offering, four times. Two bowls of *dšr.t*-beer.

146.

89a, To say: Osiris N., take to thyself the eye of Horus; the '*iśśnw* come by means of it.

89b. To say four times: For N., a lifting up of the offering, four times. Two bowls of *dśr.t*-Theban (beer?)

147.

89c. To say: Osiris N., take to thyself the eye of Horus, which they put out for him.

89d. To say four times: For N., a lifting up of the offering, four times. Two bowls of *ḥnmś*-beer.

148.

90a. To say: Osiris N., equip thyself with the liquid, which goes forth from thee.

End of 148.

90b. To say four times: For N., a lifting up of the offering, four times. Two bowls of beer.

149.

90c. To say: Osiris N., equip thyself with the liquid, which goes forth from thee.

90d. To say four times: For N., a lifting up of the offering four times. Two bowls of *šhp-t*.

150.

90e. To say: Osiris N., equip thyself with the liquid, which goes forth from thee.

90f. To say four times: For N., a lifting up of the offering, four times. Two bowls of *ph*.

Utterances 151-153.

151.

91a. To say: Osiris N., equip thyself with the liquid, which goes forth from thee.

91b. To say four times,: For N., a lifting up of the offering, four times. Two mugs of Nubian beer.

152.

91c. To say: Osiris N., take to thyself the breast of Horus, which they taste.

91d. To say four times: For N., a lifting up of the offering, four times. Two baskets of figs.

153.

92a. To say: Osiris N., open thy mouth with it.

End of 153.

92b. To say four times: For N., a lifting up of the offering, four times. Two jars of wine of the North. Wine: Two bowls of the North; two jars of *'bš*; two bowls of Buto; two bowls of (wine) Of *ḥȝmw*; two bowls of Pelusium.

154.

92c. To say: Osiris N., take to thyself the eye of Horus, which they spat out. Prevent him from swallowing it.

92d. To say four times: For N., a lifting up of the offering, four times. Two jars of wine of *'bš*.

155.

93a. To say: Osiris N., take to thyself the damsel who is in the eye of Horus; open thy mouth with her.

End of 155.

93b. To say four times: For N., a lifting up of the offering, four times. Two jars of wine of Buto.

156.

93c. To say: Osiris N., take to thyself the eye of Horus, which he fished up. Open thy mouth with it.

93d. To say four times: For N., a lifting up of the offering, four times. Two jars of wine of *ḥꜣmw*.

157.

94a. To say: Osiris N., take to thyself the eye of Horus. It shall not again be separated from thee.

94b. To say four times: For N., a lifting up of the offering, four times. Two jars of wine of Pelusium.

Utterances 158-160.

158.

94c. To say: Osiris N., take to thyself the eye of Horus; honour it.

94d. To say four times: For N., a lifting up of the offering, four times. Two baskets of *ḥbnn.t-*(fruit?).

159.

95a. To say: Osiris N., take to thyself the eye of Horus, which he carried about with him (?), (or, which he swallowed?).

95b. To say four times: For N., a lifting up of the offering, four times. Two baskets of *ḥnfw*-cakes (fruit ?).

160.

95c. To say: Osiris N., take to thyself the eye of Horus, which he took from Set.

End of 160.

95d. To say four times: For N., a lifting up of the offering, four times. Two baskets of *'išd*-fruit.

161.

96a. To say: Osiris N., take to thyself the white eye of Horus; prevent him from tearing it out.

96b. To say four times: For N., a lifting up of the offering, four times. Two baskets of *šh.t*-fruit.

162.

96c. To say: Osiris N., take to thyself the green eye of Horus; prevent him from tearing it out.

96d. To say four times: For N., a lifting up of the offering, four times. Two baskets of *šh.t*-fruit.

Utterances 163-165.

163.

97a. To say: Osiris N., take to thyself the eye of Horus; prevent him from carrying it off.

97b. To say four times: For N., a lifting up of the offering, four times. Two baskets of *sw.t-'g.t*-corn.

97c. To say: Osiris N., take to thyself the eye of Horus; prevent him from carrying it off.

97d. To say four times: For N., a lifting up of the offering, four times. Two baskets of '*g.t*-corn.

165.

98a. To say: Osiris N., take to thyself the eye of Horus, which is like *nḥȝšḥȝ*.

Utterances 165-167.

End of 165.

98b. To say four times: For N., a lifting up of the offering, four times. Two baskets, of *ḥȝḥȝ.t*-seedy-fruit.

166.

98c. To say: Osiris N., take to thyself the eye of Horus, which they swallowed.

98d. To say four times: For N., a lifting up of the offering, four times. Two baskets of *nbš*-fruit.

167.

99a. To say: Osiris N., open thine eyes that thou mayest see with them.

99b. To say four times: For N., a lifting up of the offering, four times. Two baskets of *ṭȝ-nbš*-fruit.

168.

99c. To say: Osiris N., take to thyself the eye of Horus; prevent him from seizing it.

99d. To say four times: For N., a lifting up of the offering, four times,. Two baskets of *wḥ*-fruit.

169.

100a. To say: Osiris N., take to thyself the sweet eye of Horus; cause it to stay with thee.

100b. To say four times: For N., a lifting up of the offering, four times. Two baskets of every sweet thing (fruit ?).

170.

100c. To say: Osiris N., take to thyself the eye of Horus; reclaim it for thyself.

Utterances 170-171.

End of 170.

100d. To say four times: For N., a lifting up of the offering, four times. Two baskets of all fresh plants.

171.

100e. To say: Osiris N., O may it be pleasing to thee, for thee, with thee.

100f. To say four times,: For N., a lifting up of the offering, four times. A *ḥnk.t*-offering.

Utterance 172.

Heading

101a. To say four times: An offering of a meal to N.

101b. To say: May Geb make an offering to N.

101c. I give to thee every festal offering, every oblation of food and drink, which thou canst desire,

101d. wherewith thou shalt be happy with the god for ever and ever.

Utterance 173.

101e. To say: Osiris N., Horus is come to take care of thee; thou art his father.

101f. 'h.t-barley.

Utterances 174-176.

174.

101g. To say: Betake thee to Geb. Two pots of natron.

175.

102a. Geb has given to thee thy two eyes, that thou mayest be satisfied. One table of offerings.

176.

102b. To say: Osiris N., thou art his *ka*. One *ḫ3*-loaf.

177.

103a. To say: Take the two eyes, Great One, Osiris N. Two *wr.t*-loaves.

178.

103b. To say: Be satisfied with them. Two tables of offerings of the broad-hall.

179.

103c. To say: Be thou satisfied with Horus; thou art his father. One offering of bread.

180.

104a. To say: Nekhbet takes the eye of Horus, *nb3b3..ś*; Horus. has given (it) to thee. Two baskets of *b3b3.t*-fruit.

181.

104b. To say: Nekhbet takes the eye of Horus which they swallow. Horus has given (it) to thee. Two baskets of *nbś*-fruit.

182.

105a. To say: Take the eye of Horus, which he seized; [Horus] has given (it) to thee. One basket of *wˁḥ*-fruit.

183.

105b. To say: Take to thyself the liquid which goes out of Osiris. Two jugs of ḥbi.t.

184.

106a. To say: Osiris N., take the water which is in thee; Horus has given (it) to thee.————of tnm.

185.

106b. To say: Take to thyself the eye of Horus; open thy mouth with it. Two bowls of wine of the North.

186.

107a. To say: Osiris N., take the green eye of Horus, which he carried off: Horus has given (it) to thee. Two dishes of fresh bread.

Utterances 187-196.

187.

107b. To say: Take the eye of Horus; honour (?) it; Horus has given (it) to thee. Two baskets of ḥbn.t-fruit

188.

108a. To say: Take the eye of Horus, which he possesses; Horus has given (it) to thee. Two baskets of ḫrḫnf, or, ḫnfw-fruit-cake.

108b. To say: Take the white eye of Horus, which he tore out; Horus has given (it) to thee. Two baskets of white *šh.t*-fruit.

108c. To say: Take the green eye of Horus, which he tore out; Horus has given (it) to thee. Two baskets of green *šh.t*-fruit.

109a. To say: Take the eye of Horus, which he recognized; Horus has given (it) to thee. Two *np3.t*-cakes.

109b. To say: Take the eye of Horus, which he hastily carried off; Horus has given (it) to thee. Two pots of corn.

110. To say: Osiris N., take to thyself the eye of Horus; regale thyself with (it). Two baskets of figs.

111a. To say: O Osiris N., this eye of Horus which is sweet, cause it to stay with thee. Two baskets of every sweet fruit,

111b. To say: Reclaim it for thyself. Two baskets of all fresh (fruit?).

112. To say: O may it be pleasing to thee. Two libations.

Utterances 197-198.

197.

113a. To say: Osiris N., this hard eye of Horus, take it for thyself, in thyself, in thyself,

113b. that thine enemy may fear thee————he who carried (thee), during his time.

198.

114. To say: Osiris N., Horus has completely filled thee with his eye, as an offering.

Utterance 199.

115a. To say: O Osiris N., turn thyself towards this thy bread;

115b. receive it from (my) hand. To say four times: May the eye of Horus flourish (?) for thee.

115c. A *wdb* offering-which-the-god-gives of bread, cake and liquid.

Utterance 200.

116a. Homage to thee, Incense; greetings to thee, Divine Brother; greetings to thee *mnwr* (incense), in the limbs of Horus.

116b. Be great, my father; propagate thyself in thy name of *p3d* (pellet of incense).

116c. Thine odour is for N.; thy perfume is f or N.

116d. Eye of Horus, thou art higher, thou art greater than N. Incense.

201.

117a. To say: Father N., take to thyself the eye of Horus, the bread of the gods with which they nourish themselves.

202.

117b. To say: Father N., take to thyself the liquid (?) which comes from Osiris.

203.

117c. To say: Osiris N., take it; the eye of Horus belongs to thee.

3.
A GROUP OF PRAYERS AND CHARMS,
UTTERANCES 204-212.

Utterance 204.

118a. Rejoice, O hoers; let the heart in the breasts of men be lifted up.

118b. They have swallowed the 'bright eye of Horus which is in Heliopolis.

118c. The little finger of N. draws out that which is in the navel of Osiris.

119a. N. thirsts not, he hungers not; the heart of N. faints (?) not,

119b. for it is in the hands of *Ḥȝ:* which hold off his hunger. O fill (him), O fillers of hearts.

Utterance 205.

120a. To say: O ye who preside over food, ye who are attached to plentifulness (*ȝgb*)

120b. commend N. to *Ftk.ȝ*, the cup-bearer of Rꜥ', that he may commend him to Rꜥ' himself,

120c. that Rꜥ' may commend him to the chiefs of the provisions of this year,

120d. that they may seize and give him, that they may take and give him barley, spelt, bread, beer.

121 a. For as to N., it is his father who gives, to him; it is Rꜥ' who gives to him barley, spelt, bread, beer.

121b. For he (N.) is indeed the great bull which smote *Kns.t.*

121c. For to N. indeed belong the five portions of bread, liquid, cake, in the mansion,

121d. of which three are in heaven with Rç', and two on earth with the Ennead.

122a. For he is one who is unbound, he is indeed set free; for he is one who is seen, he is one who is indeed observed.

122b. O Rç', he (N.) is better today than yesterday.

123a. N. has copulated with *Mw.t*; N. has kissed *Šw-ś.t*;

123b. N. has united with *Nḥbw.t*.

123c. N. has copulated with his beloved, deprived of *tbtb* (grain?, seed?) and of *śśś*.

123d. But as to the beloved of N., she gives bread to N.;

123e. she did well by him in that day.

Utterance 206.

123f. To say: O ye who preside over food, ye who are attached to plentifulness,

123g. commend N. to *Ftk.ß*, the cup-bearer of Rç', that he may commend N. to Rç' himself,

123h. that Rç' may commend N. to the chiefs of the provisions.

123i. That which he (Rç') bites, he gives to N.; that which he nibbles, he gives to N.,

123k. that N. may sleep and be well every day.

Utterance 207.

124a. To say: An offering of the butcher; an offering of the butcher; an offering of that which is in the eye of Rç';

124b. an offering of the bird-catcher, who is in the eye of the god. the cup-bearer who offers water.

124c. Let the fire be hot; let the joint (of meat) be with the pastry',
124d. four hands (full) of water.

Utterance 208.

A Variant of Utterance 207.

124e. To say: An offering to Atum; an offering to Atum; an offering of that which is in the eye of the boat of the god.
124f. Let the joint (of meat) be with pastry;
124g. four hands (full) of water.

Utterance 209.

125a. Shu is well (green); N. has not taken his food (meal).
125b. N. is well (green); Shu has not taken his food (meal).
125c. Let the eastern messengers repeat (double) thy bread.

Utterance 210.

126a. To say: The judge is awake; Thot is up;
126b. the sleepers are awake; they that are in *Kns.t* bestir themselves
126c. before the great bittern, which comes forth from the marsh and Wepwawet who comes forth from the tamarisk-bush.
127a. The mouth of N. is pure; the Two Enneads purify N.;
127b. pure is this tongue which is in his mouth.
127c. The abomination of N. is dung; N. rejects urine.
127d. N. loathes his abomination.
128a. The abomination of N., it is dung; he eateth not that abomination,
128b. just as at the same time Set shrinks from these two companions who voyage over the sky.
128c. Rç' and Thot, take N. with you,

129a. that he may eat of that which ye eat, that he may drink of that which ye drink,

129b. that he may live on that which ye live, that he may sit on that which ye sit,

129c. that he may be mighty by that whereby ye are mighty, that he may voyage in that wherein ye voyage.

130a. The booth of N. is an arbour among the reeds;

130b. the abundance of N. is in the Marsh of Offerings;

130c. his food is among you, ye gods; the water of N. consists of wine like that of Rç',

130d. N. compasses the sky like Rç'; N. traverses the sky like Thot.

Utterance 211.

131a. To say: The abomination of N. is hunger; he does not eat it;

131b. the abomination of N. is thirst; he does not drink it.

131c. It is N. who gives food to those who exist.

131d. His nurse is *'i3.t*;

131e. it is she who makes his life (through nourishment?); it is she who gave birth to N.

132a. N. was conceived in the night; N. was born in the night.

132b. He belongs, to the Followers of Rç', who are before the morning star.

132c. N. was conceived in Nun; he was born in Nun.

132d. He has come; he has brought to you (some) bread of that which he found there.

Utterance 212.

133a. To say: The eye of Horus drips on the tuft of the *dn.w*-plant.

133b. Ḫnti-'imntiw came to him;

133c. he brought food to him, an offering of Horus who is chief of the houses,

133d. (for) he lives on that on which N. lives,

133e. he eats that which N. eats, he drinks, that which N. drinks.

133f. One joint of meat and pastry, that is his meal.

4.

A SERIES OF OLD HELIOPOLITAN TEXTS PARTLY OSIRIANIZED, UTTERANCES 213-222.

Utterance 213.

134a. O N., thou didst not depart dead; thou didst depart living,

134b. (so) thou sittest upon the throne of Osiris, thy '*b3*-sceptre in thy hand, thou commandest the living;

134c. (thy) *mkś*-sceptre and thy *nḥb.t*-sceptre in thy hand, commanding those of secret places.

135a. Thine arm is like that of Atum; thy shoulders are like those of Atum; thy body is like that of Atum; thy back is like that of Atum;

135b. thy seat is like that of Atum; thy legs are like those of Atum; thy face is like that of Anubis.

135c. Thou travelest over the regions of Horus; thou travelest over the regions of Set (or, the regions of Horus serve thee; the regions of Set serve thee).

Utterance 214.

136a. O N., beware of the ocean (sea?). To say four times.

136b. The messengers of thy *ka* are come for thee; the messengers of thy father are come for thee; the messengers of Rç' are come for thee.

137a. Go after (pursue) thy sun (days); purify thyself,

137b. (for) thy bones are (those of) female-falcons, goddesses, who are in heaven,

100

137c. that thou mayest be at the side of the god; that thou mayest leave thy house to thy son

137d. who is thine heir. Everyone who speaks, evil against the name of N.,

138a. when he ascends, Geb reckons him as an evil-doer in his own city,

138b. so that he weakens, he falters. Thou purifiest thyself in the dew of the stars;

138c. thou descendest on firm (copper?) cables, on the shoulders of Horus in his name of "He who is in the *Ḥnw*-boat."

139a. The blessed dead (?) lament for thee (after) the imperishable stars bore thee (away).

139b. Enter the abode of thy father, to the abode of Geb,

139c. that he may give to thee that which is on the brow of Horus, that thou mayest be a *ba* thereby, that thou mayest be a *šḥm* thereby,

139d. that thou mayest be a *Ḫnti-'imntiw* thereby.

Utterance 215.

140a. O N.,

140b. let thy messengers go; let thine envoys hasten to thy father, to Atum.

140c. Atum, let him ascend to thee; enfold him in thine embrace,

141a. (for) there is no god, (who has become) a star, who has not his companion. Shall I be thy companion?

146. Look (at me); thou hast regarded the form of the children of their fathers,

141c. who know their speech. (They are now) imperishable stars.

141d. (So) shalt thou see those who are in the palace, (that is) Horus and Set.

142a. Mayest thou spit in the face of Horus; mayest thou drive away the injury from him.

142b. Mayest thou catch the testicles of Set; mayest thou drive away his mutilation.

142c. That one was born to thee; this one was conceived by thee.

143a. Thou art born, O Horus, as one whose name is "Him at whom the earth quakes." [Thou art conceived, O Set, as one whose name is] "Him at whom heaven trembles."

143b. That one (Horus) has not a mutilation; this one (Set) has not an injury; this one (Set) has not an injury; that one (Horus) has not a mutilation.

144a. Thou art born, Horus, of Osiris; thou art more *ba* than he, thou art more *shm* than he.

144b. Thou art conceived, Set by Geb; thou art more *ba* than he, thou art more *shm* than he.

145a. No seed of a god, which belongs to him, goes to ruin; so thou who belongest to him wilt not go to ruin.

145b. Rç'-Atum does not surrender thee to Osiris. He judges (lit. numbers) not thy heart; he gains not power over thy heart.

145c. Rç'-Atum does not surrender thee to Horus. He judges (lit. numbers) not thy heart; he gains not power over thy heart.

146a. Osiris, thou dost not gain power over him (Set); thy son gains not power over him.

146b. Horus, thou dost not gain power over him (Set); thy father gains not power over him.

147a. Thou belongest, O *mn*, to that god, of whom the twin-children of Atum said (to him):

147b. "Arise," said they, "in thy name of god"———and so thou becomest an Atum to (of) every god:

148a. Thy head is (that of) Horus of the *Dꜣ.t*, O Imperishable.

148b. Thy face is that of *Mhnti-'irti*, O Imperishable.

148c. Thine ears are the twin-children of Atum, O Imperishable. Thine eyes are the twin-children of Atum, O Imperishable.

148d. Thy nose is (that of) Anubis, O Imperishable. Thy teeth are (those of) Sopdu, O Imperishable.

149a. Thine arms are *Hp* and *Dw3-mw.t.f*, which thou needest to ascend to heaven, when thou ascendest;

149b. thy legs are *'Imś.ti* and *Ḳbḥ-śn.w.f*, which thou needest to descend to the lower heaven (underworld) when thou descendest.

149c. Thy (other) members are the twin-children of Atum, O Imperishable.

149d. Thou perishest not, thy *ka* perishes not, (for) thou art a *ka*.

Utterance 216.

150a. To say: I had come to thee Nephthys; I am come to thee Boat of the Evening (*mśkt.t*-boat);

150b. I am come to thee *M3'-ḥri-tr.wt*;

150c. I am come to thee *Mśḥ3.t-k3.w*; remember him————N.

151a. *Ś3ḥ* is enveloped by the *D3.t*, pure and living, in the horizon;

151b. So this is enveloped by the *D3.t*, pure and living, in the horizon;

151c. N. is enveloped by the *D3.t*, pure and living, in the horizon.

151d. He is content because of them; he is cool because of them,

151e. in the arms of his father, in the arms of Atum.

Utterance 217.

152a. To say: Rç'-Atum, N. comes to thee, an imperishable spirit, lord (by) decree of the places of the four papyrus-pillars.

152b. Thy son comes to thee; N. comes to thee,

152c. that ye may stride over the sky (way), reunited in obscurity;

152d. that ye may arise in the horizon, in a place which is pleasing to you.

153a. Set and Nephthys, hasten, announce to the gods of Upper Egypt and their spirits:

153b. "N. comes, an imperishable spirit;

153c. if he wills that ye die, you will die; if he wills that ye live, you will live."

154a-d == 1152a-d.

155a. Osiris and Isis, hasten, announce to the gods of Lower Egypt and their spirits:

155b. "N. comes, an imperishable spirit, like the morning star over the Nile;

155c. the spirits in the waters adore him;

155d. whom he wills that he live, be lives; whom he wills that be die, he dies."

156a-d = 152a-d.

157a. Thot, hasten, announce to the gods of the West and their spirits:

157b. "N. comes, an imperishable spirit, masked to the neck like an Anubis, chief of the western highland,

157c. that he may count hearts, that he may be powerful over the best of the hearts;

157d. whom he wills that he live, he lives; whom he wills that he die, he dies."

1158a-d = 152a-d.

159a. Horus, hasten, announce to the Souls of the East and their spirits:

159b. "N. comes, an imperishable spirit;

159c. whom he wills that he live, he lives; whom he wills that he die, he dies,."

160a. Rç'-Atum, thy son comes to thee; N. comes to thee;

160b. let him ascend to thee, enfold him in thy embrace;

160c. he is thy bodily son for ever.

Utterance 218.

161a. To say: Osiris, N. comes; he is displeased (?) with the Nine (Bows?), an imperishable spirit,

161b. to count hearts, to seize *kas*, to subdue *kas*. Each of his functions

161c. obliges him whom he (himself) protected, (as well as him who) asked him (to help him). There is no one who withdraws-

162a. (such) would have no bread, his *ka* would have no bread, his bread would be withheld from him.

162b. Geb has said, and it comes out of the mouth of the Ennead:

162c. "Falcon, *m-ḫt-'iti.f*," said they, "behold, thou art *ba*, thou art *ŝḥm*."

163a. N. comes, he is displeased (?) with the Nine (Bows?), an imperishable spirit,

163b. who surpasses thee, who is more like thee, who is more weary than thou, who is greater than thou, who is fresher than thou,

163c. who is more praised than thou. Thy time of silence about it is no more.

163d. Behold what Set and Thot have done, thy two brothers, who knew not how to weep for thee.

164a. Isis and Nephthys embrace ye, embrace ye;

164b. unite ye, unite ye.

164c. N. comes, he is displeased (?) with the Nine (Bows?), an imperishable spirit.

164d. The Westerners, who are on the earth belong to N.

164e. N. comes, he is displeased (?) with the Nine (Bows?) an imperishable spirit.

165a. The Easterners who are on the earth belong to N.

165b. N. comes, he is displeased (?) with the Nine (Bows?) an imperishable spirit.

165c. The Southerners who are on the earth belong to N.

165d. N. comes, he is displeased (?) with the Nine (Bows?), an imperishable spirit.

166a. The Northerners who are on the earth belong to N.

166b. N. comes, he is displeased (?) with the Nine (Bows?), an imperishable spirit.

166c. Those who are in the underworld belong to N.

166d. N. comes, he is displeased (?) with the Nine (Bows?), an imperishable spirit.

Utterance 219.

167a. To say: Atum, this thy son is this one here, Osiris, whom thou hast made to endure and to live.

167b. He lives, N. (also) lives; he dies not, N. (also) dies not;

167c. he perishes not, N. (also) perishes not, he is not judged, N. (also) is not judged;

167d. he judges, N. (also) judges.

168a. Shu, this thy son is this one here, Osiris, whom thou hast made to endure and to live.

168b-168d = 167b-167d.

169a. Tefnut, this thy son is this one here, Osiris, whom thou hast made to endure and to live.

169b-169d = 167b-167d.

170a. Geb, this thy son is this one here, Osiris, whom thou hast made to endure and to live.

170b-170d = 167b-167d.

171a. Nut, this thy son is this one here, Osiris, whom thou hast made to endure and to live.

171b-171d = 07b-167d.

172a. Isis, this thy brother is this one here, Osiris, whom thou hast made to endure and to live.

172b-172d = 167b-07d.

173a. Set, this thy brother is this one here, Osiris, who is made to endure and to live, that he may punish thee.

173b-173d = 167b-167d.

174a. Nephthys, this thy brother is this one here, Osiris, whom thou hast made to endure and to live.

174b-174d = 167b-167d.

175a. Thot, this thy brother is this one here, Osiris, who is made to endure and to live, that he may punish thee.

175b-175d = 167b-167d.

176a. Horus, this thy father is this one here, Osiris., whom thou hast made to endure and to live.

176b-176d = 167b-167d.

177a. Great Ennead, this one here is Osiris, whom ye have made to endure and to live.

177b-177d = 167b-167d.

178a. Little Ennead, this one here is Osiris, whom ye have made to endure and to live.

178b-178d = 167b-167d.

179a. Nut, this thy son is this one here, Osiris, of whom thou hast said: "One born to your father."

179b. Thou hast wiped for him his mouth; his mouth was opened by his son, Horus, whom he loves;

179c. his limbs are counted by the gods.

180a-180c = 167b-167d.

181a. In thy name, "He who is in Heliopolis, while he remains everlastingly in his necropolis":

181b-181d = 167b-167d.

182a. In thy name, "He who is in Busiris, chief of his nomes":

182b-182d = 167b-167d.

183a. In thy name, "He who is in the House of Šerḳet, the satisfied *kȝ*":

183b-183d = 167b-167d.

184a. In thy name, "He who is in the Divine Hall, who is in fumigation,

184b. (who is in the) chest, (who is in the) portable chest, (who is in the) sack":

184c-184e = 167b-167d.

185a. In thy name, "He who is in the White Chapel of *pȝ'r*-wood":

185b-185d = 167b-167d.

186a. In thy name, "He who is in *S3ḥ*": Thou sojournest in heaven; thou sojournest on earth.

186b. Osiris, turn thy face around, that thou mayest see N.,

186c. thy seed which came forth from thee, the pointed (*špd.t*).

187a-187c = 167b-167d.

188a. In thy name, "He who is in Buto":

188b. Let thine arms be about "provisions", thy daughter; equip thyself with her.

188c-188e = 167b-167d.

189a. In thy name, "He who is in the House of the Great Ox":

189b. Let thine arms be about "provisions", thy daughter; equip thyself with her.

189c-189e = 167b-167d.

190a. In thy name, "He who is in Hermopolis of the South":

190b. Let thine arms be about "provisions", thy daughter; equip thyself with her.

190c-190e = 167b-167d.

191a. In thy name, "He who is in Hermopolis of the North":

191b. Let thine arms be about "provisions", thy daughter, equip thyself with her.

191c-191d = 167b-167d.

192a. In thy name, "He who is in the City of Waters":

192b. That which thou hast eaten is an eye; thy body is full of it; thy son, Horus, parts with it for thee, that thou mayest live by it.

192c-192d = 167b-167d.

193a. Thy body is the body of N.; thy flesh is the flesh of N.;

193b. thy bones are the bones of N.

193c. Thou goest, N. goes; N. goes, thou goest.

Utterance 220.

194a. The two doors of the horizon are open; its bolts slide.

I 94b. He has come to thee, *N.t* (Crown of Lower Egypt); he has come to thee, *Nsr.t* (Uraeus);

194c. he has, come to thee, Great One; he has come to thee, Great-in-magic (Crown of Lower Egypt).

194d. He is pure for thee; he is in awe of thee.

195a. Mayest thou be satisfied with him; mayest thou be satisfied with his purity;

195b. mayest thou be satisfied with his word, which he speaks to thee:

195c. "How beautiful is thy face, when it is peaceful, new, young, for a god, father of the gods, has begotten thee!"

195d. He has come to thee, Great-in-magic (Crown of Lower Egypt).

195e. It is Horus, who has fought in protection of his eye, Great-in-magic.

Utterance 221.

196a. To say: O *N.t* (Crown of Lower Egypt), O * Inw* (Crown of Lower Egypt), O Great One (Crown of Lower Egypt),

196b. O Great-in-magic (Crown of Lower Egypt), O Nsr.t (Uraeus),

197a. make thou the terror of N. to be like the terror of thee;

197b. make thou the awe of N. to be like the awe of thee;

197c. make thou the respect for N. to be like the respect for thee;

197d. make thou the love for N. to be like the love for thee;

197e. make thou that his *'ḥз*-sceptre be at the head of the living; make thou that his *šḥm*-sceptre be at the head of the spirits;

197f. make thou that his blade be firm against his enemies.

198a. O *Inw*-Crown, thou has come forth from him as he came forth from thee.

198b. The great *Iḥ.t* has given birth to thee, the *Iḥ.t-wt.t* has adorned thee;

198c. the *Iḥ.t-wt.t* has given birth to thee, the great *Iḥ.t* has adorned thee,

198d. for as for thee, thou art like Horus, who fought in protection of his eye.

Utterance 222.

199a. To say: Stand thou upon it, this earth, which comes forth from Atum, the saliva which comes forth from *Ḫprr*;
199b. be thou above it; he thou high above it,
199c. that thou mayest see thy father; that thou mayest see Rç'.
200a. He has come to thee, his father; he has come to thee, Rç'.
200b. He has come to thee, his father; he has come to thee, *Ndi*.
200c. He has come to thee, his father; he has come to thee, *Pndn*.
200d. He has come to thee, his father; he has come to thee, *Dndn*.
201a. He has come to thee, his father; he has come to thee, *Šmȝ-wr*.
201b. He has, come to thee, his father; he has come to thee, *Šḫn-wr*.
201c. He has come to thee, his father; he has come to thee, Sopdu.
201d. He has come to thee, his father; he has come to thee, Sharp of Teeth.
202a. Cause thou that N. seize *ḳbḥ.w*, that he take the horizon;
202b. cause thou that N. govern the Nine Bows, that he equip the Ennead;
202c. cause thou that the shepherd's crook be in the hand of N., so that Lower Egypt and Upper Egypt may bow (before him).
203a. He accepts ("takes on") his opponent and stands up, the great chief, in his great kingdom;
203b. Nephthys praised him when he seized his opponent:
204a. "Thou hast equipped thyself as the Great-in-magic, Set, who is in Ombos, lord of the land of the South;
204b. nothing is lacking in thee; nothing ceases with thee,
204c. for behold thou art more glorious, more powerful than the gods of Upper Egypt and their spirits.

205a. Thou whom the pregnant brought forth, as thou didst cleave the night,

205b. thou art equipped like Set, who mightily broke forth". Fortunate is he whom Isis has praised:

206a. "Thou hast equipped thyself like Horus, the youthful,

206b. nor is there anything lacking in thee, nor anything ceases with thee,

206c. for behold thou art more glorious, more powerful than the northern gods and their spirits.

207a. Thou puttest away thine uncleanness for Atum in Heliopolis, thou ascendest with him;

207b. thou judgest distress in the underworld,. thou standest above the places of the abyss;

207c. thou art (king) with thy father Atum, thou art high with thy father Atum;

207d. thou appearest with thy father Atum, distress disappears.

207e. The midwife of Heliopolis (holds) thy head.

208a. Thou ascendest, thou openest thy way through the bones of Shu;

208b. thou envelopest thyself in the embrace of thy mother Nut;

208c. thou purifiest thyself in the horizon, thou puttest away thine impurity in the lakes of Shu.

209a. Thou risest, thou settest, thou settest with Rç', in obscurity with *Ndï*;

209b. thou risest, thou settest, thou risest with Rç',

209c. thou appearest with *Sḫn-wr*;

210a. thou risest, thou settest, thou settest with Nephthys, in obscurity with the *mśkt.t*-boat;

210b. thou risest, thou settest, thou risest with Isis;

210c. thou appearest with the *m'nd.t*-boat.

211a. Thou art master of thyself; there is no one in thy way.

211b. Thou art born because of (like) Horus; thou art conceived because of (like) Set;

211c. Thou didst purify thyself in the Falcon-nome; thou didst receive thy purification in the Nome of the Integral Ruler, from thy father, from Atum.

212a. Thou hast come into being, thou hast become high, thou hast become content;

212b. thou hast become well in the embrace of thy father, in the embrace of Atum.

213a. Atum, let N. ascend to thee, enfold him in thine embrace,

213b. for he is thy bodily son for ever".

5.

THE DECEASED KING RECEIVES OFFERINGS AND IS RE-ESTABLISHED IN HIS FUNCTIONS AND POSSESSIONS, UTTERANCES 223-225.

Utterance 223.

214a. To say: Awake. Turn around. O! O!

214b. O N., up, be seated before a thousand. loaves, a thousand mugs of beer;

214c. the roast, thy double-rib piece (comes) from the slaughtering-bench, the *rth*-bread from the broad-hall (*wsh̯.t*).

25a. As a god is provided with divine offerings, so N. is provided with his bread.

215b. Thou art come to thy *ba*, Osiris, a *ba* among the spirits, mighty in his domains,

215c. protected by the Ennead in the house of the prince.

216a. O N., betake thyself to me, approach thyself to me,

216b. be not far from the tomb, be not separated from me.

216c. I have given thee the eye of Horus; I have reckoned it to thee. O may it be pleasing to thee, with thee.

217a. O N., up, receive thy bread from (my) hand.

217b. To say four times: O N., I will be to thee a door-keeper.

218a. To say four times: An offering to him in all his dignities, in all his places.

218b. May Geb give an offering in all thy dignities, in all thy places.

Utterance 224.

218c. To say: Awake, N. Turn around, N.

218d. Thou hast come that thou mayest command in the regions of Horus;

218e. thou hast come that thou mayest command in the regions of Set;

218f. thou hast come that thou mayest command in the regions of Osiris.

219a. May the king make an offering: "in all thy dignities".

219b. Thy garment is a *b₃*-loin-cloth; thy garment is a *hśdd*-loincloth;

219c. thou goest in sandals; thou slaughterest an ox;

220a. thou goest in the *w₃d-'n*-boat, in all thy dignities, in all thy places.

220b. Thy *nḥb.t*-sceptre is at the head of the living, thy staff is at the head of the spirits,

220c. like Anubis, First of the Westerners; like *'nd.ti*, First of the Eastern nomes.

221a. How fortunate is thy condition! Thou art a spirit, O N., among thy brothers, the gods.

221b. How changed it is! How changed it is! (So) protect thy children; beware of

221c. thy border (limitation) which is in the earth. To say four times: Clothe thy body (and) come into their presence.

Utterance 225.

A Variant of Utterance 224.

222a. To say: Awake, N.! Turn around, N.!

222b. Thou hast come that thou mayest command in the regions of Horus; (thou hast come) that thou mayest command in the regions of Set;

222c. that thou mayest speak in the regions of Osiris.

223a. May the king make an offering: Thy son is upon thy throne; thy garment is the *ph.tï*; thy garment is a *ḥśdd*-loincloth;

223b. thou goest in sandals; thou slaughterest an ox;

224a. thou goest in the *w3d-'n*-boat, in all thy places, in all thy dignities

224b. Thy *nḥb.t*-sceptre is at the head of the living, thy staff is at the head of the spirits.

224c. The aged is come; he protects his son.

224d. May thy body be clothed, so that thou mayest come to [me]; and may [the eye of Horus] be pleasing to thee.

6.
MOSTLY SERPENT CHARMS,
UTTERANCES 226-243.

Utterance 226.

225a. To say: One serpent is encircled by another serpent,

225b. when a toothless (?) calf born on pasture-land is encircled.

225c. Earth, devour that which has come forth from thee. Monster (beast), lie down, glide away.

226a. A servant (holy person) who belongs to the Ennead (pelican) is fallen in water.

226b. Serpent, turn over that Rç' may see thee.

Utterance 227.

227a. To say: The head of the great black bull was cut off.

227b. *Hpn.w*-serpent, this is said to thee. *Ḥśrʔ-ntr*-scorpion, this is said to thee:

227c. Turn over, glide into the ground. I have said this to thee.

Utterance 228.

228a. To say: Face falls on face; face sees face.

228b. A knife, coloured black and green, goes out against it, until it has swallowed that which it has licked.

Utterance 229.

229a. To say: This is the finger-nail of Atum,

229b. which is upon the dorsal vertebra of the *Nḥb.w-kȝ.w* (serpent) and which caused the strife in *Wn.w* to cease.

229c. Fall, glide away.

Utterance 230.

230a. To say: Be thy two poison-glands in the ground; be thy two rows of ribs in the hole.

230b. Pour out the liquid. The two kites stand there.

230c. Thy mouth is closed by the hangman's tool; the mouth of the hangman's tool is closed by the *mȝfd.t* (lynx).

230d. The one made tired is bitten by a serpent.

231a. O Rç', N. has bitten the earth; N. has bitten Geb.

231b. N. has bitten the father of him who bit him.

231c. This is the being who has bitten N., (though) N. did not bite him.

232a. It is he who is come against N., (though) N. does not go against him;

232b. the second moment after he saw N., the second moment after he perceived N.

232c. If thou bitest N., he will make one (piece) of thee; if thou regardest N., he will make two of thee.

233a. The *n'w*-serpent (male) is bitten by the *n'.t*-serpent (female); the *n'.t*-serpent is bitten by the *n'w*-serpent.

233b. Heaven is protected magically; earth is protected magically; the "manly" who is behind mankind is protected magically.

234a. The god whose head is blind is protected magically; thou thyself, scorpion, art protected magically.

234b. These are the two knots (charm) of Elephantiné which are in the mouth of Osiris,

234c. which Horus knotted concerning the backbone.

235a. To say: Thy bone is a harpoon-point by which thou wilt be harpooned. Hearts are checked; the nomads are in the place of the spear,
235b. they are cast down. That is, the god *Ḥmn*.

Utterance 232.

236a. To say: *Mti, Mti, Mti, Mti;*
236b. *Tiw*, his mother, *Tiw*, his mother; *Miti, Miti.*
236c. Be thou watered (washed), O desert; (let there be) water, not sand.

Utterance 233.

237a. To say: The serpent which came forth from the earth is fallen; the flame which came forth from Nun is fallen.
237b. Fall; glide away.

Utterance 234.

238a. To say: A face is upon thee; thou who art on thy belly. Descend on thy backbone, thou who art in thy *n3w.t*-bush.
238b. Give away before the serpent who is provided with her two heads.

Utterance 235.

239a. To say: *Kwtiw, 'Imḥw, 'Imḥw.*
239b. Thou hast raped the two keepers of the stone door-jamb of *'It-ti-i-i3-i*.

240. To say: *Kbbhititibiti Šś*, son of *Hifg.t*, that is thy name.

Utterance 237.

241a. To say: Spittle, which is not dried up (in dust?), (which has not) disappeared (flown) into the house of his mother,
241b. serpent (beast), lie down.

Utterance 238.

242a. To say: The bread of thy father belongs to thee, *'Iki-nhii*;
242b. thine own bread belongs to thy father and to thee, *'Ik(i)-nhii*.
242c. jewelry, oil, *Ḫ'i-t3w*, that is thine ox, the renowned, for whose deed this is being done.

Utterance 239.

243a. To say: The white crown is gone forth; she has devoured the Great.
243b. The tongue of the white crown has devoured the Great, yet the tongue was not seen.

Utterance 240.

244a. To say: The uraeus-serpent belongs to heaven; the centipede of Horus, belongs in the earth.
244b. Horus was an ox-herd when he trod on (things). N. treads upon the walk (gliding-place) of Horus,
244c. while N. knows not him who is not known.
245a. A face is, upon thee, thou who art in his (thy) *n3w.t*-bush; mayest thou be lain on thy back, thou who art in his (thy) hole.

245b. Meat-cooker of Horus, escape into the earth. O let the beast, O desert, glide away.

Utterance 241.

246a. To say: "Spitting of the wall"; "Vomiting of the brick,"
246b. that which comes out of thy mouth is thrown back against thyself.

Utterance 242.

247a. To say: Extinguished is the flame. The flame-serpent is not found in the house of him who possesses Ombos.
247b. It is a serpent, which will bite, which has slipped back into the house of him whom it will bite, that it may remain in it.

Utterance 243.

248a. To say: Two ḥtś-sceptres and two ḥtś-sceptres are for both *dm'*-cords, (to say) twice, as bread which is withheld from thee.
248b. Art thou then really here, art thou then really there? O slave, go away.

7.

THE DECEASED KING ARRIVES IN HEAVEN WHERE HE IS ESTABLISHED, UTTERANCES 244-259

Utterance 244.

249a. To say: O Osiris N., this here is the [hard] eye of Horus.
249b. Take it to thee that thou mayest be strong, (and) that he (Set) may fear thee.
Rubric. Breaking of two red jars.

Utterance 245.

250a. This N. comes to thee Nut; this N. comes to thee Nut.
250b. He has thrown his father to the ground; he has left Horus behind him.
250c. His two wings are grown as (those of) a falcon; (his) two feathers as (those of) a *gmḥśw*-falcon.
250d. His *ba* has brought him (here); his magic power has equipped him.
251a. Thou openest thy place in heaven, among the stars of heaven;
251b. thou art the only star, the companion of *Ḥw*; thou lookest down on Osiris,
251c. as he commands the spirits. Thou standest there far from him.
251d. Thou are not of them; thou shalt not be of them.

252a. See, how N. stands there among (you), the two horns on him (like) two wild-bulls,

252b. for thou art the black ram, son of a black sheep.

252c. born of a white sheep, nursed by four sheep.

253a. The blue-eyed Horus comes against you; guard yourselves against the red-eyed Horus,

253b. furious in wrath, whose might no one withstands.

253c. His messengers go; his runner hastens.

253d. They announce to him who lifts up his arm in the East

254a. that this One passes in thee of whom *Dwn-'n.wi* said: "He shall command my (?) fathers, the gods."

254b. The gods are silent before thee; the Ennead lay their hands upon their mouth,

254c. before this One in thee (of whom) *Dwn-'n.wi* said: "He shall command my (?) fathers, the gods."

255a. Stand at the doorway of the horizon; open the double doors of ḳbḥ.*w*,

255b. that thou mayest stand at their (the gods') head, as Geb at the head of his Ennead———

255c. they (the gods) enter, they are smitten with fear; they depart, they lift up their head.

256a. They see thee like Min, chief of the two *'itr.t*-palaces.

256b. He stands, he stands behind thee, thy brother stands behind thee, thy relative (nś) stands behind thee.

256c. Thou perishest not; thou art not destroyed.

256d. Thy name remains among men; thy name has its being among the gods.

257a. To say: Thy son Horus has done (this) for thee.

257b. The great tremble when they have seen the sword which is in thy hand,

257c. as thou comest forth from the *Dw3-t*.

258a. Greetings to thee, wise one.

258b. Geb has created thee; the Ennead have engendered thee.

258c. Horus is satisfied with his father, (as) Atum is satisfied with his years.

258d. The gods of the East and West are satisfied with the great (thing) which is come to pass in the embrace of the divine mother (Nut).

259a. N., O. N., (thou) who hast seen; N., O. N., (thou) who hast regarded;

259b. N, O (thou) who hast heard; N., O N., (thou) who hast been there;

260a. N., O N., lift thee up upon thy side, (thou) doer of command;

260b. (thou) who hatest sleep, (thou) who art made tired, stand up, (thou) who art in *Ndi.t*.

260c. Thy fine bread is made (i.e. offered, cf. CT, I Spell 67, 286b) in Buto; take thy power in Heliopolis.

261a. This Horus commanded to do (this) for his father. The lord of tempest prevented the saliva of Set,

261b. when he (Set) should carry thee. It is he who will carry the one who is (again) complete.

Utterance 248.

262a. To say; N. is great. N. has come forth from between the thighs of the Ennead.

262b. N. was, conceived by Sekhmet, it is *Šsmt.t* who gave birth to N.,

263a. (as) the star with piercing front (glance) and wide of stride, who brings provisions for (his) journey to Rç' every day.

263b. N. has come to his throne, which is higher than (or, over, above) the two protective goddesses of Upper and Lower Egypt; N. appears (or, shines) as a star.

Utterance 249.

264a. To say: O ye two contestants, announce now to the honourable one in this his name:

264b. N. is this *sśsš*-plant which springs from the earth.

264c. The hand of N. is cleansed by him who has prepared his throne.

265a. N. it is who is at the nose of the powerful Great One.

265b. N. comes out of the Isle of Flame,

265c. (after) he, N., had set truth therein in the place of error.

265d. N. it is who is the guardian of laundry, who protects the uraeus-serpents,

265e. in the night of the great flood, which proceeds from the Great.

266a. N. appears as Nefertem, as the flower of the lotus at the nose of Rç';

266b. as he comes forth from the horizon every day, the gods purify themselves, when they see him.

Utterance 250.

267a. To say: "It is N. who is chief of the *kas*, who unites the hearts," so says be (or she) who is chief of the wise, the Great One,

267b. "he who is in possession of the divine book, who knows, who is at the right of Rç'."

267c. N. comes to his throne, he is chief of the *kas*, N. unites the hearts, (so says she) who is chief of the wise, the Great One,

267d. N. comes into being, he who knows, being in possession of the divine book, he who is at the right of Rç'.

268a. O thou who art vindicated by N.,

268b. it is N. who says (is saying) what is in the heart of the Great One (Nut), at the Feast of Red Clothes,

268c. (for) it is N., it is N., who knows, who is at the right of Rç';

268d. (thus) the heart of the chief of the abyss of Nun is vexed.

Utterance 251.

269a. To say: O ye, who are (set) over the hours, who are (go) before Rç', make (ready) the way for N.,

269b. that N. may pass through in the midst of the border guard of hostile mien.

270a. N. is on the way to his throne, (like) one whose places are in front, who is behind the god, with bowed head,

270b. adorned with a sharp (and) strong antelope's horn,

270c. like one in possession of a sharp knife, which cuts the throat.

270d. The driver-away (?) of suffering from the bull, the punisher of those in darkness,

270e. (is) the strong antelope's horn, which is behind the Great God.

271a. N. has reduced them to punishment; N. has crushed their head.

271b. The arm of N. will not be resisted in the horizon.

Utterance 252.

272a. To say: Lift up your head, ye gods, who are in the *Dw3.t*,

272b. for N. is come. Ye see him (how) he becomes as, a great god.

272c. Introduce N. with trembling; adorn N.,

273a. who has honoured ye all, (as) he commanded mankind (also to do).

273b. N. judges those who live in the midst of the land of Rç',

273c. as N. speaks to this pure land, wherein he has established his residence, with the judge of the two gods,

274a. N. is mighty in his presence; N. bears the ȝmś-sceptre, when he (Thot) would reject N.

274b. N. sits with those who row Rç'.

274c. N. commands the good, and he (Thot) does it, (for) N. is the Great God.

Utterance 253.

275a. To say: He is pure, who was purified in the Marsh of Reeds.

275b. Rç' is purified in the Marsh of Reeds.

275c. He is pure, who was purified in the Marsh of Reeds.

275d. This N. is purified in the Marsh of Reeds.

275e. The hand of N. is in the hand of Rç'; Nut takes his arm;

275f. Shu lifts him up; Shu lifts him up.

Utterance 254.

276a. The Great (Uraeus) burns incense to the bull of *Nḫn*.

276b. The heat of a flaming breath is against ye, who surround the chapel.

276c. O Great God, whose name is unknown, an offering is on the place (i.e. in place) for the One-lord.

277a. O lord of the horizon, make place for N.

277b. If thou makest not place for N., N. will put a curse on his father Geb:

277c. The earth will no more speak; Geb will no more be able to defend himself.

278a. Whom N. finds on his way, him he eats for himself bit by bit.

278b. The *ḥn.t*-pelican announces, the *pśd.ti*-pelican comes forth; the Great One arises,

278c. the (Three) Enneads speak: A dam shall dam up the earth,

279a. both boundaries-of-the-cultivation shall be united, both riverbanks shall be joined,

279b. roads shall be closed against passengers,

279c. stairs for those who would ascend shall be destroyed.

279d. Adjust the cable, traverse the *mśḳ.t*, hit the ball on the meadow of *Ḥȝpi*.

280a. O, thy fields tremble, O, '*iȝd*-star, at the column of the stars,

280b. when they see the column of *Kns.t*, the ox (or, bull) of heaven,

280c. and how the ox-herd is terrified (overwhelmed) at him.

281a. O, be afraid, tremble, ye criminals, before the tempest of heaven;

281b. he opened the earth with that which he knew, on the day he loved to come;

282a. so said, he————he who is rich in arable-land, he who inhabits the *Dȝt*.

282b. Behold, she comes to meet thee, the "Beautiful West," to meet thee,

232c. with her beautiful tresses, she says: "He comes whom I have borne,

283a. whose horn shines, the varnished column, the ox (or, bull) of heaven.

283b. Thy figure is, exalted, pass in peace.

284a. I have protected thee, says she, the "Beautiful West," to N.

284b. Go, voyage to the Marsh of Offerings;

284c. bring the oar to *Ḥri-ḳȝ.t.f.*

285a. So said he who is chief of his department (or, thigh offering). Thou decayest in the earth

285b. as to thy thickness, as to thy girt, as to thy length

285c. (but as spirit) thou seest Rç' in his bonds, thou adorest Rç' in-his freedom (from) his bonds,

285d. through the great protection which is in his red robes.

286a. The lord of peace gives to thee his (with W.) arm.

127

286b. O ye, his she-monkeys, who cut off heads,

286c. may N. pass by you in peace, (for) he has attached (again) his, head to his neck,

286d. (for) the neck of N. is on his trunk, in his name of "Head-attacher,"

286e. (as) he attached the head of the Apis in it (that is, in his name), the day the bull was caught with a lasso.

287a. Those whom N. has made to eat (they eat of their food); (and) in their drinking,

287b. they drink of their abundance.

287c. O that N. be respected there by those who see him.

288a. The *ḥkn-wt.t*-serpent is on her *d'm*-sceptre, the sister (?) of N. who holds Shu aloft.

288b. She makes his place wide in Busiris, in Mendes, in the necropolis of Heliopolis;

288c. she erects two standards before the Great Ones;

289a. she digs a pool (?) for N. in the Marsh of Reeds;

289b. she establishes his field in the two Marshes of Offerings.

289c. N. judges in the *Mḥ.t-wr.t*-cow between the two wrestlers,

290a. for his strength is the strength of the eye of Tbi (Rç'),

290b. his might is the might of the eye of Tbi.

290c. N. has freed himself from those who did this against him,

290d. who took from him his dinner,

291a. when it was there, who took his supper from him,

291b. when it was there, who took the breath from his nose,

291c. who brought to an end the days of his life.

291d. N. is mightier than they, appearing upon his shore.

292a. Their hearts fall into his fingers,

292b. their entrails to the inhabitants of heaven (birds), their blood to the inhabitants of earth (beasts),

292c. their inheritance to the poor,

292d. their houses to fire, their farms to high Nile (inundation).

128

293a. Let the heart of N. be glad; let the heart of N. be glad!

293b. N. is Unique, the ox (or, bull) of heaven.

293c. He has exterminated those who have done this against him, he has destroyed those who are on the earth.

294a-c. Belonging to his throne, what he will take, what he will lift up, is that which his father Shu has given him in the presence of Set.

Utterance 255.

295a. To say: The Horizon burns incense to Horus of *Nḫn*; provisions for the lords.

295b. The horizon burns incense to Horus of *Nḫn*,

295c. the heat of its flaming breath is against you who surrounded the chapel,

295d. the poison of its flaming breath is against you who wear the Great (Lower Egyptian crown).

296a. The horizon burns incense to Horus of *Nḫn*; provisions for the lords.

296b. O the ugly, the ugly of form (speech?), the ugly of form,

297a. remove thyself from thy place, lay down on the ground the dignity for N.

297b. If thou removest not thyself from thy place and layest (not) down on the ground thy dignity for N.;

297c. then will N. come, his face like the Great One, lord of the *ꜣ.t*-helmet,

297d. mighty through that in which he is, injured;

298a. then will he impart heat to his eye, which will surround you,

298b. and will let go a tempest on those who did wrong,

298c. and will let loose an inundation over the Ancients;

299a. then will he strike away the arms of Shu under Nut,

299b. and then will N. put his arm on the wall (protection) on which thou leanest.

300a. The Great (Rꜥ) stands tip in the interior of his chapel,

300b. and lays down to the ground his dignity for N.,

300c, after N. had taken command (Ḥw) and had laid hold of knowledge (Śĭꜣ).

Utterance 256.

301a. To say: N. has inherited Geb; N. has inherited Geb.

301b. He has inherited Atum; he is upon the throne of Horus, the eldest.

301c. His eye is his might; his protection consists in that which was done to him.

302a. The heat of the flaming breath of his uraeus-serpent

302b. is like that of the Rnn-wt.t-serpent on his forehead.

302c. N. has put his fear in their heart,

302d. in making a massacre among them.

303a. The gods saw (it) disrobed,

303b. and they bowed themselves before N. in homage (saying):

303c. "His mother conducts him; his home-town tows him;

303d. Hai, let go thy rope."

Utterance 257.

304a. To say: There is a clamour in heaven.

304b. "We see a new thing," say the primordial gods.

304c. O Ennead, a Horus is in the rays of the sun.

304d. The lords of form serve him,

304e. the Two Enneads entire serve him,

305a. as he sits in place of the All-lord. N. wins heaven, he cleaves its firmness.

305b. N. is led along the ways of Khepri;

306a. N. rests from life in the West, the dwellers in the *Dȝ.t* following him.

306b. (Then) N. rises renewed in the East,

306c. (and) he who judged the quarrel comes to him with obeisance.

306d. "Serve N., ye gods, as he who is elder than the Great (Rç') ";

306e. so says he, "(him) who has made himself mighty in his place."

307a. N. layeth hold on command (*Ḥw*), eternity is brought to him

307b. and knowledge (*Śȝ*) is placed at his feet.

307c. Shout for joy to N.; be hath won the horizon.

Utterance 258.

308a. To say: N. is Osiris in a dust-storm.

308b. His abomination is the earth; N. has not entered into Geb,

308c. that he might be destroyed; nor has he slept in his house on earth,

308d. that his bones might be broken. His wounds are effaced:

308e. N. has purified himself with the eye of Horus; his wound is effaced by the two mourners of Osiris;

308f. N. has let the running (of his wound) flow to the ground at Ḳuṣ.

309a. It is his sister, the lady of P, who wept for him.

309b. N. is on his way to heaven; N. is on his way to heaven; on the wind; on the wind.

309c. He is not hindered; there is no one by whom he is hindered.

309d. N., he is "on his own," the eldest of the gods.

310a. His bread comes on high with (that of) Rç';

310b. his offering comes out of Nun.

310c. N. is one who comes again;

310d. he goes, he comes with Rç'.

310e. His houses are visited by him.

311a. N. seizes *kas*; he frees *kas*;

311b. he covers up evil; he abolishes evil.

311c. N. spends the day; he spends, the night, while he appeases the two choppers in *Wn.w*.

311d. Nothing opposes his foot; nothing restrains his heart.

Utterance 259.

312a. To say: N. is Osiris in a dust-storm.

3112b. The abomination of N. is the earth; he has, not entered into Geb,

312c. that N. might perish; nor has he slept in his house on earth,

312d. that the bones of N. might be broken. His wounds are effaced;

312e. N. has purified himself with the eye of Horus; his wound is effaced by the two mourners of Osiris;

312f. N. has let the running (of his wound) flow to the ground at Ḳuṣ.

313a. It is the sister of N., the lady P, who wept for him.

313b. The two nurses (or, attendants), who wept for Osiris, wept for him.

313c. N. is on his way to heaven; N. is on his way to heaven, with Shu and Rç'.

313d. N. is not hindered; there is no one who hinders him.

313e. N. is upon his feet, the eldest of the gods.

313f. N. has no session in the divine court.

314a. The bread of N. comes on high with (that of) Rç';

314b. his offering comes out of Nun.

314c. N. is one who comes again;

314d. N. goes with Rç'; N. comes with Rç'.

3,4e. His houses are visited by him.

3,5a. He covers up evil; he abolishes evil.

315b. He seizes *kas*; he frees *kas*.

315c. N. spends the day; he spends the night; N. frees the two choppers in *Wn.w*.

315d. Nothing opposes the feet of N.; nothing restrains the heart of N.

8.

THE DECEASED KING TRIUMPHS OVER HIS ENEMIES AND IS RECOGNIZED BY THE GODS, UTTERANCES 260-262.

Utterance 260.

316a. To say: O Geb, bull of Nut, N. is a Horus, heir of his father.

316b. N. is the goer, the comer, the fourth of these four gods,

316c. who have brought water (and) made themselves clean, who rejoice over the "power" of their fathers.

316d. He desires that he be justified by that which he has done.

317a. Since *Tfn* and Tefnut have judged N.; since the Two Truths have heard (him);

317b. since Shu has been advocate (tongue); since the Two Truths have given verdict;

317c. he has encompassed the thrones of Geb, he has raised himself to that which he wished.

318a. (So now that) his limbs are united, which were hidden (in the grave),

318b. he unites himself with those who are in Nun. He puts an end to his words in Heliopolis,

318c. as N. goes forth on that day in the true form of an *ȝḥ*.

319a. N. destroys battle; he punishes revolt.

319b. N. goes forth (as) the protector of truth; he brings her, for she is with him.

319c. Those who were furious, (now) busy themselves for him; those who are in Nun, (now) give life over to him.

320a. The refuge of N. is in his eye; the protection of N. is in his eye;

320b. the power of N. is in his eye; the strength of N. is in his eye.

321a. O gods of South, North, West, East, respect N., fear him;

321b. he has sat in the *ḥtz* of the two courts.

321c. That uraeus-serpent *dnn-wt.t* might have burned you, for she attained your heart,

322a. you (they) who might have come to N. as an adversary; come to him (as a friend), come to him.

322b. N. is the *dśdś* of his father, the *nḥb* of his mother.

323a. The abomination of N. is to walk in darkness,

323b. lest he see those who are upside down.

323c. N. will come forth in this day; he will bring truth with him.

323d. N. will not be delivered up to your flame, O gods.

Utterance 261.

324a. To say: N. is a heart-beat, son of the heart of Shu,

324b. wide-outstretched, a blinding light.

324c. It is N. who is a flame (moving) before the wind to the ends of heaven and to the end of the earth,

324d. as soon as the arms of the lightning are emptied of N.

325a. He travels through Shu and strides through *ȝ*k*r*,

325b. he kisses the red crown, the divinely created.

326a. Those who are in the arbour (heaven?) open for him their arms.

326b. N. stands on the eastern side of heaven;

326c. (where) there is brought to him that which ascends to heaven.

326d. N. makes a separation of the tempest.

Utterance 262.

327a. To say: Disown not N., O god; for thou knowest him and he knows thee.

327b. Disown not N., O god; for he knows thee.

327c. To (thee) it is said: "The transitory."

328a. Disown not N., O Rç'; for thou knowest him and he knows thee.

328b. Disown not N., O Rç'; for he knows thee.

328c. To thee it is said: "The Great (One) is altogether destroyed."

329a. Disown not N., O Thot; for thou knowest him and he knows thee.

329b. Disown not N., O Thot; for he knows thee.

329c. To thee it is said: "He rests, the solitary."

330a. Disown not N., O Horus, the pre-eminent (pointed); for thou knowest him and he knows thee.

330b. Disown not N., O Horus, the pre-eminent (pointed); for he knows thee.

330c. To thee it is said: "The unfortunate."

331a. Disown not N., O thou who art in the *D3.t*; for thou knowest him and he knows thee.

336. Disown not N., O thou who art in the *D3.t*; for he knows thee.

331c. To thee it is said: "The damaged."

332a. Disown not N., O bull of heaven; for thou knowest him and he knows thee.

332b. Disown not N., O bull of heaven; for he knows thee.

332c. To thee it is said: "This *nḫḫ*-star."

333a. Behold, N. comes; behold, N. comes; behold, N. is ascended.

333b. N. is not come of himself.

333c. It is a messenger who is come to him; it is a divine word which will cause him to arise.

334a. N. has passed by his broad-house; the fury of the great sea has avoided him.

334b. His fare is not accepted in the great ship;

334c. the palace of the Great cannot ward him off from the way of the *šḥd.w*-stars.

335a. Behold, therefore, N. has attained the heights of heaven.

335b. He has seen his uraeus-serpent in the boat of the evening sun; it is N. who has journeyed in it.

335c. He has recognized (his) uraeus-serpent in the boat of the morning sun, it is N. who has bailed it out.

336a. The blessed dead (?) have witnessed to him;

336b. the hail-storm of heaven has taken him away, it (lit. they cause) causes N. to approach to Rç'.

9.
MEANS WHEREBY THE DECEASED KING REACHES HEAVEN, UTTERANCES 263-271.

Utterance 263.

337a. To say: The two reed-floats of heaven are placed for Rç', that he may ferry over therewith to the horizon.

337b. The two reed-floats of heaven are placed for Harachte that Harachte may ferry over therewith to Rç'.

337c. The two reed-floats of heaven are placed for N. that he may ferry over therewith to the horizon, to Rç'.

337d. The two reed-floats of heaven are placed for N. that he may ferry over therewith to Harachte, to Rç'.

338a. It is good for N. (to be) with his *ka*; N. lives with his *ka*.

338b. His *b3*-loin-cloth is on him; his Horus-weapon is on his arm; his sceptre is in his hands.

339a. He makes himself serviceable to those who have passed on.

339b. They bring to him those four spirits, the eldest, the first of the wearers of side-locks,

339c. who stand on the eastern side of the sky and lean upon their *d'm*-sceptres,

340a. that they may speak the good name of N. to Rç'

340b. and proclaim N. to N*ḥb-k3.w*,

340c. so that the entrance of N. may be greeted (or protected). The Marshes of Reeds were filled (with water),

340d. so that N. might ferry over the Winding Watercourse.

341a. N. will certainly ferry over to the eastern side of the horizon;

341b. N. will certainly ferry over to the eastern side of heaven.

341c. His sister is Sothis; his mother is the *Dw3.t* (morning star).

Utterance 264.

342a. To say: The two reed-floats of heaven are placed for Horus that he may ferry over therewith to the horizon, to Harachte.

342b. The two reed-floats of heaven are placed for N. that he may ferry over therewith to the horizon, to Harachte.

342c. The two reed-floats of heaven are placed for *Šsm.ti* that he may ferry over therewith to the horizon, to Harachte.

342d. The two reed-floats of heaven are placed for N. that he may ferry over therewith to the horizon, to Harachte.

343a. The *mn'*-canal is open; the Winding Watercourse is inundated;

343b. the Marshes of Reeds are filled (with water).

344a. N. will certainly ferry over to yonder eastern side of heaven,

344b. to the place where the gods will give him birth, where he will certainly be born, new and young,

345a. when this hour of the morrow comes———the hour of the fifth-day,

345b. the hour of the sixth day, the hour of the seventh day, the hour of the eighth day.

346a. N. will be summoned by Rç', he will be given something (to eat) by *Nḥb-k3.w*,

346b. like Horus, like him of the horizon,

346c. when this hour of the morrow comes, the hour of the third day, the hour of the fourth day.

347a. When N. stands there like this star which is on the under (side) of the body of the sky;

347b. he judges as a god after he has listened like a prince.

348a. N. calls to them and they bring to him those four gods,

348b. who stand on the *d'm*-sceptres of heaven,

348c. that they may speak the name of N. to Rç' and announce his name to Horus who inhabits the horizon.

349a. He has come to thee; he has come to thee,

349b. that he may be loosed from the bands and unbound from the fastenings.

350a. He (Rç') has freed N. from *Hrti*; he has not given him to Osiris.

350b. N. has not died the death;

350c. he has become an *3hw* (or, *3h*) in the horizon; he has become everlasting in the *Ddw.t*.

Utterance 265.

351a. To say: The two reed-floats of heaven are placed for Rç' that he may ferry over therewith to the horizon, to Harachte.

351b. The two reed-floats of heaven are placed for Harachte that he may ferry over therewith to the horizon to Rç'.

351c. The two reed-floats of heaven are placed for N. himself

351d. that he may ferry over therewith to the horizon, to Rç', to Harachte.

352a. The *mn'*-canal is open; the Winding Watercourse is inundated;

352b. the Marshes of Reeds are filled (with water).

353a. N. will certainly ferry over to the eastern side of heaven,

353b. to the place where the gods will be born,

353c. where N. will certainly be born with them, like Horus, like him of the horizon.

354a. N. is justified.

354b. Praise be to N.; praise be to the *ka* of N.!

355a. Let them be called to N.;

355b. let them be brought to N., those four traffic-guards, the wearers of side-locks,

355c. who stand on their *d'm*-sceptres, on the eastern side of the sky,

356a. that they may speak the name of N., the good, to Rç',

356b. (and) that they may proclaim the name of N., the good, to *Nḥb-kȝ.w.*

356c. N. is justified.

356d. Praise be to N.; praise be to the *ka* of N.!

357a. The sister of N. is Sothis; the mother of N. is the morning star.

357b. N. is that (star) which is with Rç' on the under (side) of the body of the sky.

357c. N. is justified.

357d. Praise be to N.; praise be to the *ka* of N.!

Utterance 266.

358a. To say: The two reed-floats of heaven are placed for Rç',

358b. that Rç' may ferry over with them to the horizon, to Harachte.

358c. The two reed-floats of heaven are placed for N.,

358d. that he may ferry over with them to the horizon, to Harachte.

358e. The two reed-floats of heaven are placed for Harachte,

358f. that Harachte may ferry over with them to the Horizon, to Rç'.

358g. The two reed-floats of heaven are placed for N.,

358h. that N. may ferry over with them to the horizon, to Rç'.

359a. The *mn'*-canal is open; the Marsh of Reeds is filled with water;

359b. the Winding Watercourse is inundated.

360a. N. will certainly ferry over to the horizon, to Harachte.

360b. Let there be brought to N. these four friendly ones,

360c. the traffic-guards, the wearers of side-locks,

360d. who sit on their *d'm*-sceptres on the eastern side of heaven.

361a. Ye shall say it (namely) the good name of N. to *Nḥb-kȝ.w.*

361b. Praise be to N.; praise be to his *ka*!

361c. N. is justified; the *ka* of N. is justified by the god.

362a. Rç' has [taken] N. to himself to heaven, on the eastern side of heaven;

362b. he is like Horus, of the *D3.t*; he is like that star which radiates heaven.

363a. The sister of N. is Sothis; [the mother of N. is the morning star];

363b. [N. sits between] them.

363c. Heaven will never be void of N.; never shall the earth be void of N.

363d. By command————

363e.————, bring this (boat) to N.

363f. he will be your third in Heliopolis (or, as a Heliopolitan).

Utterance 267.

364a. Thy heart belonged to thee, Osiris; thy legs belonged to thee, Osiris; thine arm(s) belonged to thee, Osiris.

364b. The heart of N. belongs to himself; his legs belong to himself; his arm(s) belong(s) to himself.

365a. A stairway to heaven shall be laid down for him, that he may ascend to heaven thereon;

365b. he ascends on the smoke (incense) of the great censing.

366a. N. flies, as a goose; he alights as a scarab;

366b. he flies as a goose; he alights as a scarab

366c. upon the empty throne which is in thy boat, O Rç'.

367a. Stand up, remove thyself, thou who knowest not the reed-thicket,

367b. that N. may sit in thy place and row (around) in heaven in thy boat, O Re.

368a. N. pushes off from the earth in thy boat, O Rç';

368b. so when thou goest forth from the horizon, he (N.) has his sceptre in his hand,

368c. as navigator of thy boat, O Rç',

369. Thou (N.) mountest up to heaven; thou separatest thyself from the earth, a separation from wife and office (royal-apron).

Utterance 268.

370a. To say: N. washes himself, Rç' appears, the Great Ennead sparkles;

370b. the Ombite is high as chief of the '*itr.t*-palace;

371a. N. puts humanity off from him as a limb;

371b. N. seizes the *wrr.t*-crown from the hand of the Ennead.

371c. Isis nurses him, Nephthys suckles him,

372a. Horus takes him by his fingers (to his side),

372b. he purifies N. in the lake of the jackal,

372c. he makes, the *ka* of N. clean in the lake of the *D3.t.*

372d. He rubs down the flesh of the *ka* of N. and his own

372e. with that which is near Rç' in the horizon, that which he (Rç') took,

373a. when the two lands beamed and when he bared the face of the gods.

373b. He brings the *ka* of N. and himself to the great palace,

373c. after offices (?) were made for him and the *hm3tt* was knotted for him.

374a. N. leads the imperishable stars,

374b. he ferries over to the Marshes of Reeds,

374c. the inhabitants of the horizon row him, the inhabitants of *kbh.w* navigate him.

375a. N. is very capable (mighty), his arms will not desert him;

375b. N. is very excellent (foremost), his *ka* comes to him (to his aid).

Utterance 269.

376a. To say: The fire is laid, the fire shines;

376b. the incense is laid on the fire, the incense shines.

376c. Thy fragrance comes to N., O Incense; the fragrance of N. comes to thee, O Incense.

377a. Your fragrance comes to N., O ye gods; the fragrance of N. comes to you, O ye gods.

377b. May N. be with you, O ye gods; may you be with N., O ye gods.

377c. May N. live with you, O ye gods; may you live with N., O ye gods.

378a. May N. love you, O ye gods; love him, O ye gods.

378b. The *p3k*-pellet (of incense) comes, the *p3d*-pellet (of incense) comes, (they) come forth from the thigh (or lap, *m3ś.t*) of Horus.

379a. Those who have ascended are come, those who have ascended are come; those who have climbed are come, those who have climbed are come.

379b. Those who lifted themselves up like Shu are come; those who have lifted themselves up like Shu are come.

379c. N. ascends on the hips of Isis; N. climbs up on the hips of Nephthys.

380a. The father of N., Atum, lays hold of the arm of N.; he assigns N.

380b. to those gods, who are the nimble, the wise, the imperishable stars.

381a. Mother of N., 'Ipii,

381b. give to N. thy breast,

381c. that N. may pass it over his mouth (taste it),

381d. and that N. may suck thy milk, which is white, light and sweet.

382a. That (yonder) land in which (where) N. goes,

382b. N. will not thirst in it, N. will not hunger in it for ever.

Utterance 270.

383a. To say: Awake thou in peace, (thou) whose face is behind him in peace, (thou) who seest behind him in peace,

383b. ferryman of heaven in peace, ferryman of Nut in peace,

383c. ferryman of the gods in peace.

384a. N. comes to thee,

384b. that thou mayest ferry him over in that ferry in which thou ferriest the gods over.

385a. N. comes to his side as a god comes to his side,

385b. he comes to his temple as a god comes to his side,

385c. N. comes to his temple as a god comes to his temple.

386a. There is no accuser of the living who is against N., there is no accuser of the dead who is against N.;

386b. there is no accuser of a goose who is against N., there is no accuser of an ox who is against N.

387a. If thou dost not ferry N. over, he will spring up

387b. and set himself upon the wing of Thot.

387c. He it is who will ferry N. over to yonder side.

Utterance 271.

388a. It is N. who inundated the land after it had come out of the ocean; it is N. who pulled up the papyrus;

388b. it is N. who reconciled the two lands; it is N. who united the two lands;

388c. it is N. with whom his mother, the great wild-cow, will be united.

389a. Mother of N., thou wild-cow, who is upon the herb (-overgrown) hill, who is upon the hill of the *shsh*-bird.

389b. the two *dd*-pillars are standing, the broken steps are falling down.

390a. N. ascends on the ladder which his father Rç' made for him,

390b. Horus and Set lay hold of the arm of N.; they take him to the *D₃.t.*

391a. He (Horus) to whom it was signalled (winked): "Guard thyself against him to whom (this) is ordered";

391b. he (Set) to whom it was ordered: "Guard thyself against him to whom (this) is signalled (winked)."

391c. The face of god is open (revealed) to N.; N. sits (takes his place) upon the great throne at the side of the god.

10.
THE DECEASED KING IN HEAVEN,
UTTERANCES 272-274.

Utterance 272.

392a. To say: O Lofty-one, which is not sharpened, thou Door of Nun,
392b. N. comes to thee. Cause this (door) to be opened for him.
392c. N., he is small,
392d. (yet) N. is chief of the Followers of Rç'; he is not chief of the evil
    gods (demons).

Utterances 273-274.

393a. To say: The sky is overcast, the stars are darkened,
393b. the bows are agitated, the bones of the earth-gods quake.
393c. The agitations cease
394a. after they have seen N. dawning (as) a *ba,*
394b. as a god, who lives on his fathers and feeds on his mothers.
394c. N. is lord of craftiness, whose name his mother knows not.
395a. The honour of N. is in heaven, his might is in the horizon,
395b. like his father, Atum, who begat him. He has begotten him mightier
    than he.
396a. The *kas* of N. are behind him, his maid-servants are under his feet,
396b. his gods are over him, his uraeus-serpents are upon his brow;
396c. the leader-serpent of N. is on his forehead, she who perceives the
    soul (of the enemy), (as) a diadem, a flame of fire;

396d. the might of N. is for his protection.

397a. N. is the bull of heaven, who (once) suffered want and decided (lit. gave in his heart) to live on the being of every god,

397b. who ate their entrails (?) when it came (to pass) that their belly was full of magic

397c. from the Isle of Flame.

398a. N. is equipped, he who has incorporated his spirits.

398b. N. dawns as the Great One, lord of those with (ready) hands.

398c. He sits, his side towards Geb (the earth).

399a. It is N. who judges with him whose name is hidden,

399b. (on) this day of slaying the eldest (gods).

399c. N. is lord of offerings, who knots the cord,

399d. who himself prepares his meal.

400a. N. is he who eats men and lives on gods,

400b. lords of messengers, who distributes orders.

401a. It is "Grasper-of-the-top-knot" who is in $\underline{kh}$3.w who lassoes them for N.

401b. It is "The serpent with raised head ($\underline{d}$śr-$\underline{t}p$)" who watches them (the gods) for N., who repels them for him.

401c. It is "He who is upon the willows" who binds them for N.

402a. It is "Khonsu who slaughters the lords (gods)," in that he beheads them for N.,

402b. and takes out for him what is in their body.

402c. He (Khonsu?) is the messenger whom he (N.) sends forth to punish.

403a. It is Šsm.w who cuts them up for N.,

403b. cooking for him a meal of them in his evening cooking-pots.

403c. It is N. who eats their magic and swallows their spirits;

404a. their Great Ones are for his morning meal,

404b. their middle-sized ones are for his evening meal,

404c. their little ones are for his night meal,

146

404d. their old men and old women are for his incense-burning (or, fire).

405a. It is "The Great Ones in the north side of heaven" who lay for him the fire

405b. to the kettles containing them, with the thighs of their eldest (as fuel).

406a. The inhabitants of heaven wait on N.,

406b. when the hearth was constructed for him with (out of) the legs of their women.

406c. He has completely encircled the two heavens; he has revolved about the two lands.

407a. N. is the great mighty one, who has power over the mighty ones.

407b. N. is the ʾḥm-falcon, who surpasses the ʾḥm-falcons————the great falcon.

407c. Whom he finds on his way, he eats for himself bit by bit.

407d. The respect of N. is before (first of) all noble ones, who are in the horizon.

408a. N. is a god older than the eldest.

408b. Thousands serve him; hundreds make offering to him.

408c. A certificate as (of) a mighty, great one is given to him by Śȝḥ, father of the gods.

409a. N. has dawned again in heaven; he is crowned with the Upper Egyptian crown as lord of the horizon.

409b. He has smashed the dorsal vertebra;

409c. he has carried off the hearts of the gods;

410a. he has eaten the red crown, he has swallowed the green one;

410b. N. feeds on the lungs of the wise ones;

410c. he is satisfied by living on hearts as well as their magic.

411a. N. is disgusted when he licks the emetics which are in the red crown,

411b. (but) he is delighted when their magic is in his belly.

411'c. The dignities of N. shall not be taken from him,

411d. (for) he has swallowed the intelligence of every god.

412a. The lifetime of N. is eternity, its limit is everlastingness

412b. in this his dignity of "If he wishes he does, if he wishes not he does not,"

412c. who is within the boundary of the horizon for ever and ever.

413a. Behold, their soul (of the gods) is in the belly of N., their spirits are with N.,

413b. as his soup à la *ntr.w*, cooked for N. from their bones,

413c. Behold, their soul is, with N., their shadows are taken away from the hand of those to whom they belong.

414a. N. is as that which dawns, which dawns, which endures, which endures.

414b. The doers of evil shall not be able to destroy

414c. the favourite place of N. among the living in this land for ever and ever.

11.
CHARMS, UTTERANCES 275-299.

Utterance 275.

415a. To say: N. comes to you, ye falcons,

415b. since (?) your houses are barred off for N.,

415c. his *m'ḥ*-garment of ape-skin on his back.

416a. N. opens the double doors (of heaven); N. goes to the boundary of the horizon;

40b. N. laid down the *mśd.t*-garment on the ground;

416c. N. became like the Great One who is in Crocodilopolis.

Utterance 276.

417a. To say: Thy act is against thee, what thou doest is against thee,

417b. O *sksk*-serpent, which is in his (thy) hole?, the opponent.

Utterance 277.

418a. To say: Horus falls because of his eye; the bull (Set) collapses because of his testicles.

418b. Fall, collapse!

Utterances 278.

419a. To say: *B3bi* is arisen, he is against the chief of Letopolis,

419b. whom that spittle protected; this (spittle) protects every one beloved of me.

419c. Thou art loosed, O *wfi*-serpent. Cause N. to be protected.

Utterance 279.

420a. To say: N., I have trampled the mud of the water-courses. Thot is the protector of N.,

420b. when it is dark, when it is dark.

Utterance 280.

421a. To say: Doer, doer; passer, passer;

421b. thy face behind thee; guard thyself against the great door,

Utterance 281.

422a. To say: Punish the serpent, *Kbḥḥḥrwbi*,

422b. O lion of *phti*, O lion of *ptti*, the *phti* (and) *ptti*.

422c. Give to me now, *ḥrwtwbś*, meat, now, one pot.

422d. Go, go, serpent, serpent.

Utterance 282.

423a. To say: Lo, this foreign country of the mouth of the river, this is thy complaint:

423b. "This foreign country of the mouth of the river belongs to me, the lord of *Ḥknw*."

423c. It is *Ḫʾi-t3w* of *Ḥknw*, this thine ox-god, the renowned, against whom this has been done.

Utterance 283.

424a. To say: Truly, N. wags his thumb, the left one, against thee.

424b. He gives a sign with it to Min (with his) thunderbolt. O robber, rob not.

Utterance 284.

425a. To say: He (serpent) whom Atum has bitten has filled the mouth of N.,

425b. while he wound himself up (lit. wound a winding).

425c. The centipede was smitten by the householder, the householder was smitten by the centipede.

425d. That lion is inside this lion.

425e. Two bulls fight inside the ibis.

Utterance 285.

426a. Thy two drops of poison are on the way to thy two poison-vessels. Spit both out now,

426b. for they two are rich in water. O thou who winkest, thou who art (adorned with) a head-band, O *Š'ȝ.w*,

426c. rain, that the serpent may become cowardly and the throat (canal) of my heart may be safe;

426d. storm, that the lion may drown himself in water and the throat of the heart of the king (?) may be wide.

Utterance 286.

427a. To say: O ye, who gurgle like the young of a "water-pest" (crocodile), *tmti, thn.w,*

427b. *kbnw,* those who glide away! The red crowns (i.e. water-flowers) praise

427c. the *tiw-šii*; the *tiw-šii* belong to him who has elevated the red crowns.

427d. Hail, we two!

Utterance 287.

428a. To say: *Nni*, his mother; *Nni*, his mother.

428b. Art thou really here, art thou really here? Lion, get away.

Utterance 288.

429a. To say: *Hki*-serpent or *hkr.t*-serpent, go away

429b. (with) face on the road. Eye of N., look not at him.

429c. Thou shalt not do thy will with N. Get away.

Utterance 289.

430a. To say: A bull is fallen because of the *śdḥ*-serpent; the *śdḥ*-serpent is fallen because of the bull.

430b. Fall, glide away.

Utterance 290.

43m. To say: Face falls on face; a knife coloured and black, goes out against it, until it has swallowed that

431b. which it has seized.

Utterance 291.

432a. To say: Thine honour is effaced, O white hole, by him who has escaped the *fnt*-worm.

432b. Thine honour is robbed, O white hole, by him who has escaped the *fnt*-worm.

Utterance 292.

433a. To say: Thou art seized, thou, O *'iknhi*-serpent;
433b. thy neighbour (?) has seized thee, *'iknhi*-serpent.

Utterance 293.

434a. To say: Back, hidden serpent; hide thyself,
434b. and let N. not see thee.
434c. Back, hidden serpent; hide thyself,
434d. and come not to the place where N. is,
434e. lest he pronounce against thee that name of thine, *Nmi* son of *Nmi.t*.
435a. A servant (holy person) as the Ennead's pelican (once) fell into the Nile, (so) flee, flee.
435b. Serpent (beast), lie down.

Utterance 294.

436a. To say: N. is Horus who comes forth from the acacia, who comes forth from the acacia,
436b. to whom it was commanded: "Be thou aware of the lion," he comes forth to whom it was commanded: "Be thou aware of the lion."
437a. N. has come forth from his *dni.t*-jar, after he had passed the night in his *dni.t*-jar,
437b. and N. appears in the morning.
43 7c. He has come forth from his *dni.t*-jar, after he had passed the night in his *dni.t*-jar,
437d. and N. appears in the morning.

Utterance 295.

438a. To say: The *m3fd.t*-lynx springs on the neck of the *'in-di-f*-serpent.

438b. It repeats it on the neck of the serpent with the raised head (*dśr-tp*).

438c. Who is it who will remain? It is N. who will remain.

Utterance 296.

439a. To say: *Tt.w*-serpent, where to? Thou shalt not go. Stand by N.

439b. N. is Geb. *Hmt*-serpent, brother of *hmt.t*-serpent,

439c. should thy father, the *d"miw*, die?

Utterance 297.

440a. The hand of N. which is come upon thee————

440b. it is a violent one which is come upon thee,

440c. it is the *m3fd.t*-lynx, which is in the house of life.

440d. She strikes thee in thy face; she scratches thee in thine eyes,

441a. so that thou fallest in thy dung and glidest in thy urine.

441b. Fall, lie down, glide away, so that thy mother Nut may see thee.

Utterance 298.

442a. To say: Rç' dawns, his uraeus on his head,

442b. against this serpent, which is come out of the earth, (and) which is under the fingers of N.

442c. He (N.) cuts off thy head with this knife, which was in the hand of the *m3fd.t*-lynx, [which lives in the house of life];

443a. he draws, (the teeth) which are upon (in) thy mouth; he saps thy poison

443b. with those four strings, which were in the service of the sandals of Osiris.

443c. Serpent (beast), lie down; bull, glide away.

Utterance, 299.

444a. To say: The uraeus-serpent is for heaven; the centipede of Horus is for the earth.

444b. Horus had a sandal as he advanced (towards) the master of the house, the bull of the hole,

444c. the combat-serpent. N. will not be beaten,

444d. (for) his protective sycamore is the protective sycamore of N., his refuge is the refuge of N.

444e. Whom N. finds in his way, him he eats for himself bit by bit.

12

THE FERRYMAN AND THE DECEASED KING'S ASCENSION, UTTERANCES 300-311.

Utterance 300.

445a. To say: O *Hrti* of *Ns3.t*, ferryman of the *Ikh.t*-boat, made by Khnum,

445b. bring this (boat) to N. N. is Seker of *R-St3.w*.

445c. N. is on the way to the place of Seker, chief of *Pdw-š*.

445d. It is our brother who is bringing this (boat) for these bridge-girderers (?) of the desert.

Utterance 301.

446a. To say: Thy established-offering is thine, O *Niw* (Nun) together with *Nn.t* (Naunet),

446b. ye two sources of the gods, protecting the gods with their (your) shade.

446c. Thy established-offering is thine, O Amŭn together with Amŭnet,

446d. ye two sources of the gods, protecting the gods with their (your) shade.

447a. Thy established-offering is thine, O Atum together with the two lions, ye double power of the gods, yourselves, who created yourselves,

447b. that is, Shu together with Tefnut, (who) created the gods, begat the gods, established the gods.

448a. Say ye to your father (Ptah)

448b. that N. has given to you your established-offering, that N. has satisfied you with your due.

448c. Ye shall (or, should) not hinder N. when he ferries to the horizon to him.

449a. N. knows him, knows his name. *Nḥi* is, his name, *Nḥi* lord of the year is his name;

449b. he with the warrior's arm, Horus who is over the *śhd.w* of heaven, who causes Rç' to live every day.

450a. He will rebuild N.; he will cause N. to live every day.

450b. N. comes to thee, Horus of *Ḥȝ.t*; N. comes to thee, Horus of *Šsm. t*;

450c. N. comes to thee, Horus of the East.

451a. Behold, N. brings to thee thy great left eye as healer.

451b. Take it, the intact (one), to thyself from N.; its water is in it, being intact;

451c. its blood is in it, being intact; its breath is in it, being intact.

452a. Enter into it; take possession of it, in this thy name of "Sacred *Ḥkȝš*" (a god),

452b. that thou mayest approach to it in this thy name of "Rç"".

453a. Put it on thy brow, in this, its name of "choice oil",

453b. that thou mayest rejoice in it, in this its name of "willow-tree",

454a. that thou mayest sparkle thereby among the gods, in this its name of "that which sparkles", (or, "*ṯḥnw.t*-oil"),

454b. that thou mayest be pleased with it in this its name of "oil of pleasure", (or, "*ḥkn.w*-oil").

454c. (Then) will the *Rnn-wt.t*-serpent love thee.

455a. Stand there, great reed-float, like *Wp-wȝ.wt*,

455b. filled with thy splendour, come forth from the horizon,

455c. after thou hast taken possession of the white crown in the water-springs, great and mighty, which are in the south of Libya,

456a. (like) Sebek, lord of *Bȝḥ.w*.

456b. Thou journeyest to thy fields, thou passest through thy *kśb.t*-woods,

456c. thy nose breathes the fragrance of the *Śsmt.t*-land.

456d. Thou causest the *ka* of N. to approach his side,

456e. like as thy Wig (deified) approaches thee.

457a. Purify N., make N. bright

457b. in this thy jackal-lake, O jackal, where thou purifiest the gods.

457c. Thou art become a soul, thou art become pre-eminent (sharp), (like.) Horus lord of the green-stone————(to say) four times————(like) the two green falcons.

Utterance 302.

458a. To say: Heaven is serene (?); Sothis lives, for it is N. who lives, the son of Sothis.

458b. The Two Enneads have purified themselves for him

458c. as (in the form of) the *mśḥtiw*-hook-star, the imperishable.

458d. The house of N. in heaven will not go under, the throne of N. on earth will never be destroyed.

459a. Men bury themselves (in their grave (?); the gods fly up.

449b. Sothis caused N. to fly to heaven among his brothers the gods.

449c. Nut, the great, uncovered her arms for N.

460a. The two souls who are at the head of the souls of Heliopolis, who genuflected at sun-rise,

460b. passed the night, while they did this, weeping for the god.

460c. The throne of N. is by thee, O Rç'; he will not give it to anyone else.

461a. N. ascends to heaven, to thee, O Rç';

461b. the face of N. is as (that of) falcons;

461c. the wings of N. are as (those of) geese;

461d. his claws are as the fangs of the god of the *Dw.f*-nome.

462a. There is not a word among men on earth against N.;

462b. there is no condemnation of him among the gods in heaven.

462c. N. has removed the word against him; N. has destroyed (it) so as to mount up to heaven.

463a. *Wp-w3.wt* has caused N. to fly to heaven among his brothers, the gods.

463b. N. moved (flapped) his arms like a *śmn*-goose;

463c. N. flaps his wings like a kite.

463d. He flies who flies, O men; N. also flies away from you.

Utterance 303.

464a. To say: Gods of the West, gods of the East, gods of the South, gods of the North————

464b. these four pure reed-floats, which ye placed for Osiris,

464c. for his ascension to heaven,

465a. that he might ferry over to *ḳbḥ.w*, while his son Horus was at hand (at his fingers),

465b. (whom) he reared and whom he caused to dawn as a great god in *ḳbḥ.w*,

465c. place them for N.

466a. Art thou Horus, son of Osiris? Art thou, O N., the god, the eldest, son of Hathor?

466b. Art thou the seed of Geb?

467a. Osiris has ordained that N. dawn as a second Horus.

467b. Those four souls (spirits), who are in Heliopolis, have written it

467c. in the register of the two Great Gods who are in *ḳbḥ.w*.

Utterance 304.

468a. To say: Greetings to thee, O daughter of Anubis, who is at the windows, of heaven,

468b. thou friend of Thot, who is at the double rail (end) of the ladder.

468c. Open the way for N., that N. may pass.

469a. Greetings to thee, O ostrich, who is on the shore of the Winding Watercourse.

469b. Open the way for N., that N. may pass.

470a. Greetings to thee, O ox of Rꜥ', with four horns,

470b. thy horn in the West, thy horn in the East, thy horn in the South, thy horn in the North.

470c. Incline thy western horn for N., that N. may pass.

47m. Art thou a pure westerner? I come from the falcon city.

471b. Greetings to thee, O Marsh of my Offerings (or, O Marsh of my Peace);

471c. greetings to the honourable ones (dead?) who are in thee. N. will honour those who are there.

471d. Comfortable are the pure who are in me.

Utterance 305.

472a. To say: The ladder is fastened by Rꜥ' in the presence of Osiris;

472b. the ladder is fastened by Horus in the presence of his father Osiris,

472c. as he goes to his ꜣḥ (spirit).

472d. One of them is on this side, one of them is on this side, while N. is between them.

473a. Art thou then a god, pure in dwellings (places)? (I am) come from a pure (place).

473b. Stand (here), O N., says Horus; sit (here), O N., says Set;

473c. Take his arm (certificate), says Rꜥ'.

474a. The spirit belongs to heaven; the body belongs to the earth.

474b. That which men receive when they are buried

474c. are their thousand loaves of bread, their thousand mugs of beer from the offering-table of Ḥnti-'imnti.w.

475a. If the heir is poor because he has no testament,

475b. then shall N. (really, "he") write with his great finger;

475c. but he shall not write with his little finger,

Utterance 306.

476a. To say: "How beautiful indeed is the sight, how pleasant indeed is the view," say they, say the gods,

476b. "'the ascension of this god to heaven, the ascension of N. to heaven,

477a. his renown over him, his terror on both sides of him,

477b. his magic preceding him!'"

477c. Geb has done for him as was done for himself; (and)

478a. the gods, the Souls of Buto come to him, (and) the gods, the Souls of Hierakonpolis, the gods who are in heaven, the gods who are on the earth;

478b. they make for thee (they serve thee as), N., supports of their arms,

479a. and thou ascendest, N., to heaven, and thou climbest on it in this its name of "ladder."

479b. "Let heaven be given to N.; let the earth be given to him," said Atum.

480a. He who had spoken (with Atum) about it was Geb.

480b. The regions of the kingdom, the kingdom of Horus, the kingdom of Set, (and)

480c. the Marshes of Reeds, they adore thee

480d. in this thy name of *Dw3.m*, as Sopdu, (who lives) under his *kšb. t-*trees.

481a. Has he killed thee after his heart had said that thou shouldst die for him?

481b. But, behold, thou for thy part become in spite of him as the remaining bull of the wild-bulls.

481c. There remains, there remains the remaining bull,

481d. (so) thou art remaining, O N., as their chief, as chief of the spirits, eternally.

Utterance 307.

482a. To say: A Heliopolitan is in N., O god; a Heliopolitan as thou (art) is in N. O god;

482b. a Heliopolitan is in N., O Rç'; a Heliopolitan as thou (art) is in N. O Rç'.

482c. The mother of N. is a Heliopolitan; the father of N. is a Heliopolitan.

483a. N. himself is a Heliopolitan, who was born in Heliopolis,

483b. when Rç' ruled the Two Enneads, (when) Nefertem ruled men,

483c. (as) one without an equal, the heir of his father Geb.

484a. Any god who puts out his arm (menacingly),

484b. when the face of N. turns to thee to adore thee,

484c. (and) when N. calls to thee on behalf of his person, O god, on behalf of his nose, O god,

484d. he shall have no bread, he shall have no cake among his brothers, the gods;

485a. he shall send no message, he shall not cover in heat among his brothers, the gods;

485b. the double doors of the *mśkt.t*-boat shall not be opened for him, the double doors of the *m'nd.t*-boat shall not be opened for him;

485c. his speech shall not be judged as (that of one) in his city; the double doors of the destroyer ("Hell") shall not be open (again) for him.

486a. N. comes to thee.

486b. N. is the wild-bull of the highlands, the bull with the large head, which comes from Heliopolis.

486c. N., wild-bull of the highlands, comes to thee.

486d. Henceforth N. is he who has given birth to thee and who gives birth to thee.

Utterance 308.

487a. To say: Greetings to thee, O Horus, in the regions of Horus;

487b. greetings to thee, O Set, in the regions of Set;

487c. greetings to thee, O * Iȝr.w*, in the Marshes of Reeds;

488a. greetings to you, ye two harmonius (goddesses), daughters of the four gods, who dwell in the great palace (Heliopolis),

488b. ye who are come forth at the voice of N., naked.

489a. N. has looked to you, as Horus looked to Isis;

489b. N. has looked to you, as the *Nḥb.w-kȝ.w* (serpent) looked to *Śrḳ.t-ḥtw*,

489c. N. has looked to you, as Sebek looked to Neit;

489d. N. has looked to you, as Set looked to the two harmonius (goddesses).

Utterance 309.

490a. To say: N. is the *dḥȝ.i* of the gods, who is behind the house of Rç',

490b. born of the wish of the gods, which is in the prow of the boat of Rç'.

490c. N. sits before him;

491a. N. opens his boxes; N. breaks open his edicts;

491b. N. seals his rolls (of papyrus);

491c. N. sends forth his messengers, the indefatigables.

491d. N. does, that which he (Rç') says to N.

Utterance 310.

492a. To say: If N. should be bewitched, so will Atum be bewitched.

492b. If N. should be slandered, so will Atum be slandered.

492c. If N. should be beaten, so will Atum be beaten.

492d. If N. should be hindered on this road, so will Atum be hindered.

493a. N, is Horus. N. comes after his father (in time); N. comes after Osiris.

493b. O thou, whose face is before him, whose face is behind him,

494a. bring this (boat) to N. Which boat shall I bring to thee, O N.?

494b. Bring to N. that which flies up and alights.

Utterance 311.

495a. To say: Look at N., O Rç'; recognize N., O Rç'.

495b. He belongs to those who know thee. He knows (that)

495c. when his lord (Rç') goes forth, he should not forget the *ḥtp-di*,

496a. so that she "who excludes whom she will exclude" may open the doors of the horizon for the going forth of the boat of the morning-sun.

496b. (N.) knows the hall of the royal throne, which is in the midst of the platform of *'iskn*, whence thou goest forth,

497a. that thou mayest enter (step down into) the boat of the evening-sun.

497b. Commend N.; commend him, commend him————to say four times one after another————to those four raging ones (winds),

497c. who are around thee (Rç') who see with two faces, who speak with two mouths (?),

498a. who are evil with those who are unfortunate, with those who would destroy them (the winds?),

498b. that they put not out their arm, when N. turns to thee, when N. comes to thee,

499a. as one who says to thee this thy name of "great flood," which proceeds from the great (one).

499b. N. will not be blind when thou leavest him in darkness;

499c. he will not be deaf when he does not hear thy voice.

500a. Mayest thou take N. with thee, with thee;

500b. he who drives away the storm for thee; be who chases off the clouds for thee; he who breaks up the hail for thee.

500c, N. will do homage (upon) homage to thee; he will cause acclamation (upon) acclamation to thee.

500d. Mayest thou set N. over *dt3.t.*

13.
A SERIES OF FIVE CHARMS, UTTERANCES 312-316.

Utterance 312.

501. To say: The bread flies, the bread flies to my houses, the houses of the Lower Egyptian crown.

Utterance 313.

502a. To say: The phallus of *B3-bíí* is drawn; the double doors of heaven are opened.

502b. The double doors of heaven are locked; the way goes over the flames under that which the gods create,

503a. which allows each Horus to glide through, in which N. will glide through, in this flame under that which the gods create.

503b. They make a way for N., that N. may pass by it. N. is a Horus.

Utterance 314.

504a. To say: Back, thou ox, which shall be killed, on whose horns the fingers of the earth-god shall be.

504b. Fall, glide away.

Utterance 315.

505a. It is N., O *'i'n*-ape, O *htt*-ape, O *p3tt*-ape.

505b. The death (?) of N. is upon the desire of N.; the beatitude of N. (has come) on N. (of himself).

505c. N. will do homage, the same homage (which ye do); he will sit among you, O ye $ḥꜣ.tiw$.

Utterance 316.

506a. O $Ḥmi$; O $Šḥd$, N. has not given to you his magic.

506b. N. will sit on the side of him who is revered in Heliopolis.

506c. Take N. with (you) to heaven.

14.

MISCELLANEOUS UTTERANCES ON THE CAREER OF THE DECEASED KING IN THE HEREAFTER, 317-337.

Utterance 317.

507a. To say: N. is come forth today at the head of the inundation of the flood.

507b. N. is a crocodile god, with green feather, with vigilant countenance, with forehead erect;

507c. effervescent, proceeding from leg and tail of the Great (One) who is in splendour.

508a. N. is come to his watercourses, which are in the land of the flood, in *Mḥ.t-wr.t*,

508b. to the places of satisfaction, with green fields, which are in the horizon,

509a. that N. may make green the herbs in both lands of the horizon,

509b. (and) that N. may bring the green to the great eye which is in the midst of the field.

509c. N. takes his throne which is in the horizon;

510a. N. appears as Sebek, son of Neit;

510b. N. eats with his mouth, N. urinates, N. cohabits with his phallus;

510c. N. is lord of semen, which women receive from their husband.

510d. wherever N. wishes, according to the desire of his heart,

Utterance 318.

511a. To say: N. is the *n'w*-serpent, the bull which leadeth, which swallowed its seven uraeus-serpents,

511b. through which came into being its seven neck-vertebrae,

511c. which commands its Seven Enneads who hear the words of the king.

511d. And the mother of N. is *Ḥnw.t*; N. is her son.

512a. N. has come that he may swallow myrrh,

512b. that N. may take myrrh, his nostrils (?) being full of myrrh; the finger-nail of N. being full of myrrh.

512c. N. has taken away your neck, O gods;

512d. Serve N. who will confer (upon you) your valour.

Utterance 319.

513a. To say: N. is the bull of the two splendours which are in the middle of his eye.

513b. The mouth of N. is immune because of a flaming breath, the head of N. because of horns, (as) lord of the South (Haroëris of Ḳuṣ).

513c. N. leads the god; N. rules over the Ennead.

5 1 3d. N. makes the lapis lazuli grow; N. causes the Upper Egyptian *twn*-plant to sprout.

514a. N. has tied the cords of the *šmšm.t*-plant.

514b. N. has united the heavens; N. rules over the lands, the southern and the northern,

514c. (as) the gods who were before.

514d. N. built a divine city, according to its merits.

514e. N. is the third in his dawning.

515a. To say: N. has regulated the night; N. has sent the hours on their
way.
515b. The powers (stars) dawn; they proclaim N. as *B3-bii.*
515c. N. is that son of her who knew not that
515d. she had borne N., to him of powerful visage, as lord of nights.
516a. Humble (?) yourselves, ye lords; hide yourselves, ye subjects, in the
presence of N.,
516b. (for) N. is *B3-bii*, lord of night,
516c. the bull, without whom life would cease.

517a. To say: O Thou-whose-back-is-behind-him, bring to N. the *śfr.t-
ḥtp.t*, which was upon the back of Osiris,
517b. that N. may ascend to heaven upon it; that N. may do service of
courtier to Rç' in heaven.

518a. To say: Heaven is open; earth is open.
518b. The double doors of *ś3t* are open to Horus; the double doors of
ś3 b.wt are open to Set.
518c. Turn thou for him as he who is in his fortress; N. has passed over
you (*ś3b.wt*) as Atum.
518d. N. is Ḫ'ii-t3w, who is (lives?) in the midst of the *Ng3*-mountains.

Utterance 323.

519a. To say: N. has purified himself with Rç' in the sea of reeds.

519b. Horus dries thy skin, O N.; Thot dries thy feet, O N.

519c. Shu, lift N. up on high; Nut, give thine arm to N.

Utterance 324.

520a. To say: Greetings to thee, doorkeeper of Horus, who art at the portal of Osiris,

520b. announce now the name of N. there to Horus,

521a. (for) he is come with temple-saliva for this his temple (of the head),

521b. which is painful at the [beginning] of the months, which becomes bald at the beginning of half months.

521c. Wilt thou cool it with the magic, [which thou didst make for the Great One] among the gods,

521d. in his former state, which is come upon him?

522a. Greetings to thee, O hippopotamus, from everlasting.

522b. [Art] thou [come] to N. as hippopotamus from everlasting,

522c. after he had brandished one of the two *3mś*-clubs of Horus against thee and slain thee therewith?

522d. Greetings to thee in his former state, which is come upon him.

523a. Greetings to thee, [braying] ass.

523b. Art thou come to N. as a braying ass,

523c. after he had slain thee with the————tail, [which grows] in the sea of Osiris?

524a. Greetings to thee, O Khnum, who was made harmless though he built N.

524b. Thou art his *'m'*-plant, which his foot [trod upon],

524c. which cannot straighten up under his toes.

524d. Thou art one of the two *'iwn*-pillars of the great palace.

525a. To say: The double doors of heaven are open; the double doors of
ḳbḥ.w are open

525b. for Horus of the gods, at daybreak,

525c. that he may ascend in the Marsh of Reeds and purify himself in the
Marsh of Reeds.

526a. The double doors of heaven are open; the double doors of ḳbḥ.w
are open

526b. for Harachte at daybreak,

526c. that he may ascend in the Marsh of Reeds and purify himself in the
Marsh of Reeds.

527a. The double doors of heaven are open; the double doors of ḳbḥ.w
are open

527b. for Horus of the East at daybreak,

527c. that he may ascend in the Marsh of Reeds and purify himself in the
Marsh of Reeds.

528a. The double doors of heaven are open; the double doors of ḳbḥ.w
are open

528b. for Horus of the *Šsm.t*-land at daybreak,

528c. that he may ascend in the Marsh of Reeds, and purify himself in
the Marsh of Reeds.

529a. The double doors of heaven are open; the double doors of ḳbḥ.w
are open

529b. for N. himself at daybreak

529c. that he may ascend in the Marsh of Reeds and purify himself in the
Marsh of Reeds.

530a. N. is clean; he takes his lasting (copper?) bones;

530b. he has stretched out his imperishable limbs, which were (or, are) in
the body of his mother Nut.

531a. Rç', give thine arm to N.

531b. Shu will draw him up to the "Companions of Shu,"

531c. after he has caused N. to be nourished with the milk of two black cows, the two nurses of the Souls of Heliopolis.

532a. O *Ḥpзt*, it is grievous for the body of Nut, because of the fury of the divine seed, which shall be in her.

532b. Behold also N.————N. is a divine seed which shall be in her.

533a. *Ḥpзt, Hnn, Smnn.w*,

533b. N. is purified. He has taken his divine *śwḥ*-vestment,

533c. that N. may establish himself there as a god like them.

533d. *Ḥpзt, Hnn, Smnn.w*,

533e. Take N. away; let him remain with you.

Utterance 326.

534a. To say: Collar, beloved of Horus, good-looking, which is on the neck of Rç'.

534b. If thou goest to heaven; so will N. go to heaven.

Utterance 327.

535a. To say: The messenger of Horus, whom he loves, was N., who has brought back to him his eye.

535b. The messenger of Set, whom he loves, was N., who has brought back to him his testicles.

535c. The messenger of Thot, whom he loves, was N., who has brought back to him his arm.

536a. The Two Enneads tremble for themselves,

536b. for they are the messengers, whom N. loves, who should bring N. to food.

536c. They bring N. to food.

Utterance 328.

537a. To say: N. is the exalted, who is in the forefront, who lifts up the brow;

537b. the star before which the gods bow, before which the Two Enneads tremble.

537c. It is the hand of N. which will lift him (N.) up.

Utterance 329.

538a. N. is the exalted, who is in the forefront; who lifts up the brow;

538b. the star before which the gods bow, before which the Two Enneads tremble.

538c. The face of N. is the face which sees his elevation.

538d. N. is a nose which breathes.

Utterance 330.

539a. To say: N. ascends to heaven on (or, above, or, through) the *šdšd*, which was at the separation,

539b. after its (the heaven's) sole (of the foot) was seized by the up-reached hand.

Utterance 331.

540a. To say: N. ascends to heaven on the *šdšd*, which was at the separation,

540b. after its sole (of the foot) was seized.

540c. N. is a nose which breathes;

540d. the face of N. is the face which sees his elevation.

Utterance 332.

541a. To say: this N. is he who comes forth from the *mḥn*-jar.

541b. N. has ascended as his warm breath and has returned.

541c. N. has gone, O heaven, O heaven; N. has returned, O earth, O earth.

541d. N. has walked upon the green *k3d*-herb under the feet of Geb;

541e. he treads (again) upon the paths of Nut.

Utterance 333.

542a. To say: N. purified himself upon that appearing (-mound) of the earth, on which Rç' purified himself;

542b. he placed a *ḥb-'ib*-stand and he set up the ladder.

542c. Those who are in the great (heaven), they will take the arm of N.

Utterance 334.

543a. To say: Greetings to thee, O Rç', traverser of heaven, voyager through Nut.

543b. Thou hast traversed the Winding Watercourse.

543c. N. has grasped thy tail; as to N., he is indeed a god, the son of a god.

544a. N. is a flower, which comes out of the *ka*,

544b. a golden flower, which comes out of *Ntr.w*.

544c. N. has traversed Buto; he has voyaged through *Knm.wt*.

545a. N. has traversed Buto as *Hrti*, ruler of *Nš3.t*.

545b. He has voyaged through *Knm.wt* as *Šsm.w*, who is in his ship of the oil-press. May the god be pleased

545c. that N. live as *Ftk.t* lives!

Utterance 335.

546a. To say: How beautiful is, the sight of N., adorned with the horns of Rç',

546b. his apron on him like Hathor, his feather like the feather of a falcon,

546c. when (or, as) he ascends to heaven among his brothers, the gods!

Utterance 336.

547a. To say: Greeting to thee, ox of the oxen, when thou makest the ascension.

547b. N. seizes thee by thy tail; N. takes thee by thy buttocks.

547c. When thou makest the ascension, a Great One is behind thee, a Great One is before thee.

548a. Greetings to thee, Great One among the gods, take N. to thee, he belongs to thee.

548b. Thy heart is whole; as to the parts of the corpse of N., they are young.

Utterance 337.

549a. To say: Heaven speaks, the earth quakes on account of thy fear, Osiris,

549b. when thou makest the ascension.

550a. O ye milk-cows there, O ye nurse-cows there,

550b. go around him, weep for him, praise him, lament for him,

550c. when he makes the ascension. He goes forth to heaven among his brothers, the gods.

15.

OFFERINGS FOR THE DECEASED KING, UTTERANCES 338-349.

Utterance 338.

551 a. To say: Hunger, come not to N.,

551b. go away to Nun, be off (begging) to the *ꜣgbi*-flood.

551c. N. is sated;

551d. N. hungers not by reason of that bread of Horus which he has eaten,

551e. which his head-maid made for him, with which he is satisfied, (and) whereby he wins back his (normal) condition.

552a. N. thirsts not by reason of Shu; N. hungers not by reason of Tefnut.

552b. *Ḥpi, Dwꜣ-mw.t.f, Ḳbḥ-śn.w.f, ꞌImś.ti,*

552c. they will expel this hunger, which is in the body of N.,

552d. and this thirst which is on the lips of N.

Utterance 339.

553a. To say: The hunger of N. is from the hand of Shu; the thirst of N. is from the hand of Tefnut.

553b. N. lives on the morning bread, which comes at its (appointed) time.

553c. N. lives on that on which Shu lives;

553d. N. eats, that which Tefnut eats.

176

Utterance 340.

554a. N. comes to thee, *Nḥḥ*;

554b. mayest thou fall back before N., as the east wind falls back before (behind?) the west wind;

554c. mayest thou come behind N., as the north wind comes behind the south wind.

554d. To say: Deposit (an offering?).

Utterance 341.

555a. To say: The face of Horus is opened by *ȝkr*, the face of *ȝkr* is opened by Horus.

555b. Abundance has extended her arm to N.;

555c. The arms of N. have embraced fowling.

555d. All which the marsh produces belongs to her son, *Ḥȝb*.

555e. N. has eaten with him today.

Utterance 342.

556a. To say: It is N., O Isis; it is N., O *ȝšb.t*; it is N., O Nephthys.

556b. Come, see thy son.

556c. He has passed through the nome of Athribis, after he has passed through the (region of the) *wrr.t*-crown.

557a. The handbag of N. is of *twn*-plant;

557c. N. comes; he brings what is desired and what is given.

557b. the basket of N. is of *nn.t*-plant.

Utterance 343.

558a. To say: *Bdš.t* comes; the fire-pan burns.

558b. Those with (ready) hands stand to give an offering to N.

Utterance 344.

559a. To say: Greetings to thee, O Great Flood (*3gb-wr*),

559b. cup-bearer of the gods, leader of men,

559c. mayest thou make men and gods favourable to N., that they may give an offering to him.

Utterance 345.

560a. To say: O *Wr-k3.f*,

560b. cup-bearer of Horus, chief of the dining-pavillion of Rç', chef of Ptaḥ,

560c. give generously to N.; N. eats as much as thou givest.

Utterance 346.

561a. To say: Kas are in Buto; *kas* were in Buto as of old.

561b. Kas will be in Buto; the *ka* of N. is in Buto,

561c. red as a flame, living as Khepri.

561d. Be cheerful, be cheerful. A meal (fit) for butchers.

562a. It is now thou givest, my lady, love to N., veneration to N.;

562b. it is now thou givest, my lady, veneration to N., liking to N.,

562c. in the body of all gods.

Utterance 347.

563a. To say: The mouth of N. is in incense; the lips of N. are in myrrh.

563b. Descend, O N., from the field of thy *ka* to the Marsh of Offerings.

563c. of N. is from the *n'r.t*; the meal of N. is like (that of) the divine boat.

564a. The life of N. will be more than that of *Rnp.t*; the food of N. will be more than (that of) *Ḥpi* (the inundation).

564b. O *ka* of N., bring (food) that N. may eat with thee.

Utterance 348.

565a. To say: Greeting to thee, O Great Flood,

565b. cup-bearer of the gods, leader of men,

565c. mayest thou make the gods favourable to N., that they may refresh N.,

565d. that they may love N., that they may render N. well.

Utterance 349.

566a. To say: O *Wr-k3.f.*

566b. cup-bearer of Horus, chief of the dining-pavillion of Rç', chef of Ptah,

566c. give generously to N.; N. eats as much as thou givest, a generous portion of his meat.

16.
MISCELLANEOUS UTTERANCES ON THE HEREAFTER, 350-374.

Utterance 350.

567a. To say: O thou who stridest very wide,
567b. as she sows the emerald, the malachite, the turquoise (as) stars,
567c. if thou art green (well), N. will be green, green as living plants (?).

Utterance 351.

568a. To say: A vulture is become pregnant with N. in the night;
568b. (he is) on thy horn, O pregnant cow.
568c. If thou art green (well), N. will be green, green as living plants (?).

Utterance 352.

569a. To say: A vulture has become pregnant with N. in the night;
569b. (he is) on thy horn, O pregnant cow.
569c. (He is) thy papyrus-sprout, green as the turquoise of stars; thy green papyrus-sprout is N.
569d. (He is) green as living plants (?); N. is green with thee.

Utterance 353.

570. To say: N. has come out of Buto, red as fire, living as Khepri.

Utterance 354.

571a. To say: An offering of the butcher; an offering of the cupbearer, ['iwn-nw.t.f];

571b. [cup-bearer], bring the water———

Utterance 355.

572a. The double doors of heaven open.

572b. O N.,

572c. thy head is joined for thee to thy bones; thy bones are joined for thee to thy head.

572d. The double doors of heaven are open for thee; the great bolts are drawn back for thee;

572e. a brick is drawn out of the great tomb for thee.

573a. Thy face is that of a jackal; thy tail is that of a lion;

573b. thou sittest upon this thy throne; thou commandest the spirits.

573c. Thou comest to me, thou comest to me, thou comest indeed to me,

573d. like (to) Horus after he had avenged his father, Osiris.

574a. I am thine Anubis-priest.

574b. Thou puttest thy hand on the land; thy warrior-arm is over the great region,

574c. wherein thou goest (or, passest through) among the spirits.

574d. Rise, lift up thyself like Osiris.

Utterance 356.

575a. To say: O Osiris N., Horus has come that he may seek thee.

575b. He has caused that Thot turn back for thee the Followers of Set,

575c. and that he bring them to thee all together.

576a. He has made the heart of Set timid. Thou art greater (or, elder) than he;

576b. thou didst come forth (from the womb) before him; thy qualifications are better than his.

576f. Geb has seen thy qualifications; he has put thee in thy place.

577a. Geb has brought to thee thy two sisters, to thy side, Isis and Nephthys.

577b. Horus has caused the gods to unite with thee,

577c. to fraternize with thee in thy name of "He of the two *śnw.t-* palaces,"

577d. but not to reject thee in thy name of "He of the two *'itr.t-* palaces."

578a. He has caused the gods to avenge thee.

578b. Geb has put the sole of his foot on the head of thine enemy, who is afraid of thee.

578c. Thy son Horus has smitten him;

578d. he has snatched back his eye from him; he has given it to thee,

579a. that thou mayest become glorious thereby, that thou mayest become mighty before the spirits.

579b. Horus has caused thee to seize thine enemy, that there should be none escaping among them from thee.

580a. Horus was indeed ingenious in that be recognized in thee his father, in thy name of *b3-'iti-rp.t.*

580b. Nut has established thee as god, in spite of Set, in thy name of "god";

580c. thy mother Nut has, spread herself over thee in her name of "She of *Št-p.t.*"

581a. Horus has seized Set; he has placed him under thee

581b. that be may carry thee and that he may quake under thee like the quaking of the earth,

581c. for thou art more exalted than he, in thy name of "He of the exalted land."

582a. Horus has caused that thou recognize him (Set) in himself without his getting away from thee;

582b. he has caused that thou seize him with thy hand without his escaping from thee.

582c. O Osiris N., Horus has avenged thee;

582d. he has done (it) for his *ka* in thee, that thou mayest be satisfied in thy name of "Satisfied *ka*."

Utterance 357.

583a. To say by Horus: May Geb make an offering to Osiris N., O Osiris N.,

583b. Geb has given to thee thy two eyes that thou mayest be satisfied. Take in thee the two eyes of this Great One.

583c. Geb has caused Horus to give them to thee that thou mayest be satisfied with them.

584a. Isis and Nephthys have seen thee; they have found thee.

584b. Horus has taken care of thee; Horus has caused Isis and Nephthys to protect thee.

584c. They have given thee to Horus that he may be satisfied with thee.

585a. It is pleasing to Horus (to be) with thee in thy name of "He of the horizon, whence Rç' goes forth,"

585b. in thine arms in thy name of "He from within the palace."

585c. Thou hast closed thine arms about him, about him,

585d. so that his bones stretch and he become proud.

586a. O Osiris N., betake thyself to Horus,

586b. approach thyself to him, do not go far from him.

587a. Horus has come, he recognizes thee;

587b. he has smitten (and) bound Set for thee, for thou art his *ka*.

587c. Horus has made him afraid of thee, for thou art greater than he;

588a. he swims under thee; he carries in thee one greater than he.

588b. His followers have noticed thee how thy strength is greater

588c. so that they dare not resist thee. than his,

589a. Horus comes; he recognizes his father in thee, for thou art young in thy name of "He of the fresh water."

589b. Horus has opened for thee thy mouth.

590a. O Osiris N., be not in distress, groan not.

590b. Geb has brought Horus to thee, that he may count for thee their hearts.

590c. He has brought to thee all the gods together; there is not one among them who escapes him.

591a. Horus has avenged thee; it was not long till he avenged thee.

591b. Horus has snatched back his eye from Set; he has given it to thee.

591c. This his eye, the sweet one, cause it to stay with thee, reclaim it for thyself. O may it be pleasing to thee.

592a. Isis has taken care of thee.

592b. The heart of Horus is glad because of thee in thy name of "He who is First of the Westerners."

592c. It is Horus who will avenge what Set has done to thee.

Utterance 358.

593a. To say: N. thou art the eldest (son) of Shu.

593b. Thy fetters are loosed by the two lords of Nun.

Utterance 359.

594a. To say: Horus has moaned because of his eye; Set has moaned because of his testicles.

594b. The eye of Horus sprang up as he fell on yonder side of the Winding Watercourse,

594c. to protect itself against (or, free itself from) Set.

594d. Thot saw it on yonder side of the Winding Watercourse.

594e. The eye of Horus sprang up on yonder side of the Winding Watercourse,

594f. and fell upon the wing of Thot on yonder side of the Winding Watercourse.

595a. O ye gods, ye who ferry over on the wing of Thot

595b. to yonder side of the Winding Watercourse, to the eastern side of heaven,

595c. to speak with Set about that eye of Horus,

596a. may N. ferry over with you on the wing of Thot

596b. to yonder side of the Winding Watercourse, to the eastern side of heaven,

596c. that he, N., may speak with Set about that eye of Horus.

597a. Mayest thou awake in peace, thou "face-behind", in peace;

597b. mayest thou awake in peace, thou who art within Nut, in peace, ferryman of the Winding Watercourse.

597c. Speak the name of N. to Rç'; announce N. to Rç'.

598a. N. is on the way to yonder far-off palace of the lords of *kas*,

598b. where Rç' is adored in the morning in the regions of Horus and in the regions of Set,

598c. as the god of those who are gone to their *kas*.

599a. Rç' recommends N. to the "face-behind," the ferryman of the Winding Watercourse,

599b. that he may bring to N. that ferry of the Winding Watercourse,

599c. in which he ferries the gods

599d. to yonder side of the Winding Watercourse, to the eastern side of heaven,

600a. and ferry N.

600b. to yonder side of the Winding Watercourse, to the eastern side of heaven.

600e. N. is in search of the eye of Horus which is injured.

601a. N. is on the way to the numbering of fingers.

601b. The face of N. is washed by the gods, male as well as female;

601c. '*Imś.ti, Ḥp.wi, Dwȝ-mu.t.f, Ḳbḥ-śn.w.f*,

601d. at the right side of N., which is Horus,

601e. *Ḥw-dndr.w, Ḫnti-wȝd.wi.f*, Nephthys, *Mḫnti-n-'irti*,

601f. at the left side of N., which is Set.

602a. N. is known by his seat; his helm remembers him.

602b. N. has found his seat empty,

602c. in the bottom (hold) of the boat of gold, of Rç'.

Utterance 360.

603a. To say: O lofty one, which is not sharpened (rubbed, or touched), thou Gate of Nut,

603b. N. is Shu who came forth from Atum.

603c. Nun (Nw), cause this (gate) to be opened for N.;

603d. behold, N. comes; he is spiritual (i.e. "soul-like"), he is divine.

Utterance 361.

604a. To say: Nun has recommended N. to Atum.

604b. *Pgȝ* has recommended N. to Shu,

604c. that he may cause those double doors of heaven to be opened for N., in spite of men,

604d. who have no name (or, because they have no name).

604e. Seize N. by his arm; take N. to heaven,

604f. that he die not on earth among men.

Utterance 362.

605a. To say: Father of N., father of N. in darkness,

605b. father of N., Atum, in darkness, bring N. to thy side,

606a. that he may kindle the light for thee and protect thee,

606b. as Nun protected these four goddesses,

606c. the day they protected the throne (bed
606d. Isis, Nephthys, Neit, *Śrḳt-ḥtw*.

Utterance 363.

607a. To say: Way of Horus,
607b. make ready thy tent for N., make ready thy arms for N.
607c. Rç' comes, ferry N. over to yonder side,
607d. as thou ferriest thy follower over, the *wng*-plant, which thou lovest.
608a. If thou stretchest out thine arm towards the West, so wilt thou stretch out thine arm to N.;
608b. if thou stretchest out thine arm toward the East, so wilt thou stretch out thine arm to N.,
608c. as that which thou hast done to the *bnti* (-ape), thine eldest son.

Utterance 364.

609a. To say: O Osiris N., arise.
609b. Horus comes; he reclaims thee from the gods. Horus has loved thee,
609c. he has equipped thee with his eye; Horus has adapted to thee his eye.
610a. Horus has opened for thee thine eye that thou mayest see with it.
610b. The gods have bound to thee thy face; they have loved thee.
610c. Isis and Nephthys have healed thee.
610d. Horus is not far from thee; thou art his *ka*.
611a. Thy face is gracious unto him; hasten, accept the word of Horus and be satisfied with it.
611b. Hearken unto Horus, it will not be harmful to thee; he has caused the gods to follow thee.

612a. Osiris N., awake. Geb has brought Horus to thee, and he recognizes thee;

612b. Horus has found thee; he rejoices over thee.

613a. Horus has caused the gods to ascend to thee; he has given them to thee that they may illuminate thy face (cheer thee).

613b. Horus has placed thee at the head of the gods; he has caused thee to take the *wrr.t*-crown, the lady.

613c. Horus has accustomed himself to thee; he cannot part from thee.

64a. Horus has caused thee to live in this thy name of '*nd.ti*.

614b. Horus has given thee his eye, the hard (one);

614c. (he) has placed it to thee (i.e. in thy hand), that thou mayest be strong, and that all thine enemies may fear thee.

614d. Horus has completely filled thee with his eye, in this its name of "Fullness of god."

615a. Horus has corralled the gods for thee,

615b. so that they cannot get away from thee, from the place where thou hast gone.

615c. Horus has counted the gods for thee,

615d. so that they cannot get away from thee, from the place where thou wast drowned.

616a. Nephthys has assembled for thee all thy limbs,

616b. in her name of "*ŚŚ3.t*, lady of builders."

616c. She has made them well for thee.

616d. Thou art given over to thy mother Nut, in her name of "Grave";

616e. she has embraced thee, in her name of "Grave";

616f. thou art brought to her, in her name of Maṣṭaba."

617a. Horus has united for thee thy limbs and does not allow thee to be sick;

617b. he has put thee together, so that there is no disorder in thee (or, without anything being disordered in thee).

617c. Horus has set thee up without staggering.

618a. O Osiris N., let thy heart be glad for him (Horus); thy heart is great, thy mouth is opened.

618b. Horus has avenged thee; it was not long till he avenged thee.

619a. O Osiris N., thou art the mightiest god; there is no god like thee.

619b. Horus has given to thee his children, that they may carry thee;

620a. he has given to thee all gods that they may follow thee and that thou mayest have power over them.

620b. Horus has set thee up, in his name of "Ḥnw-boat"

620c. he carries thee, in thy name of "Seker."

621a. Thou livest; thou movest every day;

621b. thou art glorious, in thy name of "Horizon whence Rꞓ' goes forth";

621c. thou art honoured, thou art pre-eminent, thou art a soul, thou art mighty for ever and ever.

Utterance 365.

622a. To say: Lift thyself up N., hurry, thou great of power;

622b. sit at the head of the gods and do what Osiris did in the princely house, which is in Heliopolis,

622c. after thou hast received thy dignity.

622d. Thy foot (step) will not be hindered in heaven; thou shalt not be restrained on earth,

623a. for thou art verily a spirit, born of Nut, nursed by Nephthys;

623b. they unite with thee.

623c. Thou shalt stand in thy place, that thou mayest do what thou wast accustomed to do before.

624a. Thou shalt be spirit more than all spirits.

624b. Thou goest to Buto; thou findest him there whom thou hast to resist;

624c. thou comest to Hierakonpolis; thou findest him there whom thou hast to resist.

625a. Thou doest what Osiris does, for thou art he who is on his throne,

625b. who stands there (as) this great and mighty spirit, N., bedecked as the great wild-bull.

625c. Thou wilt not be resisted at any place where thou goest;

625d. thy foot will not be hindered at any place where thou desirest (to be).

Utterance 366.

626a. To say: O Osiris N., stand up, lift thyself up;

626b. thy mother Nut has brought thee forth; Geb has wiped thy mouth for thee.

626c. The Great Ennead avenge thee;

626d. they put for thee thine enemy under thee.

627a. Carry thou (him who is) greater than thou, said they to him, in thy name of "He of the Great Saw Palace."

627b. Lift (him up who is) greater than thou, said they, in thy name of "He of the Great Land Nome."

628a. Thy two sisters Isis and Nephthys come to thee; they heal thee

628b. complete and great, in thy name of "Great Black,"

628c. fresh and great, in thy name of "Great Green."

629a. Behold, thou art great and round like the "Great Round";

629b. behold, thou are bent around, and art round like the "Circle which encircles the *nb.wt*";

629c. behold, thou art round and great like the "Great Circle which sets."

630a. Isis and Nephthys protected thee in Siût,

630b. even their lord in thee, in thy name of "Lord of Siût";

630c. even their god in thee, in thy name of "God."

631 a. They adore thee, so that thou shalt not (again) withdraw from them, in thy name of "*Dw3-ntr*" (or, "divine *Dw3*");

631b. they take care of thee, so that thou mayest not (again) be angry, in thy name of "*Dndr.w*-boat."

632a. Thy sister comes to thee, rejoicing for love of thee.

632b. Thou hast placed her on thy phallus,

632c. that thy seed may go into her, (while) it is pointed like Sothis.

632d. Horus the pointed has come forth from thee as Horus who was in Sothis.

633a. Thou art pleased with him, in his name of "Spirit who was in the *Dndr.w*-boat";

633b. he avenges thee, in his name of "Horus, the son, who avenges his father."

Utterance 367.

634a. To say: O Osiris N., Geb has brought Horus to thee that he may avenge thee

634b. and bring the hearts of the gods to thee,

634c. that thou mayest not be in need, that thou mayest not groan.

634d. Horus has given his eye to thee, that thou mayest take by it the *wrr.t*-crown before the gods (i.e. as chief of the gods).

635a. Horus has collected thy limbs for thee; he has put thee together,

635b. without any disorder in thee (or, without anything being disordered in thee).

635c. Thot has seized thine enemy for thee; so that he is beheaded with his followers;

635d. there is not one whom he has spared.

Utterance 368.

636a. To say: O Osiris N., this is Horus who is in thine arms;

636b. he will avenge thee.

636c. It is pleasing to him to be again with thee, in thy name of "He of the horizon whence Rç' goes forth."

636d. Thou hast closed thine arms round and round him;, he will not depart from thee.

637a. Horus does not allow thee to be sick; Horus, has placed thine enemy under thy feet,

637b. that thou mayest live. Horus has given his children to thee,

637c. that they may put themselves under thee, without one of them withdrawing, and that they may carry thee.

638d. Thy mother Nut has spread herself over thee, in her name of "She of *Št-p.ł*";

638b. she has caused thee to be as a god, in spite of thee, in thy name of "God",

638c. she protects thee against all evil things, in her name of "Great Sieve" (protectress).

638d. Thou art the greatest among her children.

639a. Geb is satisfied with thee; he has loved thee; he has protected thee;

639b. he has given (back) to thee thy head; he has caused Thot to take care of thee, so that what was against thee ceased.

Utterance 369.

640a. To say: O Osiris N., stand up. Horus has caused thee to stand up.

640b. Geb has caused Horus to see his father in thee, in thy name of "He of the royal castle."

641a. Horus has given the gods to thee; he has brought them to thee, so that they may illuminate thy face.

641b. Horus has given his eye to thee, that thou mayest see with it.

642a. Horus has placed thine enemy under thee,

642b. that he may carry thee, that thou be not far from him,

192

642c. and that thou mayest come (again) in thy (former) state. The gods have bound (again) thy face to thee.

643a. Horus has opened thine eye for thee, that thou mayest see with it, in her (the eye) name of "Opener of the way."

643b. Thine enemy is smitten by the children of Horus; they made his smiting red (bloody);

643c. they have punished him; he is severely punished, so that his smell is evil.

644a. Horus has fitted thy mouth to thee; he has adjusted for thee thy mouth to thy bones.

644b. Horus has opened thy mouth for thee;

644c. thy beloved son has re-instated thy two eyes for thee.

644d. Horus does not permit thy face to be without the power to see,

644e. in thy name of "Horus chief of his subjects."

Utterance 370.

645a. To say: O Osiris N., Horus has caused the gods to unite with thee,

645b. to fraternize with thee, in thy name of "He of the two *śnw.t*-palaces."

645c. Betake thyself to Horus, repair to him;

645d. withdraw not thyself from him, in thy name of "He of heaven."

646a. Horus has accustomed himself to thee; he cannot part from thee;

646b. he has caused thee to live.

646c. Hasten, accept his word and be satisfied with it.

646d. Hearken to him; it will not be harmful to thee.

647a. He has brought to thee the gods together; there is not one among them who escapes him.

647b. Horus has accustomed himself to his children; thou hast united thyself with those of his body (his children);

647c. they have loved thee.

647d. Horus has done it for his *ka* in thee, that thou mayest be satisfied, in thy name of "Satisfied *ka*."

Utterance 371.

648a. To say: O Osiris N., Horus has placed thee in the heart of the gods;

648b. he has caused thee to take the white crown, the lady.

648c. Horus has found thee; he rejoices over thee.

648d. Go forth against thine enemy; thou art greater than he, in thy name of "He of the great house, the '*itr.t*-palace."

649a. Horus has caused him to carry thee, in thy name of "Great carried one."

649b. He has delivered thee from thine enemy.

649c. He has avenged thee, as "He who is avenged in his time."

649d. Geb has seen thy character; he has put thee in thy place.

650a. Horus has stretched thine enemy under thee; thou art older than he, for thou wast born before him.

650h. Thou art the father of Horus, who begat him, in thy name of "Bird-begetter."

650c. The heart of Horus is glad because of thee, in thy name of "First of the Westerners."

Utterances 372.

651a. To say: O Osiris N., awake.

651b. Horus has caused Thot to bring thine enemy to thee;

651c. he has placed thee upon his back, so that he dare not resist thee.

651d. Sit down upon him.

652a. Mount; sit upon him, so that he may not escape thee.

652b. Dismount, for thou art mightier than he; do thou evil to him.

653a. Horus has loosed the hips (legs) of thine enemies;

653b. Horus has brought them to thee, cut up.

653c. Horus has chased their *ka* from them.

653d. (So then) thou mayest be powerful by means of that which thy heart will do to them, in thy name of "Powerful over the sea" (as bull god).

Utterance 373.

654a. To say: O, O, raise thyself up, N.;

654b. receive thy head, unite thy bones to thee,

654c. collect thy limbs,

654d. shake the earth (dust of the earth) from thy flesh.

655a. Receive thy bread which cannot mould, thy beer which cannot sour.

655b. Thou standest at the doors, which hold people back.

655c. He who is chief of his department (or, thigh offering) comes out to thee, he lays hold of thine arm,

655d. and takes thee to heaven to thy father Geb.

656a. He rejoices at thy approach; he gives his arm to thee;

656b. he kisses thee; he embraces thee;

656c. he places thee at the head of the spirits, the imperishable stars;

656d. they of secret places adore thee;

656e. the great assemble for thee; the watchers stand before thee.

657a. Barley is threshed for thee; spelt is reaped for thee;

657b. some is offered for the beginning of thy monthly feasts;

657c. some is offered for the beginning of thy half-monthly feasts,

657d. as something commanded to thee to be done by thy father Geb.

657e. Lift thyself up, N., thou shalt not die.

Utterance 374.

658a. To say: Thou art great, N.; thou art ferried over, N.;

658b. thy name is announced to Osiris.

658c. Thy foot (step) is great, thy foot is great, that it may traverse the great couch (sky).

658d. Thou art not seized by 3*kr.w* (earth-gods);

658e. thou art not rejected by the *šḥd.w* (planets).

659a. The two doors of heaven are open for thee, that thou mayest go forth through them,

659b. like Horus, like the jackal, on his side (belly), who concealed his forms from his enemies,

659c. thou who hast no father, among men, who conceived thee;

659d. thou who hast no mother, among mankind, who bore thee.

17.
CONJURATIONS AND CHARMS, UTTERANCES 375-400.

Utterance 375.

660a. To say: N. is he whom TW will protect; N. is he whom *Tšii* will deliver.

660b. Bring thy message, messenger of *Tšii*; bring thy message while it is fresh, messenger of *Tšii*.

660c. Mayest thou not come against N., son of a Great One, (as) a knife which castrates.

Utterance 376.

661a. To say: The knife which castrates!

661b. Brilliant, brilliant; triumphant, triumphant.

661c. Let the seaman cast off his garments (as a sail) for the boat of the sun!

Utterance 377.

662a. To say: Thou shalt land, in thy name of "Fortress";

662b. thou shalt capsize, in thy name of "*Ig3i*,"

662c. for thou art indeed the *Hpi.w*-serpent, which is on his belly,

662d. who lives on the hearts of those gods who are in Heliopolis.

662e. Give way; also, go away.

663a. To say: The uraeus-serpent belongs to heaven; the centipede of Horus belongs in the earth.

663b. It is the sandal (or, sole of the foot) of Horus which has trod upon the (dangerous) serpent,

663c. the serpent (dangerous) for Horus, a young child, his finger in his mouth.

664a. N. is also a Horus, a little child, his finger in his mouth.

664b. If it is dangerous for N., he will tread upon thee (serpent);

664c. be wise for N., so will he not tread upon thee,

665a. for thou art indeed the mysterious, the hidden, as the gods call thee,

665b. because thou hast no legs, because thou hast no arms,

665c. with which thou mayest go in the following of thy brothers, thy gods.

666a. O ye both who are unlucky, O ye both who are unlucky; O ye both who arise, O ye both who arise,

666b. ye who make the *mti*-knot of the god, protect N. that he may protect you.

Utterance 379.

667. To say: Thy water is in heaven; thy thousands are on earth; O 'išii-ḥꜣ!

Utterance 380.

668a. To say: Doer, doer; passer, passer;

668b. thy foot, behind thee; guard thyself against the "great Great,"

669a. To say: The great centipede descends after he has charmed the householder;

669b. the householder is charmed by the centipede.

Utterance 382.

670a. To say: *Ỉkr.w*-serpent or *'ỉkr.t*-serpent, go away from N. who is in the *d"miw.*

670b. Horus circulates behind his eye.

670c. Reverse-serpent, make ruin (in) the earth (decay (in) the earth).

Utterance 383.

671a. To say: *Tt.w*-serpent, *tt.w*-serpent, where to?, where wilt thou go?

671b. Stand by N.; he is the *d"miw*, should thy father, the *d"miw*, die?

671c. A servant (holy person), who belonged to the Ennead (pelican), (once) fell into this Nile. Thou who art in *hpnn*, come here.

Utterance 384.

672a. To say: This hand of N., which is come against thee,

672b. is the hand of *tt.t*, the great, who is in the "house of life."

672c. He who was seized by her has lived no longer; he who was struck by her has not fastened on his head (again).

672d. Fall, glide away.

Utterance 385.

673a. To say: Rç' dawns against thee;

673b. Horus bends his Nine Bows against this spirit which comes out of the earth,

673c. with severed head and clipped tail.

673d. *Dśr*-serpent, *Ddi*, son of *Śrk.t-ḥtw*,

674a. turn around, turn over, that one may forgive (?) thee in respect of him (the dead).

674b. *Ḥfn.w*-serpent, *ḥfnn.t*-serpent,

675a. pay attention to him, pay attention to the earth, pay attention to thy father Geb.

675b. If thou payest not attention to him, his. branding-iron which is on (over) thy head will pay attention to thee.

675c. *Śri.w*-serpent, lie down.

676a. Spring up, *ȝkr* (earth), seize him; Hole-in-the-earth, straighten thy tail.

676b. If N. moves his arm against thee thou shalt die;

676c. if the arm of N. lets thee go thou shalt not live.

677a. The (my) watercourse is thy watercourse, says Shu.

677b. Shu stands on thy fetters.

677c. Turn around, turn over.

677d. The fingers of N. which are upon thee are the fingers of the *mȝfd.t*-lynx, who lives in the "house of life,"

678a. that thou mayest spit out. Fall, flee, turn over.

678b. Horus would have struck thee down, and thou wouldst not be alive;

678c. Set would have cut thee to pieces, and thou wouldst not rise (again).

Utterance 386.

679a. To say: N. comes to thee, *'iwti.w.*

679b. Mayest thou let N. pass by through "the divided opening."

679c. If thou drivest N. back, he will drive thee, back.

679d. Horus fell because of his eye; Set suffered because of his testicles.

679e. Serpent with raised head (*dśr-tp*), who is in the *n3w.t*-bush, fall, glide away.

680a. To say: A Great One is fallen: a servant (holy person) who belongs to the Ennead (pelican) is fallen.
680b. Monster (beast), lie down.

681a. To say: Horus is risen; he escaped the combat-serpent. Behold N.,
681b. N. is Horus, who escaped the combat-serpent. Hurry;
681c.————(as) no messenger is given to him, (and) his "boy" is taken away from him————(and say):
681d. The serpent, "Fowling-with-the-phallus,"
681e. Horus has smashed its mouth with his foot (or, sole of his foot).

682a. To say: A face is upon thee, thou who art in his (thy) hole.
682b. Lay thee on thy back, thou god, who art in it (the hole), before N.
682c. N. is the great mistress (or, damsel).
682d. He whom N. sees will not live;
682e. upon whom the face of N. falls, his head will not (again) be attached.
682f. *Śri.w*-serpent, glide away, thou who art in the *n3w.t*-bush, turn over.

683a. To say: N. is pure, his *ka* is pure.
683b. How well is N., how well is N.————the bodily health of Horus!

683c. How well is N., how well is, N.————the bodily health of Set!

683d. The bodily health of N. is (to be) between you.

684a. It is N. who stretched the cord (of a bow) as Horus, who draw the string as Osiris.

684b. It is that one (the dead) who has gone; it is this one (Osiris) who comes (again).

685a. Art thou Horus? A face is upon thee; thou shalt be set on thy head.

685b. Art thou Set? A face is upon thee; thou shalt be laid on thy back.

685c. This foot of N. [which he has placed upon thee is the] foot of *M3fd.t*;

685d. [that] hand of N., which he has placed upon thee, is the hand of *M3fd.t*, who lives in the "house of life."

686a. N. strikes thee in thy face,

686b. so that thy saliva runs away. [He————so that] thy cheek————.

686c. *Śiw*-serpent, lie down; *n'w*-serpent, glide away.

Utterance 391.

687a. To say twice: On [thy] side! Thou shalt lie down.

687b. Escape, escape; hence, hence————

687c. [Deliv]er N.; protect N.

687d. Thy message is ready; thy testament is received; that which is before thee is restful.

Utterance 392.

688. To say: The water of N. is in heaven; the people of N. are on earth. The heart is sad (?)

Utterance 393.

689a. To say: Thy protective-sycamore is thy corn; thy corn is thy protective-sycamore.

689b. Thy tail shall be in thy mouth, combat-serpent. Turn thyself around thy turning, great bull.

669c.———his (?)———the Great escaped from him whom he had charmed.

689d. *S3-t3*-serpent, protect thyself against the earth; *s3-t3*-serpent, protect thyself against Geb

Utterance 394.

690. To say: A lion is behind a lion because of life. Two bulls are in (inside) the ibis.

Utterance 395.

691a. To say twice: Earth, protect thyself against the earth; *s3-t3*-serpent, protect thyself against Geb (?).

691b. Protect thyself against thy father who begat Osiris; *s3-t3*-serpent, protect thyself against Geb

Utterance 396.

692a. To say: *Tirf*-serpent, (there is a) smell of the drawing (of the plough through) the earth.

Utterance 397.

692b. To say: Art thou the *d"mw*———?

692c. He is effervescent; he is effervescent; Shu, let thy arms be about N.

Utterance 398.

693a. To say: Hoer, thou who hoest the earth, hoe not the earth.

693b. Protect thyself from the enemy.

693c. N. is conceived of *d"mw* N. is born to *d"mw*.

693d. It is *d"mw* who went to his mother with him.

Utterance 399.

694. To say: Thy water is in heaven; thy people are on earth; O *'isii-hii*!

Utterance 400.

695a. To say: The eye of Horus drips on the tuft of the *dn.w*-plant.

695b. Ye two Horuses who are chief of the houses, great lord of food in Heliopolis,

695c. mayest thou give bread to N., mayest thou give beer to N.; mayest thou refresh N.,

696a. while thou refreshest the dining-table (?) of N.,

696b. while thou refreshest the slaughtering-bench of N.

696c. If N. is hungry, so will the two lions hunger;

696d. if N. is thirsty, so will she of el-Kâb thirst.

696e. *Hdnw.t, Hdnw.t,*

696f. bring not the smell of thy *hdn* to N.;

696g. thou shalt not bring the smell of thy *hdn* to N.

18.

UTTERANCES CONCERNING WELL-BEING, ESPECIALLY FOOD AND CLOTHES, 401-426.

Utterance 401.

697a. To say: N. is come from Buto, red as a flame, living as Khepri.

697b. N. has seen the great uraeus-serpent; N. has perceived the great uraeus-serpent.

697c. The face of N. is fallen upon the great uraeus-serpent.

697d. Ḥw bowed his temples to N.,

697e. when N. ferried over his lake, his uraeus-serpent in his following.

Utterance 402.

698a. To say: The place of N. with Geb is enlarged;

698b. the *šḥd*-star of N. with Rç' will be made high,

698c. that N. may promenade in the Marshes of Offering.

698d. N. is the eye of Rç', which was conceived in the night and born each day.

Utterance 403.

699a. To say: O thou whose *ȝb*-tree becomes green, who is over his field;

699b. O thou flower-opener, who is on his sycamore;

699c. O thou with the green lands, who is over his *'iȝm*-tree;

700a. O lord of the green fields, rejoice today.

700b. N. will henceforth be among you; N. will go forth in your neighbourhood;

700c. N. will live on that on which you live.

701a. O bulls of Atum,

701b. make N. fresh, refresh N. more than the red crown which is upon his head;

701c. more than the inundation which is up to his breast (or, lap, or knee), more than the dates, which are in his fist.

Utterance 404.

702a. To say: N. juggles about with thee, O juggler————further (to say) four times————he who was over the officials of Buto.

702b. N. is greater than the Horus adorned with red, the red crown which was (once) on the head of Rç'.

702c. The green eye-paint of N. consists in the papyrus-umbel of thine eye, which is aflame;

702d. N. is green (fresh) with (or, like) thee.

Utterance 405.

703a. To say: O Rç', O *w3ḥ-ti*, O *w3ḥ-ti*, O *pnd.ti*, O *pnd.ti*,

703b. N. is thou, thou art N.

704a. Praise be to N.; praise be to the *ka* of N.

704b. Cause N. to be well, f or N. causes thee to be well;

704c. cause N. to be well, for N. causes thee to be well.

704d. Cause N. to be refreshed, for N. causes thee to be refreshed.

705a. N. is that eye of thine which was on the horn of Hathor,

705b. which repeats the repeating (successive) years for (or, upon) N.,

705c. while N. is conceived in the night and born every day.

706a. To say: Greetings to thee Rç' in thy beauty, in thy beauties,

706b. in thy places, in thy two-thirds gold.

707a. Mayest thou bring the milk of Isis to N., and the flood of Nephthys,

707b. the swishing of the lake, the primaeval flood of the ocean,

707c. life, prosperity, health, happiness,

707d. bread, beer, clothing, food, that N. may live thereof.

708a. May the brewers listen to (come to terms with) him!

708b. As they are long in days (patient at work), as they are satisfied in the nights,

708c. so he (the deceased) takes his place at the table (partakes of his meal), since they are satisfied with their nourishment (contentment).

709a. May N. behold thee when thou goest forth as Thot,

709b. when the course is set for the boat of Rç',

709c. to his fields which are in the '*i̯ꜣ.i̯.w*-part of heaven,

709d. and when thou stormest forth as he who is at the head of his *ḥi*-carriers.

Utterance 407.

710a. To say: N. is pure, so that he can receive for himself his pure place which is in heaven.

710b. N. will remain, the beautiful places, of N. will remain.

710c. N. receives for himself his pure place which is in the bow of the boat of Rç'.

711a. And the sailors who row Rç',

711b. they also will row N.;

711c. and the sailors will take Rç' round about the horizon.,

711d. they also will take N. round about the horizon.

712a. N.'s mouth is opened for him, N.'s nose is opened for him,

712b. N.'s ears are opened for him,

712c. that N. may judge words, that he may separate the two contenders,

713a. that he may command words to him who is greater than he.

713b. Rç' purifies N.; Rç' protects N. against the evil which is done against him.

Utterance 408.

714a. To say: "Born-in-the-night," come ye; N. is born.

714b. Ye two women, ye who conceived by day, that ye may be patient and bear him who dwells in the egg-city,

715a. since ye have given birth to N., ye must also nourish N.

715b. The heart of N. is glad as he who is chief of the *D₃.t*;

715c. the heart of the gods rejoices over N., as soon as they see N. how rejuvenated he is.

716a. Now the banquet of the sixth day of the month shall be for the breakfast of N.;

716b. the banquet of the seventh day of the month shall be for the supper of N.

716c. Cows shall be slaughtered for N. (at) the *w₃g*-feast.

716d. The desideratum, that which is given of it, that is the gift for N.,

716e. for N. is indeed the bull of Heliopolis.

Utterance 409.

717a. To say: N. is the bull of the Ennead,

717b. lord of the five meals, three in heaven, two on earth.

717c. It is the boat of the evening sun and the boat of the morning sun,

717d. which convey this to N. from the *nḫn*-house of the god.

718a. The abomination of N. is offal; he rejects urine;

718b. he drinks it not.

718c. N. lives on sweet-wood (i.e. sweets), and from fumigations which are in the earth.

Utterance 410.

719a. To say: O Busirite, thou *dd*, he who is in his *Grg.w-b3.f*,

719b. N. is a *wrw.t.k*; N. will be a *wrw.t.k*.

719c. N. finds thee, sitting on that fortress of Ḥ3ti,

719d. in which the gods sit (live), to which the lords of *kas* are drawn.

719e. Comes————

Utterance 411.

720a.————

720b. bring it to N.; put N. [on that side of life and joy].

Utterance 412.

721a. To say: The Great One is fallen on his side;

721b. he who is in N*di.t* stirs;

721c. his head is lifted up by Rç';

721d. his abomination is to sleep, he hates to be tired.

722a. Flesh of N.,

722b. rot not, decay not, let not thy smell be bad.

722c. Thy foot shall not pass over, thy step shall not stride through,

722d. thou shalt not tread upon the (corpse)-secretion of Osiris.

723a. Thou shalt tiptoe heaven like *S3ḥ* (the toe-star); thy soul shall be pointed like Sothis (the pointed-star).

723b. Soul shalt thou be and soul thou art; honoured shalt thou be and honoured thou art.

723c. Thy soul stands there (like a king(?)) among the gods, like Horus who lives in *Irw*.

724a. Thy dread gets into the heart of the gods,

724b. like (the dread) of the red crown which is on the head of the king of Lower Egypt, like the white crown which is on the head of the king of Upper Egypt,

724c. like the lock (of hair) which is upon the head of *Mnti.w*.

724d. Thou layest hold of the hand (lit. arm) of the imperishable stars.

725a. Thy bones will not be destroyed; thy flesh will not sicken, N.;

725b. thy limbs will not be distant from thee,

725c. for thou art as one among the gods.

725d. Buto ferries up to thee; Hierakonpolis ferries down to thee,

726a. the *śmnt.t*-woman mourns for thee; the *'imi-ḥnt*-priest robes himself for thee.

726b. A welcome comes out for thee, O N., on the part of thy father; a welcome comes out for thee on the part of Rç'.

727a. The double doors of heaven are open for thee; the double doors of the *śḥd.w*-stars are open for thee,

727b. after thou art descended (in the grave) as the jackal of Upper Egypt,

727c. as Anubis on his belly, as *Wpi.w* who resides in Heliopolis.

728a. The great damsel who lives in Heliopolis has given her arm to thee,

728b. for thou hast no mother among mankind who has borne thee,

728c. for thou hast no father among men who has conceived thee.

729a. Thy mother is the great wild-cow who lives in el-Kâb, the white crown, the royal head-dress,

729b. she with the long feathers, she with the two hanging breasts;

729c. she will nurse thee; she will not wean thee.

730a. Get up (from) on thy left side, sit (put thyself) on thy right side, O N.

730b. Thy places among the gods will remain, while Rç' leans upon thee with his arm;

730c. thy fragrance is as their fragrance;

730d. thy sweetness is as the sweetness of the Two Enneads.

731a. Thou appearest, N., in the royal head-dress (the things of the forehead),

731b. thy hand seizes the Horus-weapon (*ʒmś*), thy fist grasps the *ḥd*-mace,

731c. thou standest, N., as he who is in (or, who is chief of) the two '*itr.t*-palaces, who judges the words of the gods.

732a. Thou belongest to the *nḫḫ.w* (-stars), the servants, of Rç', who are before the morning star.

732b. Thou wilt be born (again) at thy new moons (feasts) like the moon

732c. while Rç' leans upon thee in the horizon, N.,

733a. and the imperishable stars serve (follow) thee.

733b. Command thyself until Rç' comes, N.;

733c. purify thyself; ascend to Rç'.

733d. Heaven will not be empty of thee, N., for ever.

Utterance 413.

734a. To say: Raise thyself up, O king. Thy water belongs to thee., thine abundance belongs to thee,

734b. thy milk belongs to thee, which is in the breasts of thy mother, Isis.

734c. The children of Horus raise thee up; the children of him who is in *Db'.wt-P* (Buto),

734d. like Set who is in *Ḥn.t* (Hypselis, or Ombos).

735a. This Great One slept, after he had fallen to sleep.

735b. Awake, N., raise thyself up, take to thee thy head;

735c. unite to thee thy bones; shake off thy dust.

736a. Sit thou upon thy firm throne,

736b. that thou mayest eat the leg of meat, that thou mayest pass the cutlet (over thy mouth),

736c. that thou mayest nourish thyself with thy double-rib piece in heaven among the gods.

Utterance 414.

737a. To say: O N.,

737b. take thy garment of light, take thy veil upon thee,

737c. clothe thyself with the eye of Horus, which was in *Tʒi.t,*

737d. that it may gain thy respect among the gods, that it make for thee a sign of recognition among the gods,

737e. that thou mayest take the *wrr.t*-crown by means of it among the gods,

737f. that thou mayest take the *wrr.t*-crown by means of it with Horus lord of men.

Utterance 415.

738a. To say: Greetings to thee *Tʒi.t,*

738b. thou wast on the edge of the great nest which united the god with his brother.

738c. Thou wilt be or not be; thou wilt be or not be.

739a. Protect the head of N., that it may not detach itself;

739b. collect the bones of N., that they may not separate.

739c. Mayest thou put the love for N. in the body of every god who will see him.

Utterance 416.

740. To say: This is a sound garment which Horus has made for his father, Osiris.

Utterance 417.

741a. To say: A Great One slept on his mother, Nut.

741b. Thy mother *T3i.t* clothed thee;

741c. she carried thee to heaven, in her name of "Kite,"

741d. the fondling whom she found, her Horus.

741e. Thy Horus is this one, O Isis; mayest thou bring his certificate (lit. arm) to Rç', to the horizon.

Utterance 418.

742a. To say: Greetings to thee, Fine Oil.

742b. Greetings to thee which was on the brow of Horus, which Horus put on the head (horns) of his father, Osiris.

742c. N. put thee on his head (horns), as Horus put thee on the head (horns) of his father, Osiris.

Utterance 419.

743a. To say: Greetings to thee, N., on this thy day,

743b. as thou standest before Rç', when he ariseth in the east,

743c. adorned with this thy dignity among the spirits.

743d. The arms interlace for thee; the feet agitate for thee; the hands wave for thee.

744a. Isis laid hold of thine arm; she caused thee to enter into the *min. w.*

744b. The earth is adorned; thy mourners lament.

745a. May Anubis First of the Westerners give an offering:

745b. thy thousands of loaves of bread, thy thousands of mugs of beer, thy thousands of jars of ointment,

745c. thy thousands of alabaster vases (of perfume), thy thousands of garments,

745d. thy thousands of heads of oxen.

746a. The *śmn*-goose will be beheaded for thee; the *trp*-goose will be killed for thee.

746b. Horus has exterminated the evil which was in N. in his four day (term);

746c. Set has annulled that which he did against N. in his eight day (term).

747a. The doors are open for those in secret places.

747b. Stand up, remove thy earth, shake off thy dust, raise thyself up,

748a. voyage thou with the spirits.

748b. Thy wings are those of a falcon; thy brightness is that of a star.

748c. No enemy (?) will bend over N.;

748d. the heart of N. will not be taken; his heart will not be carried off.

749a. N. is a great one with an uninjured *wrr.t*-crown.

749b. N. equips himself with his firm (or, iron, shining) limbs.

749c. N. voyages, over the sky to the Marsh of Reeds;

249d. N. makes his abode in the Marsh of Offerings,

749e. among the imperishable stars in the following of Osiris.

Utterance 420.

750a. To say: O N., be pure, cense thyself for Rç'.

750b. How beautiful is thy purity today!

750c. Today, establish thyself among the gods, today.

750d. Today, establish thyself among those who are in the *šḥ-ntr*, today.

Utterance 421.

751a. To say: N., thou climbest up, thou reachest the radiance.

751b. Thou art the brilliance which is upon the eastern(?)-quarter of the sky.

752a. To say: O N.,

752b. thou art departed that thou mayest become a spirit, that thou mayest become mighty as a god, an enthroned one like Osiris,

753a. since thou hast thy soul in thy body, since thou hast thy might behind thee,

753b. since thou hast thy *wrr.t*-crown on thy head, since thou hast thy *misw.t*-crown before thee (at hand).

753c. Thy face is before thee, thy homage is before thee;

754a. the followers of a god are behind thee, the nobles of a god are before thee;

754b. they recite: "A god comes, a god comes, N. comes (who shall be) on the throne of Osiris,

754c. that spirit comes who is in *Ndi.t*, that power which is in the Thinite nome."

755a. Isis speaks to thee; Nephthys laments for thee.

755b. The spirits come to thee, bowing down; they kiss the earth at thy feet,

755c. because the terror of thee, N., is in the cities of *Ś'₃*.

756a. Thou ascendest to thy mother Nut; she lays hold of thine arm;

756b. she shows thee the way to the horizon, to the place where Rç' is.

756c. The double doors of heaven are opened for thee, the double doors of *ķbḥ.w* are opened for thee.

757a. Thou findest Rç' standing, while he waits for thee.

757b. He lays hold of thy hand, he leads thee into the double *'itr.t*-palace of heaven,

757c. he places thee on the throne of Osiris.

758a. O N., the eye of Horus comes to thee, it addresses thee:

758b. "Thy soul which is among the gods comes to thee; thy might which is among the spirits comes to thee.

758c. A son has avenged his father; Horus has avenged Osiris."

758d. Horus has avenged N. on his enemies.

759a. Thou standest, N., avenged, equipped as a god,

759b. endued with the form of Osiris; on the throne of him who is First of the Westerners,

759c. and doest what he was accustomed to do among the spirits, the imperishable stars.

760a. Thy son stands on thy throne endued with thy form;

760b. he does what thou wast accustomed to do formerly at the head of the living

760c. by the command of Rç', the Great God.

761. He tills barley, he tills spelt, that he may present thee therewith.

762a. O N., all life and health are given to thee, eternity is thine, saith Rç' to thee,

762b. that thou thyself mayest speak after thou hast taken the form of a god,

762c. wherewith thou shalt be great among the gods who are over the lake (ḥnti.w-š).

763a. O N., thy soul. stands among the gods, among the spirits,

763b. it is thus that thy fear is in their hearts.

763c. O N., N. stands upon thy throne at the head of the living,

763d. it is thus that thy terror is in their hearts.

764a. Thy name which is upon the earth lives; thy name which is upon the earth endures;

764b. thou wilt not perish; thou wilt not pass, away for ever and ever.

Utterance 423.

765a. To say: O Osiris N., take to thyself this thy libation, which is offered to thee by Horus,

765b. in thy name of "He who is come from the cataract"; take to thyself thy natron that thou mayest be divine.

765c. Thy mother Nut has made thee to be as a god to thine enemy (or, in spite of thee), in thy name of "God."

766a. Take to thyself the efflux which goes forth from thee.

766b. Horus has made me assemble for thee the gods from every place to which thou hast gone.

766c. Take to thyself the efflux which goes forth from thee.

766d. Horus has made me count for thee his children even to the place where thou wast drowned.

767a. *Ḥr-rnp.wi* recognizes thee, for thou art made young again, ill this thy name of "Fresh water."

767b. Horus is indeed a soul, for he recognizes his father in thee, in his name of "*Ḥr-bꜣ-'iti-rp.t*."

Utterance 424.

768a. To say: O N., this thy going, these thy goings;

768b. is that going of Horus, by this his going, by these his goings,

769a. as his runners hastened, so his envoys rushed on behind,

769b. so that they might announce him to him who lifts up the arm in the East.

769c. Rejoice, N.,

769d. thine arms are like those of *Wpi.w*, thy face like that of *Wp-wꜣ-wt*.

770a. O N., may the king make an offering,

770b. that thou mayest occupy thy Horite regions, that thou mayest pass through thy Setite regions.

770c. Thou sittest on thy firm throne,

770d. thou directest their words to him who is at the head of the Great Ennead, who are in Heliopolis.

771a. O N., *Mḫnti-n-'irti* protects thee,

771b. thy herdsman, who is behind thy calves.

771c. O N., 'r———protects thee against the spirits.

772a. O N., know

772b. that thou shalt take for thyself this thy divine offering, that thou
mayest be satisfied with it every day:

773a. thousands of loaves of bread, thousands of mugs of beer, thousands
of heads of oxen, thousands of geese,

773b. thousands of all sweet things, thousands of all textures.

7 74a. O N., thy water belongs to thee, thy abundance belongs to thee,

774b. thy natron belongs to thee, (all) which is brought to thee by thy
brother, N̲ḥḥ.

Utterance 425.

775a. To say: Osiris N., thou art avenged; I have given all gods to thee,

775b. together with their inheritance, together with their food,

775c. together with all their things. Thou shalt not die.

Utterance 426.

776a. To say: Osiris N., thou hast dawned as king of Upper and Lower
Egypt,

776b. for thou hast gained power over the gods together with their *kas*
(attributes).

19.
IN PRAISE OF NUT, UTTERANCES 427-435

Utterance 427.

777a. To say: Nut, spread thyself over thy son, Osiris N.;

777b. hide him from Set; protect him, Nut.

777c. Thou art come, that thou mayest protect (lit. hide) thy son; come now, protect this Great One.

Utterance 428.

778a. To say: Nut, fall upon thy son, Osiris N.;

778b. protect him, Great Sieve (protectress), this Great One among thy children.

Utterance 429.

779a. To say by Geb: Nut, thou art become (spiritually) mighty:

779b. thou wast (already physically) mighty in the womb of thy mother, Tefnut, before thou wast born.

779c. Protect N. with life and well-being. He shall not die.

Utterance 430.

780a. To say: Mighty was, thy heart,

780b. when thou wast in the body of thy mother, in thy name of "Nut".

781a. (To say:) Thou art the daughter, who has gained (physical) power over her mother, who dawned as king of Lower Egypt.

781b. Make N. (spiritually) mighty in thy womb. He shall not die.

Utterance 432.

782a. To say: Great lady, who didst become heaven, thou didst become (physically) mighty,

782b. thou art become victorious, thou hast filled every place with thy beauty.

782c. The whole earth lies (lit. is) under thee; thou hast taken possession of it;

782d. thou encompassest the earth and all things (therein) in thine arms;

782e. mayest thou establish this N. in thee as an imperishable star.

Utterance 433.

783a. To say: I have fertilized thee as Geb, in thy name of "Heaven";

783b. I have united to thee the whole earth in every place.

Utterance 434.

784a. To say: High one over the earth, thou art above thy father Shu, who hast the mastery over him.

784b. He has loved thee in that he has set himself under thee; all things are thine.

785a. Thou hast taken each god to thyself with his boat;

785b. thou hast educated them as "She of a thousand souls,"

785c. so that they will not disappear from thee like stars.

785d. So let not N. leave thee, in thy name of "Far off one" (or, "High one").

Utterance 435.

786a. To say: I am Nut, "the Granary." I have proclaimed the name of Osiris N.,

786b. namely, "Horus, beloved of the two lands, N."; "King of Upper and Lower Egypt, N.";

786c. "*nb.ti*, beloved of the Corporation, N."; "falcon over gold, N. ";

787a. "heir of Geb, his beloved N.", "beloved of all the gods, N.";

787b. given all life, stability, prosperity, health, joy like Rç', thou livest for ever.

20.

MISCELLANEOUS TEXTS—SOME LARGELY OSIRIAN, UTTERANCES 436-442.

Utterance 436.

788a. To make a libation. To say: Thy water belongs to thee; thine abundance belongs to thee;

788b. the efflux goes forth from the god, the secretion which comes out of Osiris,

788c. so that thy hands may be washed, so that thine ears may be open.

789a. This power is spiritualized by means of its soul.

789b. Wash thyself for thy *ka* washes itself. Let thy *ka* be seated,

789c. that it may eat bread with thee, without ceasing eternally.

790a. Thy going is as a successor of Osiris;

790b. thy face is before thee; thine homage is before thee.

791a. It is agreeable to thy nose on account of the smell of *Iḥ.t-wt.t*;

791b. for thy feet when they hit thy feast (carry thee to thy feast);

791c. for thy teeth, for thy finger-nails when thy bread is broken.

792a. Thou ferriest over as the great bull, the pillar (or, column) of the Serpent nome,

792b. to the fields of Rç' which he loves.

792c. Raise thyself up, N. Thou shalt not die.

Utterance 437.

793a. To say: Wake up for Horus; stand up against Set;

793b. raise thyself up as Osiris, like the spirit, son of Geb, his first (-born);

793c. and stand up as Anubis, who is on the *min-w* (-shrine),

794a. before whom the Ennead tremble. The three beginnings (of the divisions of the year) will be celebrated for thee;

794b. thou purifiest thyself on the day of the new-moon, thou dawnest on the first of the month.

794c. The great *min.t* (-stake) mourns for thee

794d. as for "Him who stands without being tired," who resides in Abydos.

795a. Earth, hear that which the gods have spoken,

795b. what Rç' says as he spiritualizes N.,

795c. that he may receive his spirituality as one at the head of the gods, like Horus, son of Osiris,

795d. while he gives him his spirituality among the watchers Of Buto,

795e. while he dignifies him as a god among the watchers of Hierakonpolis.

796a. The earth speaks:

796b. The double doors of Aker are open for thee; the double doors of Geb are open for thee.

796c. Thou goest forth at the voice of Anubis, while he has spiritualized thee, like Thot,

797a. that thou mayest judge the gods, that thou mayest set a boundary to the Bows,

797b. between the two sceptres, in this thy dignity of spirit, commanded by Anubis.

798a. If thou goest, Horus, goes; if thou speakest, Set speaks.

798b. Thou approachest the sea (lake); thou advancest to the Thinite nome;

798c. thou passest through Abydos.

799a. A portal is open for thee in heaven, towards the horizon;

799b. the heart of the gods rejoices at thy approach.

799c. They take thee to heaven in thy (capacity as) soul; thou art a soul (mighty) among them.

800a. Thou ascendest to heaven like Horus, who is over the *šdšd* of heaven,

800b. in this thy dignity issuing from the mouth of Rç',

800c. as Horus among the spirits,

800d. whilst thou sittest on thy firm throne.

801a. Thou withdrawest thyself to heaven;

801b. the ways, of the Bows, which lead up to Horus, are made firm for thee;

801c. the heart of Set fraternizes with thee as (with) the Great One of Heliopolis.

802a. Thou hast voyaged over the Winding Watercourse in the north of Nut

802b. as a star, which ferries over the ocean, which is under the body of Nut.

802c. The *D₃.t* strikes (takes) thy hand, towards the place of *S₃ḥ*,

803a. after the bull of heaven had given thee his arm.

803b. Thou nourishest thyself with the food of the gods, with which they nourish themselves.

803c. The odour of *Ddwn* is on thee, the Upper Egyptian youth, who is come from Nubia;

803d. he gives thee the incense wherewith the gods cense themselves.

804a. The two children (twin?) of the king of Lower Egypt, who are on his head, the possessors of the great (crown), have given birth to thee.

804b. Rç' has called thee out of the *'iskn* of heaven,

804c. as Horus who is chief of his department (or, presides over his thigh-offering) he of *S₃tw-t*, lord of *Šbw.t* (the rebel city),

804d. as the jackal god, nome-governor of the Bows, as Anubis who presides over the pure (holy) land.

805a. He appoints thee as the morning star (god of the morning) in the midst of the Marsh of Reeds,

805b. and thou sittest upon thy throne.

805c. Thy dismembered limbs are collected by the two mighty ones, the crowns of Upper and Lower Egypt, as lord of the Bows.

805d. Thine abundance is in the field of the gods where they nourish themselves.

806a. Thou hast thy spiritualization; thou hast thy messengers;

806b. thou hast thine understanding; thou hast thine earthly servants.

806c. May the king give an offering, may Anubis give an offering (of) thy thousand of the young of antelopes

806d. from the desert, as they come to thee with bowed head.

807a. May the king give an offering, may Anubis give an offering (of) thy thousand loaves of bread, thy thousand mugs of beer,

807b. thy thousand large loaves, which come from the broad-hall, thy thousand of all sweet things,

807c. thy thousand of oxen, thy thousand of all things which thou eatest, on which thy heart is set.

808a. The *'im3*-tree serves thee, the *nbś*-tree bows its head to thee,

808b. such as Anubis will do for thee.

Utterance 438.

809a. To say: O, O, I will do it for thee, O, my father,

809b. for thou hast no father among men, thou hast no mother among mankind;

809c. thy father is the great wild bull, thy mother is the young cow (lit. girl, or damsel).

810a. Live a life, and thou shalt certainly not die a death,

810b. like Horus lived, who dwelt in Letopolis,

810c. after the great grave (hole) of Heliopolis was opened for him.

811a. The great one of the *ḥtś.t*-sedan-chair-man and the great one of the '-sedan-chair-man of *Ḥnti-'imn.tiw*,

811b. they give thee water on the beginning of the month and on the beginning of the half-month,

811c. that thou mayest give to the great and lead the small.

811d. Thou hast thy double-rib piece (*śbti.w*) from the slaughtering-bench of *Ḥnti-'imn.tiw*,

811e. in accordance with thy dignity among the lords of the *'imȝḥ*.

Utterance 439.

812a. To say: N. is Satis who has taken possession of both lands,

812b. the burning one who has seized her two lands.

812c. N. has ascended to heaven;

812d. he has found Rç' standing; he approaches him;

813a. he sits down beside him;

813b. Rç' allows him not to throw himself on the ground,

813c. knowing that he (the king) is indeed greater than he (Rç').

813d. N. is more spiritual than the spirits,

813e. more excellent than the excellent ones;

813f. N. is more enduring than the enduring ones.

814a. N. has triumphed over the lady of the *ḥtp.t*;

814b. N. has taken his stand with him in the north of the sky;

814c. N. has taken possession of both lands as king of the gods.

Utterance 440.

815a. To say: If thou desirest to live, Horus, who is in charge of his life-staff (?) of truth,

815b. then shalt thou not shut the double doors of heaven, then shalt thou not binder (with) its (the heaven's) hindrances,

815c. as soon as thou hast taken the *ka* of N. to heaven,

815d. among the august-ones of the god, unto the beloved ones of the god,

816a. who lean upon their *d'm*-sceptres, who guard the land of Upper Egypt,

816b. who clothe themselves in purple (?), who live on figs,

816c. who drink wine, who anoint themselves with *ḥ3t.t*-oil,

816d. that he (the *ka*) may speak for N. to the Great God, and cause N. to climb up to the Great God.

Utterance 441.

817a. To say: The earth has been hoed for thee; the *wdn.t*-offering before thee has been made for thee,

817b. as thou goest on that way whereon the gods go.

818a. Turn thou and see this offering,

818b. which the king has made for thee, which the First of the Westerners has made for thee,

818c. as thou goest to those gods in the north, the imperishable stars.

Utterance 442.

819a. To say: That Great One is certainly fallen on his side; he who is in *Ndi.t* is thrown down.

819b. Thine arm is seized by Rç'; thy head is lifted up by the Two Enneads.

819c. Behold, he is come (again) as *Ś3ḥ*; behold, Osiris is come as *Ś3ḥ*.

820a. lord of the wine-cellar at the *W3g*-feast,

820b. "good," as his mother said; "heir," as his father said,

820c. conceived by heaven, born of the *Dw3.t*.

820d. Heaven conceives thee together with *Ś'3ḥ*;

820e. N. is born in the *Dw3.t* together with *Ś'3ḥ*.

821a. He lives who lives at the command of the gods; so wilt thou live.

821b. Thou ascendest with *S'ȝḥ* on the eastern side of the sky;

821c. thou descendest with *S'ȝḥ* on the western side of the sky.

822a. Your third is Sothis of the pure places,

822b. she is your leader (or, who will lead you) by the beautiful ways in heaven,

822c. in the Marsh of Reeds.

21.
SECOND SERIES IN PRAISE OF NUT,
UTTERANCES 443-452.

Utterances 443.

823a. To say: Nut, two eyes are come forth from thy head.

823b. Thou hast taken possession of Horus and his Great-in-charms;

823c. thou hast taken possession of Set and his Great-in-charms.

823d. Nut, thou hast numbered thy children, in thy name of "*rp.t*-sedan-chair of Heliopolis."

823e. Thou shalt reclaim N. also for life; he shall not perish.

Utterances 444-445.

824a. To say: Nut, thou hast dawned as king of Lower Egypt, because thou hast gained power over the gods,

824b. together with their *kas*, together with their heritage,

824c. together with their food, together with all their possessions.

824d. Nut, him thou causest to endure, he will live.

824e. Nut, if thou livest, N. will live.

Utterance 446.

825a. To say: Osiris N., thy mother, Nut, has spread herself over thee,

825b. that she may hide thee from all evil things.

825c. Nut has guarded thee from all evil;

825d. thou art the greatest among her children.

826a. To say: He is gone who went to his *ka*; Osiris is gone to his *ka*; Set is gone to his *ka*;

826b. *Mḫnti-'irti* is gone to his *ka*; thou thyself art gone to thy *ka*.

827a. O N., he who comes, comes, thou shalt not be in need;

827b. thy mother comes, thou shalt not be in need; Nut, thou shalt not be in need;

827c. protectress of the great, thou shalt not be in need; protectress of the fearful, thou shalt not be in need.

828a. She protects thee, she prevents thy need, she gives back thy head to thee;

828b. she collects thy bones for thee;

828c. she brings thy heart into thy body for thee.

829a. Thou art (henceforth?) chief of those who were before thee;

829b. thou commandest those who will be after thee.

829c. Thou causest thy house to prosper after thee; thou protectest thy children from sorrow.

829d. Thy purity is the purity of the gods, who have gone to their *kas*;

829e. thy purity is the purity of the gods who have passed on, and so do not suffer hardship.

Utterance 448.

830a. To say: Thot, heal N., that he may live,

830b. that what is against him may cease. Thot, give him the eye of Horus.

Utterance 449.

831. To say: Horus, who art in Osiris N., take the eye of Horus to thyself.

Utterance 450.

832a. To say: He is gone, who went to his *ka*; Osiris is gone to his *ka*; Set is gone to his *ka*;

832b. *Mḫnti-'irti* is gone to his *ka*; N. is gone to his *ka*.

833a. O N., thou art gone, that thou mayest live; thou art gone, that thou mayest not die;

833b. thou art gone, that thy spirit may be at the head of the spirits, that thou mayest be powerful at the head of the living;

833c. that thou mayest be mighty (a soul), and thou art mighty (a soul); that thou mayest be honoured, and thou art honoured.

834a. He who comes, comes; thou shalt not be in need.

834b. Thy mother comes to thee, thou shalt not be in need; Nut comes to thee, thou shalt not be in need;

834c. the protectress of the great comes to thee, thou shalt not be in need.

835a. She protects thee, she prevents thy need, she gives back thy head to thee;

835b. she assembles thy bones for thee, she unites thy limbs for thee;

835c. she brings thy heart into thy body for thee.

836a. Thou art (henceforth?) chief of those who were before thee;

836b. thou commandest those who were before thee;

836c. thou protectest thy children from sorrow.

836d. Thy purity is the purity of the gods,

836e. the lords of want, who have gone to their *kas*.

Utterance 451.

837a. To say: O N., awake, raise thyself up,

837b. stand up, that thou mayest be pure, that thy *ka* may be pure,

837c. that thy soul may be pure, that thy might may be pure.

838a. Thy mother comes to thee, Nut comes to thee, the great protectress comes to thee;

838b. she purifies thee, N., she protects thee, N.,

838c. she prevents thy need.

839a. O N., thou art pure, thy *ka* is pure,

839b. thy might which is among the spirits is pure, thy soul which is among the gods is pure.

840a. O N.,

840b. "Thy bones are united for thee; take to thee thy head," says Geb.

840c. Let him efface the evil which is in thee, N., says Atum.

Utterance 452.

841a. To say: O N., stand up, that thou mayest be pure, that thy *ka* may be pure.

841b. Horus purifies thee in *ḳbḥ.w*.

842a. Thy purification is the purification of Shu, thy purification is the purification of Tefnut,

842b. thy purification is the purification of the four spirits of the houses,

842 C. when they rejoice in Buto because thou art pure.

842d. Thy mother Nut purifies thee, the great protectress, she protects thee.

843a. "Take to thee thy head; thy bones are united for thee," says Geb.

843b. "Effaced be the evil which is with N., destroyed shall be the evil which is with him," says Atum.

22

A MISCELLANEOUS GROUP, UTTERANCES 453-486.

Utterance 453.

844a. To say: O N., stand up,

844b. put on thee the eye of Horus, take it to thyself,

844c. that it may stick to thee, that it may stick to thy flesh,

845a. that thou mayest go out in it, and that the gods may see thee adorned with it,

845b. that thou mayest take the great *wrr.t*-crown among the Great Ennead of Heliopolis.

846a. O N., live,

846b. for the eye of Horus is brought to thee; it will not depart from thee for ever and ever.

Utterance 454.

847a. To say: Osiris N., thou hast encircled every god in thine arms,

847b. their lands, all their possessions.

847c. Osiris N., thou art great, thou art bent around like the circle which encircles the *nb.wt.*

Utterance 455.

848a. To say: The watercourses are full, the canals are inundated

848b. on account of the purification (which) comes forth from Osiris.

848c. *Sm*-priest, hereditary-prince, ye ten great ones of the palace, ye ten great ones of Heliopolis,

849a. Great Ennead, be seated,

849b. behold this purification of the king, this Osiris N.,

849c. who is being purified by *smn* (-natron) and by *bd* (-natron),

850a. the spittle which went out of the mouth of Horus, the sputum which went out of the mouth of Set,

850b. whereby Horus was purified,

850c. whereby the evil, which was in him, was poured to the ground, after Set had done (it) to him,

850d. whereby Set was purified,

850e. (whereby) the evil, which was in him, was poured to the ground, after Horus had done (it) to him.

851a. N. is thereby purified, and the evil which was in him is poured to the ground,

851b. which *Nwtknw* has done to thee, together with thy spirits.

Utterance 456.

852a. To say: Greetings to thee, Great One, son of a Great One!

852b. The *š3w* of the *pri-wr* run for thee;

852c. the *pri-nsr* work for thee;

852d. the apertures of the (heavenly) windows are open for thee;

852e. the steps of light are revealed for thee.

853a. Greetings to thee, sole one, of whom it is said, he will live always!

853b. Horus comes, he with the long stride comes;

853c. he comes, he who wins power over the horizon, who wins power over the gods.

854a. Greetings to thee, soul, who is in his red blood,

854b. sole one, as his father named him, wise one, as the gods called him,

854c. who took his place, as the sky was separated (from the earth), at the place where thy heart was satisfied,

854d. that thou mayest stride over the sky according to thy stride,

854e. that thou mayest traverse Lower and Upper Egypt in the midst of that which thou stridest!

855a. He who really knows it————this saying of Rç',

855b. he who uses them————those charms of Harachte,

855c. he shall be indeed an intimate of Rç',

855d. he shall be a friend of Harachte.

856a. N. knows this saying of Rç';

856b. N. uses them————these charms of Harachte.

856c. N. shall be an intimate of Rç',

856d. N. shall be a friend of Harachte.

856e. The arm of N. will be taken to heaven in the following of Rç'.

Utterance 497.

857a. To say: The watered fields are satisfied, the canals are inundated

857b. for N. on this day,

857c. when his spirit is given to him, when his might is given to him.

858a. Raise thyself up, N., take to thyself thy water; gather to thee thy bones.

858b. Stand up upon thy feet; spirit art thou at the head of the spirits.

859a. Raise thyself up for this thy bread, which cannot mould,

859b. for thy beer, which cannot become sour,

859c. by which thou shalt become spiritually mighty, by which thou shalt become pre-eminent, by which thou shalt become physically mighty,

859d. by which thou shalt give thereof to him who was, before thee. O N., thou art glorious and thy successor is glorious.

860a.————
860b.————
861a. The keeper (*min.w*) stands up before thee, so that the feast of the new-moon may be celebrated for thee,
861b. so that the feast of the month may be celebrated for thee, so that the feast of the half-month may take place for thee,
861c. so that the feast of the sixth day may be celebrated for thee, so that [the feast of———] may take place [for thee].
862a.————
862b.————
862c.————.
863a. Arms are given to thee, the dance comes down to thee,
863b. the great *mni.t* speaks to thee————
863c.————

Utterance 459.

864a. To say: O N.,
864b. take to thyself this thy pure water, which is come forth out of Elephantiné,
864c. thy water from Elephantiné, thy natron from *'Irw,*
864d. thy *ḥsmn* (natron) from the Oxyrhynchus nome, thine incense from Nubia.
865a. Thou sittest upon thy firm throne,
865b. thy forepart being as, that of a jackal, thy hinderpart as that of a falcon;
865c. thou consumest the meat of the slaughtering-bench of Osiris and the double-rib piece of the slaughtering-bench of Set;
866a. thy bread is the bread of the god out of the broad-hall (*wsḥ.t-*hall).

866b. Thou strikest with the '*ḥꜣ*-sceptre, thou directest with the '*iꜣꜣ.t*-sceptre;

866c. thou commandest the gods;

866d. thou layest hold for thyself of the arm of the imperishable stars.

867a. Thou ascendest in the Thinite nome; thou descendest in the great valley.

867b. Stand up, raise thyself up.

Utterance 460.

868a. To say: O N.,

868b. thy water, thy cool water-libation is the inundation of the Great One (who) which is come forth from thee.

868c. Now be still, hear it, this word which is said: "N.,

869a. he shall be a spirit at the head of the spirits, he shall be mighty at the head of the living,

869b. be shall sit at the side (temple, of the head) of the *Ḥnti-'imnti.w*."

869c. Thy two *psn*-cakes come out of the broad-hall; thy two ribs from the slaughtering-bench of the god.

870a. O N., raise thyself up.

870b. Receive for thyself this thy fresh bread, this thy fresh beer,

870c. which is come from thy house, which is given to thee.

Utterance 461.

871a. To say: O N.,

871b. thou ascendest (or, goest forth) as the morning star, and voyagest as the *ḥnti* (master of the heavenly ocean).

871c. Those who are in Nun fear thee;

871d. thou commandest the spirits.

872a. Isis laments for thee, Nephthys bemoans thee,

872b. the great *mni.t* smites evil for thee,

872c. as for Osiris in his suffering.

872d. "Nunite," "Nunite," guard thee against the great sea.

873a. Be seated on this thy firm throne,

873b. that thou mayest command those of secret places.

873c. The double doors of heaven are open for thee, the double doors of *ḳbḥ.w* are open for thee,

873d. that thou mayest ferry over (pull the oar) to the Marsh of Reeds,

874a. and till the barley and reap the spelt,

874b. that thy livelihood may be secured thereby, like Horus, son of Atum.

Utterance 462.

875a. To say: O N., thou who wast great in waking and who art great in sleep,

875b. sweetness is too sweet for thee.

875c. Raise thyself up, N., thou shalt not die.

Utterance 463.

876a. To say: The double doors of heaven are open for thee, the double doors of *ḳbḥ.w* are open for thee,

876b. those which hold people back.

876c. The *mni.t* laments for thee, *ḥnmm.wt* bemoan thee;

876d. the imperishable stars stand up for thee.

877a. Thine air is incense, thy north-wind is (incense-) smoke.

877b. Thou art great in the Thinite nome;

877c. thou art the only star, which comes forth in the eastern side of heaven,

877d. which does not surrender himself to Horus of the *Dꜣ.t*.

Utterance 464.

878a. Further, to say: Thou who art very high among the stars, the imperishable stars,

878b. thou wilt not perish (go down), eternally.

Utterance 465.

879a. To say: O ye gods of the horizon, who (live) at the end of the sky,

879b. as true as ye wish that Atum lives,

879c. that ye anoint yourselves with ointment, that ye clothe yourselves in linen,

879d. that ye receive your offering-cakes,

880a. so shall ye take (lit. to yourselves) the arm of N.

880b. and put him in the Marsh of Offerings,

880c. after ye have caused him to be a spirit among the spirits,

880d. after ye have caused him to be mighty among the gods,

880e. that he may prepare for you a great meal and a great offering.

881a. He voyages over the sky; N. leads those who are in the "settlements" ("colonies");

881b. N. takes possession of the *wrr.t*-crown as Horus, son of Atum.

Utterance 466.

882a. To say: O N.,

882b. thou art the great star, the companion of *S3ḥ*,

882c. who traverses the sky with *S3ḥ*, who voyages over the *D3.t* with Osiris.

883a. Thou, N., ascendest on the eastern side of the sky,

883b. renewed in thy time, rejuvenated in thine hour.

883c. Nut has borne thee, N., together with *S3ḥ*;

883d. the year has adorned thee together with Osiris.

884a. Arms are given to thee, the dance comes down to thee, a meal is given to thee.

884b. The great *mni.t* laments for thee, as for Osiris in his suffering.

885. O N., sail, arrive, protect thyself against the great sea.

Utterance 467.

886a. To say: O Rç' concerning these things which thou hast said (about it), Rç', "O that I had a son," as thou wast king, Rç',

886b. "who is (spiritually) mighty, (physically) mighty, honoured,

886c. with carrying arms, with wide stride."

887a. Behold N., Rç', N. is thy son;

887b. N. is (spiritually) mighty, N. is honoured, N. is, (physically) mighty;

887c. the arms of N. are carrying, the stride of N. is long.

888a. N. shines in the East like Rç';

888b. he goes in the West like Khepri.

888c. N. lives on that which Horus, lord of heaven, lives, by the command of Horus, lord of heaven.

888d. N. purifies Rç';

889a. N. mounts upon his throne;

889b. N. takes his helm (oar).

889c. N. sails (rows) Rç', as him who strides over the sky,

889d. the *šḥd*-star of gold, the adornment of the bull of light,

889e. the bifork (brother) of gold, the companion of him who strides over the sky.

890a. He flies, who flies; N. also flies away from you, O men.

890b. He belongs not to the earth; N. belongs to heaven.

891a. O thou his city-god, may the *ka* of N. be at thy fingers.

891b. N. has flown as a cloud to heaven like the heron;

891c. N. has kissed the sky like a falcon;

891d. N. has reached the sky as the grasshopper, which makes the sun invisible.

892a. N. has not reviled the king,

892b. he has not respected Bastet.

892c. There is not an 'iḫзb.w, which N. has done as chief of the sedan-chairmen.

893a. If it is the son of Rç', for whom he will prepare his place, then will he prepare a place for N.;

893b. if it is the son of Rç' who will be well, then N. will be well,

893c. who will hunger, then N. will hunger.

Utterance 468.

894a. To say: A Great One is awake beside his *ka*, after this Great One had fallen asleep by his *ka*;

894b. N. is awake beside his *ka*, after this N. had fallen asleep by his *ka*;

894c. this Great One is awake; N. is awake;

894d. the gods are awake, awakened are the mighty ones.

895a. O N., raise thyself up, stand up.

895b. The Great Ennead, who are in Heliopolis, have assigned thee to thy great position,

895c. that thou mayest sit, N., at the head of the Ennead,

895d. like Geb, the hereditary prince of the gods, like Osiris at the head of the mighty ones, as Horus lord of men and gods.

896a. O N., who keeps secret his form like Anubis,

896b. take to thee thy face as jackal.

896c. The keeper, who presides in the two 'itr.t-palaces, stands up before thee, as before Anubis, who presides in *ḥ-ntr*.

897a. Thou causest the Followers of Horus to be satisfied.

897b. Horus avenges thee, N.; Horus causes thee to be satisfied, N., with the offering which he hath,

897c. that thy heart, N., may be satisfied with it, on the feast of the month and on the feast of the half-month.

897d. The joyful rejoices for thee, as for Anubis, who presides in *ḥ-ntr*.

898a. Isis laments for thee, Nephthys bemoans thee, as Horus who avenged his father, Osiris.

898b. A son who avenged his father, Horus has avenged N.

899a. Osiris lives, the spirit who is in *Ndi.t* lives, N. lives.

899b. O N., thy name lives among the living;

899c. thou wilt be a spirit, N., among the spirits; thou wilt be mighty among the mighty.

900a. O N., thy fear (i.e. the fear of thee) is the sound eye of Horus,

900b. that white crown, (which is) the *wt.t*-uraeus, which is in el-Kâb (N*ḫb*).

900c. She puts thy fear, N., in the eyes of all gods,

900d. in the eyes of the spirits, the imperishable stars, those of secret places,

900e. in the eyes of all things (beings), who will see thee and who will hear thy name.

901a. O N., equip thyself with the red eye of Horus, the red crown,

901b. which is great in fame (spirits), which is rich in appearances (beings),

901c. that it may protect thee, N., as it protected Horus.

902a. It gives thee fame, N., among the Two Enneads,

902b. through the two *wt.t*-uraeuses, which are on thy forehead.

902c. They lift thee up, N.;

902d. they lead thee to thy mother Nut; it (the uraeus of the North) lays hold of thine arm,

903a. that thou be not in need, that thou mayest not moan (like a cedar), that thou perish not.

903b. Horus has caused thee to be a spirit at the head of the spirits, that thou mayest be mighty at the head of the living.

903c. How beautiful is that which Horus has done for N.,

903d. for this spirit, who was conceived by a god, who was conceived by two gods!

904a. O N., thou wilt be a soul like the Souls of Heliopolis;

904b. thou wilt be a soul like the Souls of Hierakonpolis; thou wilt be a soul like the Souls of Buto;

904c. thou wilt be a soul like the star of life, which is at the bead of his brothers.

905a. O N., I am Thot. May the king give an offering: Thy bread and thy beer are given to thee;

905b. these are thy two *p3d*-cakes, which are delivered by Horus, which are in the broad-hall,

905c. that he may cause thy heart to be satisfied thereby, N., for ever and ever.

Utterance 469.

906a. N. purifies himself;

906b. N. has taken his helm (oar); he occupies his seat;

906c. N. seats himself in the bow of the boat of the Two Enneads;

906d. N. rows Rç' to the West.

906e. He (Rç') establishes the seat of N. ever the lords of *kas*;

906f. he writes (the name) of N. over the living.

907a. The double doors of the *b3-k3*, which is in *kbḥ.w*, are open for N.;

907b. the double doors of *bi3*, which is in *śḥd.w*, are open for N.

907c. This N. goes through,

907d. with his panther-skin loin-cloth on, and the *3mś*-sceptre of N. in his hand.

906a. N. is unhurt (well) with his flesh; N. is pleased (is good) with his name.

906b. N. lives with his *ka*;

908c. it (the *ka*) expels the evil which is before N.;

908d. it drives away the evil which is behind N.;

908e. like the boomerangs of him who presides over Letopolis,

908f. which drove away the evil which was before him,

908g. which expelled the evil which was behind him.

909a. N. sees what the *nḥḥ.w* (-stars) do, because (to be) on their side is so good;

909b. N. is pleased (to be) with them; they are pleased.

909c. I am a (*nḥḥ.w*)-star, the side-locks of a (*nḥḥ.w*)-star; N. is a (*nḥḥ.w*)-star, a (*nḥḥ.w*)-star indeed.

909d. This N. will not suffer eternally.

Utterance 470.

910a. To say: N. knows his mother; N. forgets not his mother;

910b. the white crown, the shining, the broad, which dwells in el-Kâb, the lady of the great house,

910c. the lady of the land worthy of honour, the lady of the secret land,

910d. the lady of the marsh of fishermen, the lady of the valley of *ḥtp. tiw,*

911a. the red-coloured, the red crown, the lady of the lands of Buto.

911b. "Mother of N.," so said I,

911c. "give thy breast to N., that N. may suck therewith."

912a. "(My) son N.," so said she, "take to thee my breast; that thou mayest suck it" said she,

912b. "that thou mayest live again," so said she, "that thou mayest be (again) small," so said she.

913a. "Thou shalt ascend to heaven as a falcon,

913b. thy feathers shall be as those of a goose," so said she.

913c. *Ḥdḥd,* bring this to N.;

913d. he is the great wild-bull.

914a. "Bull of offerings, bow thy horn,

914b. let N. pass by; it is N."

914c. "Where goest thou?" "N. goes to heaven, in possession of life and joy,

915a. that N. may see his, father; that N. may see Rç'."

915b. "Thou are on the way to the high places, to the places of Set."

916a. The high places will put him on the places of Set;

916b. (even) on that high sycamore cast of the sky, it having bent down, on which the gods sit;

917a. for N. is indeed the living falcon, who has explored *ḳbḥ.w*;

917b. for N. is indeed the great helmsman, who has voyaged over the two *ḫзtз*-parts of heaven;

917c. for N. is indeed he of the great foot, with long stride.

918a. N. purifies himself in the Marsh of Reeds;

918b. N. dresses himself in the field of Khepri;

918c. N. finds Rç' there.

919a. If Rç' comes forth in the East, he finds N. in the horizon;

919b. if Rç' comes to the West, he finds N. in the possession of life and endurance;

919c. every beautiful place where Rç' goes, he finds N. there.

Utterance 471.

920a. To say: N. is the being of a god, the son of a god, the messenger of a god.

920b. N. comes, and N. purifies himself in the Marsh of Reeds,

920c. N. comes down to the field of *Kns.t.*

921a. The Followers of Horus purify N.

921b. they bathe N., they dry N.,

921c. they recite for N. the chapter of the right way,

921d. they recite for N. the chapter of those who ascend for life and joy.

922a. N. ascends to heaven for life and joy.

922b. N. embarks (descends) for life and joy into the boat of Rç';

922c. N. commands for him those gods who transport him.

923a. Every god shall rejoice at the approach of N.,

923b. as they rejoice at the approach of Rç',

923c. when he comes forth on the eastern side of the sky, in peace, in peace.

Utterance 472.

924a. To say: Heaven thunders, the earth trembles before N.
924b. N. is a magician; N. is he who is possessed of magic.
925a. N. comes that he may glorify *S̱ȝḥ*,
925b. that he may cause Osiris to be at the head, that he may put the gods in their places.
925c. *Mȝ-ḥȝ.f*, bull of the gods, bring this (boat?) to N.,
925d. set N. on that side for life and joy.

Utterance 473.

926a. To say: The two reed-floats of heaven are placed by the morning-boat for Rꜥ,
926b. that Rꜥ may ferry over on them to Horus who inhabits the horizon, to the horizon.
926c. The two reed-floats of heaven are placed by the evening-boat for Horus who inhabits the horizon,
926d. that Horus who inhabits the horizon may ferry over on them to Rꜥ, to the horizon.
927a. The two reed-floats of heaven are caused to descend for N. by the morning-boat,
927b. that N. may mount on them to Rꜥ, to the horizon.
927c. The two reed-floats of heaven are caused to descend for N. by the evening-boat,
927d. that N. may mount on them to Horus, who inhabits the horizon, to the horizon.
928a. N. mounts on high on this eastern side of heaven where the gods are born;

246

928b. N. will be born (anew there) like Horus, like him of the horizon.

929a. N. is justified; the *ka* of N. is justified;

929b. the sister of N. is Sothis; the mother of N. is the morning star.

930a. N. hath found the spirits well-equipped by reason of their mouth,

930b. sitting on the two shores of the *ḥsḥ*-lake,

930c. the drinking-bowl of each spirit well-equipped by reason of his mouth.

930d. "Hast thou no eyes?", so said they to N.,

930e. the spirits well-equipped by reason of their mouth.

930f. Said he, "a spirit well-equipped by reason of his mouth."

931a. "How has this happened to thee?", so said they to N.,

931b. the spirits well-equipped by reason of their mouth,

931c. "that thou art come to this place which is more august than any place?"

931d. N. is come to this place which is more august than any place.

932a. The two reed-floats of heaven are placed by the morning-boat for Rç',

932b. that Rç' may ferry over on them to Horus who inhabits the horizon, to the horizon.

932c. The two reed-floats of heaven are placed by the evening-boat for Horus who inhabits the horizon,

932d. that Horus who inhabits the horizon may ferry over on them to Rç', to the horizon,

933a. because the two reed-floats of heaven were caused to descend for N. by the morning-boat,

933b. that N. may mount on them for life and joy to Rç', to the horizon;

933c. because the two reed-floats of heaven were caused to descend for N. by the evening-boat,

933d. that N. may mount on them to Horus who inhabits the horizon, to the horizon.

934a. N. mounts on high on this eastern side of heaven, where the gods are born;

934b. N. was born (anew there) like Horus, like him of the horizon.

935a. N. is justified; the *ka* of N. is justified.

935b. Praise be to N.; praise be to the *ka* of N.

935c. The sister of N. is Sothis; the mother of N. is the morning star.

936a. N. comes (to be) with you:

936b. N. walks with you in the Marsh of Reeds;

936c. he pastures as you pasture in the field of malachite;

937a. N. eats of that which you eat;

937b. N. lives on that on which you live;

937c. N. clothes himself with that wherewith you clothe yourselves;

937d. N. anoints himself with that wherewith you anoint yourselves;

937e. N. takes water with you out of the mn-canal (or, lake of the nurse) of N.,

937f. the drinking-bowl of each spirit well-equipped by reason of his mouth.

938a. N. sits as he who lives in the great '*itr.t*-palace;

938b. N. commands (each) spirit well-equipped by reason of his mouth;

938c. N. sits on the two shores of the *šḥšḥ*-lake;

938d. N. commands (each) spirit well-equipped by reason of his mouth.

Utterance 474.

939a. To say: "How beautiful indeed it is to see," says she, said Isis;

939b. "how fortunate indeed it is to see," says she, said Nephthys

939c. to the king, to this Osiris N.,

940a. as he ascends to heaven among the stars, among the imperishable stars,

940b. the lion-helmet (renown) of N. on his head,

940c. his terror on both sides of him, his magic preceding him!

941a. N. goes therewith to his mother Nut;

941b. N. climbs upon her, in this her name of "Ladder."

941c. The gods who inhabit heaven are brought to thee; they unite for thee with the gods who inhabit the earth,

941d. that thou mayest be with them, that thou mayest go on their arms.

942a. The Souls of Buto are brought to thee; the Souls of Hierakonpolis are united for thee.

942b. "All belongs to N.,"

942c. so said Geb, who has spoken thereof with Atum. So it was done for him.

943a. "The Marshes of Reeds,

943b. the Horite regions, the regions of Set

943c. all belongs to N.,"

943d. so said Geb, who has spoken thereof with Atum. So it was done for him.

944a. He came against thee; he said he would kill thee.

944b. He has not killed thee; it is thou who wilt kill him.

944c. Thou holdest thine own against him, as the surviving bull of the wild-bulls.

945a. Further, to say four times: N., thou remainest in life and joy;

945b. N., thou shalt certainly remain in life and joy.

Utterance 475.

946a. To say: O ferryman,

946b. who has brought this (boat) to Horus, that his, eye may be brought back,

946c. who has brought this to Set, that his testicles may be brought back,

947a. the eye of Horus sprang up as he fell on the eastern side of the sky.

947b. Dost thou spring up with it, that thou mayest fall on (come to) the eastern side of the sky?

948a. N. goes that he may do service of courtier to Rç'
948b. in the place of the gods, who are gone to their *kas*,
948c. who have lived in the places of Horus, who have lived in the places of Set.
949a. Behold N. is come, behold N. is ascended for life and joy;
949b. N. has attained the heights of heaven;
949c. N. is not warded off by the palace of the Great Ones, from the way of the *šḥd.w*-stars.
950a. The morning-boat calls N.; it is, N. who bails it out.
950b. Rç' appoints N. as lord of life and joy.

Utterance 476.

951a. To say: Heaven purifies itself for Rç'; the earth purifies itself for Horus.
951b. Every god who is between them purifies N.;
951c. N. adores the god.
952a. O thou keeper of the way of N., who art at the great gate,
952b. certify N. to these two great and powerful gods,
952c. for N. is indeed the wng-plant, the son of Rç',
952d. which supports, the sky, which leads (governs) the earth, which will judge the gods.
953a. N. will sit among you, ye stars who inhabit the *D3.tiw*.
953b. You shall carry N. like Rç', you shall serve N. like Horus;
953c. You shall cause N. to be high like *Wp-w3.wt*, you shall love N. like Min.
954a. Scribe, scribe, break thy writing-kit,
954b. break thy two pens, tear up thy papyrus-rolls.
955a. Rç', expel him from his post, put N. in his place, living eternally,
955b. that N. may be happy in possession of the staff of office.
955c. Rç', expel him from his post, put N. in his place.
955d. It is N., for life.

956a. To say: The sky shakes, the earth quakes.

956b. Horus comes; Thot appears. They raise Osiris from on his side;

956c. they cause him to stand (as chief) among the Two Enneads.

957a. Remember, Set, put in thy heart

957b. this word which Geb spoke, this threat which the gods made against thee

957c. in the house of the prince, in Heliopolis, because thou didst strike Osiris to the ground,

958a. as thou, Set, didst say: "I have not done this against him,"

958b. that thou mayest prevail thereby, having been acquitted, that thou mayest prevail in spite of Horus.

959a. As thou, Set, didst say: "It is he who defied me"

959b.———and so arose his name of "*Ik̠-w-t̠ʒ*";

959c. as thou, Set, didst say: "It is he who came too near to me"

959d.———and so arose his name of "*S̠ʒḥ*"

959e. he with outstretched leg, with long stride, who inhabits the land of Upper Egypt.

960a. Raise thyself up, Osiris; Set raised himself up,

960b. after he had heard the threat of the gods, who spoke concerning the father of the god.

960c. Isis has thine arm, Osiris; Nephthys has thy hand; thou goest between them.

961a. Heaven is given to thee, earth is given to thee, the Marsh of Reeds,

961b. the Horite regions, the Setite regions,

961c. the cities are given to thee, the nomes are united for thee, saith Atum.

961d. It is Geb who has spoken about it.

962a. Whet thy knife, Thot, the sharp, the cutting,

962b. which removes heads, which cuts out hearts.

963a. It shall remove the heads, it shall cut the hearts

963b. of those who would place themselves in the way of N., when he goes to thee, Osiris;

963c. of those who would restrain N., when he goes to thee, Osiris.

963d. Give him life and joy.

964a. N. comes to thee, lord of heaven; N. comes to thee, Osiris,

964b. that N. may wipe thy face, that he may clothe thee with the clothes of a god,

964c. serving as priest to thee in the *Ddi.t* (necropolis).

965a. It is Sothis, thy daughter, who loves thee,

965b. who secures thy livelihood (or, makes thy yearly offerings), in this her name of "Year",

965c. who conducts N., when N. comes to thee.

966a. N. comes to thee, lord of heaven; N. comes to thee, Osiris,

966b. that N. may wipe thy face, that N. may clothe thee with the clothes of a god,

966c. while N. serves as a priest to thee in the *'I3di*,

966d. that he may eat a limb of thine enemy,

966e. that he may cut it in pieces for Osiris, so that he may make him as he who is at the head of the butchers.

967a. N. comes to thee, lord of heaven; N. comes to thee, Osiris,

967b. that N. may wipe thy face, that N. may clothe thee with the clothes of a god,

967c. that N. may do for thee that which Geb commanded that he should do for thee,

967d. that he fasten thine arm on the *'nh*-sceptre, that he lift up thine arm on the *w3ś*-sceptre.

968a. N. comes to thee, lord of heaven; N. comes to thee, Osiris,

968b. that N. may wipe thy face, that N. may clothe thee with the clothes of a god,

968c. while N. serves as priest to thee.

969a. It is Horus thy son, whom thou hast conceived; he has not put N. over the dead,

969b. he puts him among the gods, for he is divine.

970a. Their water is the water of N., their bread is the bread of N.,

970b. their purification is the purification of N.

970c. What Horus has done for Osiris, he has done for N.

Utterance 478.

971a. To say: Greetings to thee, Ladder of god;

971b. greetings to thee, Ladder of Set.

971c. Stand up Ladder of god;

971d. stand up Ladder of Set; stand up Ladder of Horus

971e. which was made for Osiris, that he may ascend upon it to heaven and do service of courtier to Rç'.

972a. Thou art come in search of thy brother, Osiris,

972b. after his brother Set had cast him on his side,

972c. on yonder side of *Gḥś.ti*.

973a. Horus comes, his lion-helmet on his head; his face he turns towards his father, Geb.

973b. N. is thy son, N. is Horus.

974a. Thou hast conceived N. as thou hast conceived the god, lord of the ladder,

974b. to whom thou hast given the ladder of the god, to whom thou hast given the ladder of Set,

974c. that N. may ascend to heaven on it and do service of courtier to Rç'.

975a. Let also the ladder of god be given to N., let the ladder of Set be given to N.

975b. that N. may ascend to heaven on it, and do service of courtier to Rç',

975c. just like gods who are gone to their *kas*.

976a. The eye of Horus glowers (?) on the wing of Thot,

976b. on the left side of the ladder of the god.

976c. O men, a uraeus-serpent (goes) to heaven. N. is the eye of Horus.

976d. After its foot has been stopped at every place where it was, N. goes as the eye of Horus goes.

977a. Be pleased that N. come among you, ye his brothers, the gods;

977b. rejoice at the approach of N., ye his brothers, the gods,

977c. as Horus rejoiced at the approach of his eye,

977d. after his eye was given (back) to him in the presence of his father, Geb.

978a. Every spirit, every god, who shall oppose his arm to N.,

978b. when he ascends to heaven on the ladder of the god,

978c. the earth shall not be hoed for him, the *wdn.t*-offering shall not be made for him,

978d. he shall not ferry over to the evening meal in Heliopolis,

978e. he shall not ferry over to the morning meal in Heliopolis.

979a. He shall guard himself, he has obligated himself, (he) who will see, (he) who will hear,

979b. that he (the deceased) ascends to heaven on the ladder of the god,

979c. appearing like the uraeus-serpent which was on the forehead of Set.

980a. Every spirit, every god who shall open his arms to N. (will be) on the ladder of the god.

980b. United for N. are his bones, assembled for him are his limbs;

980c. N. has sprung up to heaven on the fingers of the god, lord of the ladder.

Utterance 479.

981a. To say: The double doors of heaven are open; the double doors of *ḳbḥ.w* are open for Horus of the gods,

981b. that he may ascend at daybreak and purify himself in the Marsh of Reeds.

982a. The double doors of heaven are open; the double doors of $ḳbḥ.w$ are open for Horus of the East,

982b. that he may ascend at daybreak and purify himself in the Marsh of Reeds.

983a. The double doors of heaven are open; the double doors of $ḳbḥ.w$ are open for Horus of the $Šsm.t$-land,

983b. that he may ascend at daybreak and purify himself in the Marsh of Reeds.

984a. The double doors of heaven are open; the double doors of $ḳbḥ.w$ are open for Osiris,

984b. that he may ascend at daybreak and purify himself in the Marsh of Reeds.

985a. The double doors of heaven are open; the double doors of $ḳbḥ.w$ are open for N.,

985b. that he may ascend at daybreak and purify himself in the Marsh of Reeds.

956a. Truly,

986b. he Who ascended, ascended at daybreak and he has purified himself in the Marsh of Reeds,

986c. Horus of the gods ascended at daybreak and he has purified himself in the Marsh of Reeds.

987a. He who ascended, ascended at daybreak and he has purified himself in the Marsh of Reeds,

987b. Horus of the $Šsm.t$-land ascended at daybreak and be has purified himself in the Marsh of Reeds.

988a. He who ascended, ascended at daybreak and he has purified himself in the Marsh of Reeds.

988b. Osiris ascended at daybreak and be has purified himself in the Marsh of Reeds.

989a. He who ascended, ascended at daybreak and he has purified himself in the Marsh of Reeds,

989b. N. ascended at the beginning of day and has purified himself in the Marsh of Reeds.

990a. Rç', impregnate the body of Nut with the seed of the spirit, which shall be in her.

990b. The earth shall rise under the feet of N.; Tefnut shall lay bold of the arm of N.

990c. It is Seker who will purify N.; it is Rç' who will give his certificate (lit. arm) to N.

991a. N. will be more at the head than he who is at the head of the Ennead.

991b. N. takes his place-he is in *ḳbḥ.w*.

991c. *Hnni, Hnni, 'Ip3ti, 'Ip3ti,*

991d. Take N. with you, living eternally.

Utterance 480.

992a. To say: How beautiful indeed is the sight; how elevating indeed is the sight,

992b. the ascension of this god, N., to heaven, like the ascension of father Atum to heaven,

992c. his renown over him, his magic on both sides of him, his terror before him,

993a. after he (Atum) has brought to N. the cities, assembled for N. the nomes,

993b. united for N. the *mśm.w*-lands!

993c. He who had spoken concerning it is Geb, hereditary prince of the gods.

994a. The regions of Horus, the regions of Set, the Marsh of Reeds—

———

994b. they praise N., as *Dw3.w*,

994c. as *Ꜣḥś*, who is chief of the land of Upper Egypt,

994d. as *Ddwn*, who is chief of the land of Nubia,

994e. as Sopdu, (who lives) under his *kśb.t*-trees.

995a. They bring the ladder for N.;

995b. they set up the ladder for N.;

995c. they raise up the ladder for N.

995d. The *mꜣḳ.t*-ladder comes; the *pꜣḳ.t*-ladder comes, thy name comes (as) the gods named (it).

996a. Those who have ascended are come, those who have ascended are come; those who have climbed up are come, those who have climbed' up are come;

996b. those who have lifted themselves up like Shu are come, those who have lifted themselves up like Shu are come.

996c. N. ascends on the hips of Isis; N. climbs up on the hips of Nephthys.

997a. The father of N., Atum, lays bold of the arm of N.;

997b. he appoints N. as, chief of those gods,

997c. the nimble, the wise, the imperishables.

998a. Behold this which you have said, ye gods, that N. would not again be at your head.

998b. Behold, N. remains as he who is at your head, as the surviving bull of the wild bulls.

Utterance 481.

999a. To say: Look-out, His-face-behind-him, ferry N. over.

999b. The two reed-floats of heaven are placed, that N. may ferry over therewith to Rꜥ', to the horizon.

999c. The two reed-floats of heaven were placed for Rꜥ', that he might ferry over therewith to Horus of the gods, to the horizon.

1000a. The two reed-floats of heaven are placed for N.,

1000b. that N. may ferry over therewith to Rꜥ', to the horizon.

1000c. N. will ferry over to his station on the eastern side of the sky,

1000d. in its northern region, among the imperishable stars,

1000e. who stand on (by?) their *d'm*-sceptres, who stand (?) on their eastern standard.

1001a. N. will stand among them.

1001b. The brother of N. is the moon, the mother (*mśtw*) of N. is the morning star.

1001c. Give thine arm to N., that he may live.

Utterance 482.

1002a. To say: O father, Osiris N.,

1002b. raise thyself from thy left side, put thyself on thy right side,

1002c. toward this fresh water, which I have given to thee.

1003a. O father, Osiris N.,

1003b. raise thyself from thy left side, put thyself on thy right side,

1003c. toward this warm bread, which I have made for thee.

1004a. O father, Osiris N.,

1004b. the double doors of heaven are open for thee; the double doors of the bows are open for thee.

1004c. The gods of Buto are filled with compassion

1004d. when they come to Osiris at the voice of lamentation of Isis and Nephthys.

1005a. The Souls of Buto dance for thee;

1005b. they beat their flesh for thee; they smite their arms for thee;

1005c. they dishevel their hair for thee;

1005d. they say to Osiris:

1006. "Thou art gone, thou art come; thou art awake, thou wast asleep; thou remainest alive.

1007a. Stand up, see this; stand up, hear this,

1007b. what thy son has done for thee, what Horus has done for thee.

1007c. He beats him who beats thee; he binds him who binds thee;

1008a. he puts him under his great daughter who is in *Ḳdm*.

1008b. (it is) thy great sister who collected thy flesh, who gathered thy hands,

1008c. who sought thee, who found thee upon thy side on the shore of N*di.t*,

1009a. so that mourning ceased in the two '*itr.t*-palaces."

1009b. Ye gods, speak to him, bring him to you.

1009c. But thou shalt ascend to heaven; thou shalt become *Wp.w3.wt*.

1010a. Thy son Horus leads thee on the ways of heaven.

1010b. Heaven is given to thee; earth is given to thee; the Marsh of Reeds is given to thee,

1010c. together with those two great gods who come from Heliopolis.

Utterance 483.

1011a. To say: The libation is poured which should be poured. *Wp.w3.wt* is up.

1011b. The sleeping ones are awake, awakened are those who should awake; Horus is awake.

1012a. Raise thyself up, Osiris N., son of Geb, his, first(-born),

1012b. before whom the Great Ennead tremble.

1012c. Thou purifiest thyself on the first of the month, thou dawnest on the day of the new moon, for thee will be celebrated the three beginnings (of the divisions of the year).

1012d. The great *min.t* mourns for thee, as for "Him who stands there without being tired," who resides at Abydos.

1013a. Earth, hear that which Geb said, that he spiritualized Osiris as god,

1013b. as the watchers of Buto appointed him, and the watchers of Hierakonpolis proclaimed him,

1013c. like Seker, who is at the head of *Pdw-š*,

1013b. (like) Horus-*Ḥ3*, and (like) *Ḥmn*.

259

1014a. The earth speaks: "The portal of the *Dȝ.t* (var. *ȝkr*) is open."

1014b. The double doors of Geb are open for thee, before thee. Thy speech goes forth before Anubis;

1015a. thy dignity, which is come out of the mouth of Anubis, is Horus, who is chief of his department (or, thigh-offering),

1015b. he of *Śȝtw.t*, the lord of *S'bw.t* (the rebel city),

1015c. the Upper Egyptian jackal god, nome-governor of the Great Ennead.

1016a. Thou withdrawest thyself to heaven on thy firm throne;

1016b. thou ferriest over the Winding Watercourse, while thy face is in the north of Nut.

1016c. Rç' calls thee out of the *'iskn* of heaven;

1016d. thou approachest the god; Set fraternizes with thee.

1017a. The odour of *Ddwn* is on thee, the Upper Egyptian youth;

1017b. he gives thee his pure incense wherewith he censes the gods,

1017c. at the birth of the two children (twins?) of the king of Lower Egypt, who are on the head of the lord of the great (crown).

1018a. Thou hast abundance in the green herb,

1018b. where abundance came to the children of Geb.

1018c. Thy dismembered limbs are collected, thou who hast might over the Bows.

1019a. May Anubis give an offering: The *'imȝ*-tree serves thee; the *nbś*-tree turns its head to thee;

1019b. thou encirclest the sky like *Swntw* (or, *Swnt*).

Utterance 484.

1020a. To say: N. is the Great One who is ascended to heaven

1020b.———

1021a.———[a god is come] in peace, so says she,

1021b. my son, N., is come in peace, so says she, Nut,

1021c. he on whose back no strap (?) has fallen; he on whose hands nothing evil has fallen.

1021d. I will also not permit him to fall; I will also not permit him to leave me.

1022a. N. is the appearing (-mound) of the earth in the midst of the sea, whose hand the inhabitants of the earth have not grasped;

1022b. the inhabitants of the earth have not grasped the hand [of N].

1022c.————the inhabitants of the earth.

1022d. Shu bends the earth under the feet————

1022e.————

1023a. Also that which he has done is that

1023b. he separates N. from his brother 'n.ti; he unites him with my brother 'f.ti.

1024a. His name lives on account of natron-offerings and he is divine.

1024b. N. lives also on that which he lives, on the wr.t-loaf, behind the god.

1024c. It is N. who has transgressed the order; it is N. who has transgressed the order, who is at your feet, ye gods.

Utterance 485.

1025a. To say: [The two doors of heaven] are open, [the two doors of *ḳbḥw* are open].

1025b.————

1025c.————

1025d. [take N. to heaven to the house] of Horus, which is in heaven.

1026a. Each god who will take N. to heaven, living, enduring,

1026b. for him oxen shall be slaughtered, to him legs shall be offered,

1026c. and he shall ascend to the house of Horus, which is in heaven.

1027a. Each god who will not take him to heaven,

1027b. he shall not be respected, he shall have no *ba*-loin-cloth, he shall smell (taste) no *p3ḳ*-cake,

1027c. he shall not ascend to the house of Horus, which is in heaven, on the day of the hearing of the word (trial).

1028a.————

1028b.————

1028c.————

1029a. [N. has come] to thee, Rç',

1029b. calf of gold, born of heaven,

1029c. fattened (calf) of gold, created by the *Ḥ₃.t*-cow.

1030a. Horus, take N. with thee, living, enduring;

1030b. Horus, let not N. be without a boat.

1030c. N. comes to thee, father; N. comes to thee, Geb.

1030d. Give thine arm to N., that N. may ascend to heaven to his mother Nut.

1031a.————

1031b.————

1031c.————

1032a. that we, the Two Enneads, may find an avenger beside him (lit. at his hand),

1032b. although we, the Two Enneads, did not find him who (seized him) from behind (lit. on his hinder part).

1032c. Geb comes, (his) lion-helmet on his head, his two (angry) eyes (lit. yellow eyes) in his face,

1033a. that he may smite you and count (search) foreign lands in search of Osiris.

1033b. He found him lying on his side in *Ghś.ti*.

1033c. Osiris, stand up for thy father, Geb, that he may protect thee against Set.

1034a. Nun————

1034b.————

1035a.————[I have protected] Osiris against his brother, Set.

1035b. I am that which bound his feet, bound his hands,

1035c. which laid him on his side in *T₃-rw*.

1036a. Horus who is over the *šdšd* of heaven, give thou thine arm to N.,

1036b. that N. may ascend to heaven to Nut; (Nut) give thine arm to N., in life and satisfaction,

1036c. that thou mayest unite his bones and collect his limbs.

1037a. Thou unitest his bones [to]————

1037b.————

1037c.————

1037d. [There is not a limb to N] which is without a god,

1038. when he ascends, when he lifts himself up to the sky as the great star which is in the east.

Utterance 486.

1039a. To say: Greetings to you, Waters, which were brought by Shu and lifted up by the two sources,

1039b. in which Geb bathed his limbs,

1039c. so that hearts were in the following of fear and hearts were in the following of terror.

1040a. N. was born in Nun,

1040b. when the sky had not yet come into being, when the earth had not yet come into being,

1040c. when the two supports (of the sky) had not yet come into being, when unrest had not yet come into being,

1040d. when fear had not yet come into being, which came into being on account of the eye of Horus.

1041a. N. is one of that great corporation who was born before (all others) in Heliopolis,

1041b. who will not be taken away for (on account of?) a king

1041c. who (lit. they) will (not) be confiscated for (on account of?) high officials,

1041d. who will not be executed, who will not be pronounced guilty.

1042a. N. is such as has not been executed;

1042b. he has not been taken away for (on account of?) a king,
1042c. he has not been confiscated for (on account of?) high officials,
1042d. his enemy has not been justified against him;
1043a. N. has not become poor, his fingernails have not become long,
1043b. no bones of N. have been broken.
1044a. If N. descends into the water,
1044b. Osiris raises him up and the Two Enneads bear him up;
1044c. Rꜥ' gives his arm to N. to the place where a god should be.
1045a. If N. descends into the earth,
1045b. Geb raises him up and the Two Enneads bear him up;
1045c. Rꜥ' gives his arm to N. to every place where a god should be.

23.
A SERIES OF FOOD TEXTS,
UTTERANCES 487-502.

Utterance 487.

1046a. To say: O my father, Osiris N.,

1046b. thou art spiritualized on the horizon, thou endurest in the *Ddi.
t*;

1046c. thou commandest (with) words as he who is at the head of the living, eternally.

1047a. Get (lit. stand up) from thy left side, put thyself on thy right side;

1047b. take this thy bread, which I am giving thee; I am thy son and thine heir.

Utterance 488.

1048a. To say: O N., (free) course is given to thee by Horus;

1048b. thou art adorned as the only (unique) star in the sky.

1048c. Thy two wings are grown as (those of) a falcon; great of breast

1048d. like the *gnh.św*-falcon, whose descent was seen, after he had traversed the sky.

1049a. Thou voyagest the *ḳbḥ.w* by the watercourse of Rç'-Harachte.

1049b. Nut gives [to thee] her arm————

1049c.————

1050a. To say: If thou desirest that N. say————who sees the tribute of the land,
1050b. then mayest thou be————
1051 .see, order————

1052. To say:————
1053. N. is the bull-herd————
1054. Since you two have given birth to————

1055a. To say: When N. dies [his] *ka* will gain power————
1055b.————
1056a. [who descend into the earth] as two serpents, and I descend on [their] coi[ls].
1056b.————
1057a. It is N. who knelt in Nun; it is N. who sat in *M3* [————]
1057b.————
1058a. [Horus gives me this his bread], with which he has satisfied his subjects,
1058b. and I eat of it with them.

1058c. To say:————

1059a. To say: Greetings to you, who rule over abundance,

1059b. who look after food, who reside as ruler of the green field,

1059b + 1 (N. XIV 1055 + 47). near the lord of splendour.

1059b + 2 (Nt. XXVII 701-702). Cause N. to eat of the corn which originates there,

1059b + 3 (N. 1055 + 48). like the equipment which was made in *Mḥt-wr.t*

1059b + 4 (N. 1055 + 48). by him who sees with his face.

1059b + 5 (N. 1055 + 48). It (the corn) will be brought in for N. and for him who eats with his mouth.

1059c-1060a. Those who are attached to the offerings of the oldest gods————

1060a-b. they introduce me to abundance, they introduce me to food,

1060b + 1 (N. 1055 + 49). that N. may eat with his mouth like him who separates *Wp-šn.wi* (the two tuffs (of hair),

1061a (Nt. XXVII 704). and drop with my (or, his) anus like Śerḳet.

1061a + 1 (Nt. 704). I give offerings and distribute food

1061a + 2 (N. 1055 + 50). like him with the long wings who lives in the Marsh of Reeds.

1061b. Wind is in my nose; seed is in my phallus,

1061c. as (seed is in the phallus) of him of mysterious form, who lives in splendour.

1061c + 1 (N. 1055 + 50. N. sees Nun,

1061c + 2 (Nt. 705). when she appears on her way.

1061c + 3 (N. 1055 + 51). Honour will be given to N.;

1061c + 4 (Nt. 706). N. will be great because of her power; there will be a six days' feast in *Hri-'ḥ3*;

1062. (Nt. 706). N. will eat of the pregnant cow like those who are in Heliopolis.

Utterance 494.

1063a. He sat, who was seated to eat bread; Rç' sat to eat bread.

1063b. Water was given by the Two Enneads.

1063c. [The flood] stood [on the bank].

1063d. (Firth-Gunn, 235, 19; Lacau TR 4). I come to thee, O Flood,

1063e. (Firth-Gunn, 235, 19-20; Lacau TR 4). that thou mayest give me bread when I am hungry; that thou mayest give me beer when I am thirsty.

Utterance 495.

1064a. To say: O Great Ennead in Heliopolis,

1064b. lady of the (Three) Enneads,

1064c. his meal (shall be) as his who is chief of the *'itr.t*-palace

1064d. Two of N.'s meals (shall be) in the *Ddi.t*;

1064e. [three of his meals (shall be) in the horizon————]

Utterance 496.

1065a. To say: Greetings to thee, O Food; greetings to thee, O Abundance;

1065b. greetings to thee, O Corn; greetings to thee, O Flour.

1065c. Greetings to you, ye gods, who put the meal before Rҫ',

1065d. who————with *Ḥw*, who are at the *Mḥ.t-wr.t*;

1065e. I will eat of the morsel of Rҫ', sitting on the throne of splendour.

1066a. I am she of Tentyra; I am come from Tentyra;

1066b. Shu is behind N.; Tefnut is before him;

1066c. it is *Wp-wȝ.wt*, who serves as a protection (?) on the right of N.

1066d. They cause this field-of-food of Rҫ' to keep me alive so that I may eat,

1066e. after it is collected for me, as for him who rules over the Ennead, who lives at (or, on) *Mḥ.t-wr.t*.

1067a. [To say: O N., stand up], be seated, shake the earth (i.e. dust of the earth) from thee;

1067b. remove the two arms from behind thee, as (those of) Set.

1067c. The eye of Horus will come to thee at the beginning of the decade, because thou art eager for it.

1067d.————

Utterance 498.

1068a. To say: Awake, Osiris, awake.

1068b. O N., stand up, be seated, shake the earth (i.e. the dust of the earth) from thee.

1068c. I come, I give [the eye] of Horus to thee; it will be lasting with thee (or, it will be pleasing to thee).

1068d.————

1069a. [Stand up] for this joint of (*św.t-*) meat, which is from the broad-hall; come out, receive this thy bread from my hand.

1069b. O Osiris N., I am thy son, conceived of thee;

1069c. I am come with————

Utterance 499.

1070a. To say: Back, O Spittle, which is not fallen (discharged).

1070b. It (the serpent) is lying outstretched. Protect thyself. Stand (firm). Smite.

Utterance 500.

1071a. To say: A heart is there, a heart is there, one who will lock himself in, one who will lock himself in is there.

1071b. Back, thou great hidden one, who has come out of a hidden member.

1071c. A man sees it. Protect thyself. Bar the way (?).

Utterance 501.

1072a. To say:————for me three meals,

1072b. one in heaven, two on earth.

1072c. A lion-helmet————green————

Utterance 502.

1073————four————

1074.————a point————

1075.————darkness————

1076.————be not————

1077. come————

24.

A SERIES OF REED-FLOATS AND FERRYMAN TEXTS, UTTERANCES 503-522.

Utterance 503.

1078a. To say: The door of heaven is open, the door of earth is open,

1078b. apertures of the (heavenly) windows are open,

1078c. the steps of Nun are open,

1078d. the steps of light are revealed

1078e. by that one who endures always.

1079a. I say this to myself when I ascend to heaven,

1079b. that I may anoint myself with the best ointment and clothe myself with the best linen,

1079c. and seat myself upon (the throne) of "Truth which makes alive";

1080a. while my side is against the side of those gods who are in the north of the sky,

1080b. the imperishable stars, and I will not set,

1080c. the untiring (in swimming), and I will not tire (in swimming),

1080d. the one not drawn out of the water, and I will not be drawn out of the water.

1081a. If *Mnt.w* (a star?) is high, I will be high with him,

1081b. If *Mnt.w* hastens away, I will hasten away with him.

1082a. To say: The sky is pregnant with the wine juice of the vine;

1082b. Nut has given birth to (it) as her daughter, the morning star.

1082c. I also arise;

1082d. the third is Sothis of the pure places.

1083a. I have purified myself in the lakes of the dancers(?) singers(?) or, panegyrists(?),

1083b. I have cleansed myself in the lakes of the jackal.

1083c. Thorn-bush, remove thyself from my way,

1084a. that I may take the south side of the Marsh of Reeds.

1084b. The m3'-canal is opened, the Winding Watercourse is inundated.

1084c. The two reed-floats of heaven are placed for Horus,

1084d. that he may ferry over to Rç', to the horizon.

1085a. The two reed-floats of heaven are placed for him of the horizon,

1085b. that he may ferry over to Rç', to the horizon.

1085c. The two reed-floats of heaven are placed for Horus *S̀sm.t,*

1085d. that he may ferry over to Rç', to the horizon.

1085e. The two reed-floats of heaven are placed for Horus of the East,

1085f. that he may ferry over to Rç', to the horizon,

1086a. The two reed-floats of heaven shall be placed for me, I, Horus of the gods,

1086b. that I also may ferry over to Rç', to the horizon,

1086c. and that I may take my throne, which is in the Marsh of Reeds.

1087a. I descend to the south side of the Marsh of Offerings.

1087b. I am a Great One, son of a Great One;

1087c. I am come forth from between the thighs of the Two Enneads.

1087d. I have adored Rç'; I have adored Horus of the East;

1087e. I have adored Horus of the horizon,

1088a. as he girded himself with the apron,

1088b. that he might be gracious to me, that he might be gracious to
"Horus-on-his-throne(?)."

1088c. that he might be gracious to "Horus-on-his-throne(?)," that he
might be gracious to me.

Utterance 505.

1089a. To say: I am come forth from Buto, to the Souls of Buto,
1089b. adorned with the adornment of Horus,
1089c. clothed with the clothes of Thot.
1089d. Isis is before me; Nephthys is behind me;
1090a. *Wp-w3-wt* opens the way for me;
1090b. Shu lifts me up;
1090c. the Souls of Heliopolis construct a stairway for me,
1090d. to unite with the Above (i.e. to reach the top);
1090e. Nut gives her arm to me as she did for Osiris
1090f. the day that he landed there.
1091a. O thou whose face is behind thee, ferry me over to the Marsh of
Reeds.
1091b. Whence art thou come here? I am come from *3w3r.t*;
1091c. my companion is the uraeus-serpent, who comes forth from the
god, the *'i'r.t*-serpent, who comes forth from Rç'.
1092a. Ferry me over; put me in the Marsh of Reeds————
1092b. those four spirits who are with me————
1092c. *Ḥpi, Dw3-mw-t-f, 'Imś.ti, Ḳbḥ-śn.w.f*————
1092d. two on this side, two on that side
1093a. (and) I will be the rudder. I find the Two Enneads.
1093b. It is, they who give me their arm;
1093c. I sit between them to give judgment;
1093d. I command those whom I find there.

1094a. To say: I am *St.ti*, I am *Sti-sti*;

1094b. I am the *Sw-sw*-lake;

1094c. I am Swnt, the chest of heaven;

1095a. I am *'Ir-k3*, the most spiritual of the kings of Lower Egypt;

1095b. I am "he who shall remain hidden," the *'Imn* of this land;

1095c. I am he who made (?) the two lands;

1095d. I am *krkr*, I am *krkrw*;

1096a. I am Praise; I am Appearance;

1096b. I am Hathor-symbol-of-the-female-soul, who has two faces;

1096c. I am he who is to be delivered; I have delivered myself from all evil things.

1097a. Further, to say: I am *Wnš.t* (the female wolf); I am he who belongs to the female wolf;

1097b. I am *Hpi*; I am *Dw3-mu.t.f.*;

1097c. I am *'Imš.ti*, I am *Kbh-śn.w.f.*;

1098a. I am (*Dwn-'n.wi*) he who stretches out the wings;

1098b. I am those great gods who rule over the lake.

1098c. I am the *B3-'nh* (living soul) with bearded (?) face,

1098d. who has stretched his head high, who has freed himself, who has removed himself,

1099a. (by) the interruption of the action of him who would act,

1099b. (by) putting to sleep the action of him who would act, the command of him who would command.

1099c. I do (good) to him who does what is good; I command (good) to him who commands what is good;

1100a. my lips are as the Two Enneads;

1100b. I am the great spoken word;

1100c. I am a delivered one; I am one worthy of deliverance;

1100d. I am delivered from all evil things.

1101a. Further, to say: Men and gods, your arms under me,

274

1101b. while you raise me and lift me up to heaven,

1101c. as the arms of Shu (were) under the sky as he lifted her up———

1101d. to heaven, to heaven, to the great seat, among the gods!

Utterance 507.

1102a. To say: *Ḥmti*, say to him who had what is, and to him who has it not: "The entrance of

1102b. the *b'n*-canal is open,

1102c. the Marsh of Reeds is inundated,

1102d. the Winding Watercourse is full of water;

1103a. the two reed-floats of heaven are placed for Horus that he may ferry over therewith to Rç';

1103b. the two reed-floats of heaven are placed for Rç' that he may ferry over therewith to Horus who inhabits the horizon."

1104a. He (*Ḥmti*) commends N. to his father, the moon,

1104b. (and to) the mother of N., the morning star;

1104c. he commends N. to those four youths,

1104d. who sit on the eastern side of the sky;

1105a. he commends N. to those four youths,

1105b. who sit on the eastern side of the sky;

1105c. to those four youths with hair black as coal,

1105d. who sit in the shade (shadow) of the fortress *Ḳзti*.

1106a. Further, to say: Great is the father of N.; great is the father of N.;

1106b. N. is great like his father (or, in the greatness of his father).

Utterance 508.

1107a. To say: He ascends, who ascends; N. ascends.

1107b. Let the lady of Buto rejoice; let the heart of her who dwells in el-Kâb be glad

1107c. the day that N. ascends there in the place of (or, as representative of) Rç'.

1108a. N. has trodden down for himself thy splendour,

1108b. as stairs under his feet,

1108c. that N. may ascend thereon to his mother, the living uraeus which is on the head of Rç'.

1109a. Her heart has pity for him; she gives her breast to him, that he may suck it.

1109b. "My son," says she, "take to thee my breast, that thou mayest suck it," says she,

1109c. "since thou comest not on every one of thy days."

1110a. Heaven speaks, the earth quakes; the gods, of Heliopolis shudder

1110b. at the voice of the *wdn.t*-offering (made) before N.

1111a. His mother has nourished him-she of Bubastis;

1111b. she who dwells in el-Kâb has reared him;

1111c. she who dwells in Buto has given him her arm.

1112a. Behold, he is come; behold, he is come;

1112b. behold, N. is come, for life and joy,

1112c. and he makes his repast on figs

1112d. and on wine which is in the divine vineyard.

1113a. The chef who is beside him, he prepares a repast of it for him.

1113b. N. runs; his herdsman runs;

1113c. his sweetness is the sweetness of Horus; his fragrance is the fragrance of Horus.

1114a. To heaven, to heaven, together with the gods of the house of the lion and the falcon;

1114b. to heaven, together with the gods of the house of the lion and the falcon,

1114c. those at my side accompanying me!

1115a. So says Geb, as he seizes N. by his arm,

1115b. and as, he guides him through the portals of heaven.

276

1115c. The god is on his throne; it is well that the god is on his throne.

1116a. Satis has washed him

1116b. with her four *ȝbt*-pitchers from Elephantiné.

1116c. Ho, whence, pray, art thou come, my son, O king?

1116d. He is come to the Ennead, to heaven, that he may eat of its bread.

1117a. Ho, whence, pray, art thou come, my son, O king?

1117b. He is come to the Ennead, to the earth, that he may eat of its bread.

1117c. Ho, whence, pray, art thou come, my son, O king?

1117d. He is come to the *dnddndr*-boat.

1118a. Ho, whence, pray, art thou come, my son, O king?

1118b. He is come to these his two mothers, the two vultures,

1118c. They of the long hair and hanging breasts,

1118d. who are on the hill of *šḥšḥ*.

1119a. They draw their breasts over the mouth of N.,

1119b. but they do not wean him for ever.

Utterance 509.

1120a. To say: Heaven speaks; the earth quakes:

1120b. Geb trembles; the two nomes of the god shout;

1120c. the ground is hoed; the *wdn.t*-offering is made before N., living, enduring,

1121a. when he ascends to heaven, when he ferries over the vault, for life and joy:

1121b. also when he traverses the foaming sea, destroying the walls of Shu.

1122a. He ascends to heaven,

1122b. the tip of his wings being like (that of) a great bird,

1122c. his entrails having been washed by Anubis;

1122d. the services of Horus having been rendered (lit. served) in Abydos, (even) the embalming of Osiris.

1123a. He ascends to heaven among the imperishable stars;

1123b. his sister is Sothis; his guide is the morning star;

1123c. they two take his arm as far as the Marsh of Offerings.

1124a. He sits upon that (his) firm throne,

1124b. whose knobs are lions,

1124c. whose feet are the hoofs of a great wild-bull.

1125a. He stands (or, he is erect) upon his elevated throne, which is between the two great gods,

1125b. with his sceptre '*b*3, the *mnḥi*, in his hand.

1126a. When he lifts his arm toward the blessed dead (?)

1126b. the gods come to him bowing,

1126c. and the two great gods watch at their side.

1127a. They find him between the Two Enneads in giving judgment:

1127b. "A prince of all princes this is," they say of him;

1127c. (and) they appointed N. among the gods.

Utterance 510.

1128a. To say: It is certainly not N. who asks to see thee

1128b. in the form which has become thine;

1128c. Osiris asks to see thee in the form which has become thine;

1129a. it is thy son who asks to see thee in the form which has become thine;

1129b. it is Horus who asks to see thee in the form which has become thine.

1130a. When thou sayest, "statues", in respect to these stones,

1130b. which are like fledglings of swallows under the river-bank;

1130c. when thou sayest, "his beloved son is coming," in the form which had become that of "his beloved son"

1131a. they (the "statues") transport Horus; they row Horus over,

1131b. as Horus ascends (lit. in. the ascent of Horus) in the *Mḥt-wr.t-* cow.

1132a. The double doors of heaven are open, the double doors of *ḳbḥ.w* are open for Horus of the East,

1132b. at day-break, that he may descend and purify himself in the Marsh of Reeds.

1133a. The double doors of heaven are open, the double doors of *ḳbḥ. w* are open for N.,

1133b. at daybreak, that N. may descend and purify himself in the Marsh of Reeds.

1134a. The double doors of heaven are open, the double doors of *ḳbḥ.w* are open for Horus of the *Dꜣ.t,*

1134b. at daybreak, that he may descend and purify himself in the Marsh of Reeds.

1135a. The double doors of heaven are open, the double doors of *ḳbḥ. w* are open for N.,

1135b. at daybreak, that be may descend and purify himself in the Marsh of Reeds.

1136a. The double doors of heaven are open, the double doors of *ḳbḥ.w* are open for Horus. of the *Šsm.t*-land,

1136b. at daybreak, that he may descend and purify himself in the Marsh of Reeds.

1137a. The double doors of heaven are open, the double doors of *ḳbḥ. w* are open for N.,

1137b. at daybreak, that N. may descend and purify himself in the Marsh of Reeds.

1138a. The ground is hoed for him; the *wdn.t*-offering is made for him,

1138b. when he dawns as king and takes charge of his throne.

1138c. He ferries over the *ptr.ti*-sea;

1138d. he traverses the Winding Watercourse.

1139a. *'Imt.t* lays hold of the arm of N.,

1139b. beginning with her chapel, beginning with her hidden place, which the god made for her,

1139c. for N. is pure (a priest), the son of a pure one (a priest).

1140a. N. is purified with these four *nmś.t*-jars,

1140b. filled at the divine-lake in *Ntr.w*;

1140c. (he is dried) by the wind of the great Isis, together with (which) the great Isis dried (him) like Horus.

1141a. Let him come, he is pure,

1141b. so said the priest of Rˁ concerning N. to the door-keeper of *ḳbḥ.w*,

1141c. (who) was to announce him to these four gods, who are over the lake of *Kns.t*.

1142a. They recite: "How just is N. to his father, Geb!"

1142b. They recite: "How just is N. to Rˁ!"

1142c. His frontiers exist not; his boundary stones are not to be found.

1142d. Also, Geb, whose (one) arm (reaches) to heaven, whose (other) arm is on earth,

1142e. announces N. to Rˁ.

1143a. N. leads the gods; N. directs the divine boat;

1143b. N. seizes heaven, its pillars and its stars.

1144a. The gods come to him bowing;

1144b. the spirits escort N. to his *ba*;

1144c. they reckon (gather up) their war-clubs;

1144d. they destroy their weapons;

1145a. for behold N. is a great one, the son of a great one, whom Nut has borne;

1145b. the power of N. is the power of Set of Ombos.

1145c. This N. is the great wild-bull, who comes forth like *Ḫnti-'imnti.w*.

1146a. N. is the pouring down of rain; he came forth as the coming into being of water;

1146b. for he is the *Nḥb-kȝ.w*-serpent with the many coils;

1146c. N. is the scribe of the divine book, who says what is and causes
to exist what is not;

1147a. N. is the red bandage, who comes forth from the great *Iḥ.t*;

1147b. N. is that eye of Horus,

1147c. stronger than men, mightier than the gods.

1148a. Horus carries N., Set lifts him up.

1148b. Let N. make an offering which a star gives;

1148c. he satisfies the two gods, let them be satisfied; he satisfies the two
gods, and so they are satisfied.

Utterance 511.

1149a. To say: Geb laughs, Nut smiles

1149b. before him, (when) N. ascends to heaven.

1150a. Heaven rejoices for him; the earth quakes for him;

1150b. the tempest roars (lit. drives) for him.

1150c. He howls (or, roars) like Set;

1151 a. the guardians of the parts (?) of heaven open the doors of heaven
for him.

1151b. He stands on Shu;

1151c. he upholds the stars, in the shadow of the walls of god.

1152a. He crosses the sky like Swnt;

1152b. the third (with him) is Sothis of the pure places,

1152c. for he purifies himself in the lakes of the *Dw3.t*.

1153a. The *nmt-š*-cow will make his ways pleasant;

1153b. she will guide him to the great seat, which the gods made, which
Horus made, which Thot begat.

1154a. Isis will conceive him; Nephthys will bear him.

154b. Then he will take his seat on the great throne which the gods
made.

1155a. *Dw3-w* in jubilation and the gods in homage will come to him;

1155b. the gods of the horizon will come to him on their face,

1155c. and the imperishable stars, bowing.

1156a. He takes the offering table; he directs the mouth of the gods;

1156b. he supports the sky in life; he sustains the earth in joy;

1156c. his right arm, it supports the sky in satisfaction (might

1156d. his left arm, it sustains the earth in joy.

1157a. He finds *Štt*,

1157b. the crier, the door-keeper of Osiris.

1157c. His abomination is ferrying over without doing *'isnw.t*.

1158a. He receives the wind of life, he breathes joy,

1158b. and he abounds in divine offerings;

1158c. he inhales wind and breathes out the wind of the North;

1158d. he prospers among the gods.

1158a. He is sharp like the great *Śpd*;

1159b. he advances towards the two *'itr.t*-palaces;

1159c. he strikes with the *'bȝ*-sceptre and directs with the *'iȝȝ.t*-sceptre.

1160a. He puts his record among men, and his love among the gods,

1160b. saying: "Say what is; do not say what is not;

1161a. the abomination of a god is a deceitful word."

1161b. Let him be tested! Thou shalt not speak (thus of) him.

1161c. This N. is thy son; this N. is thine heir.

Utterance 512.

1162a. To say: My father made for himself his heart, after the other (heart) was taken from him, since it was opposed thereto,

1162b. as he ascended to heaven,

1162c. and traversed the billows of the Winding Watercourse.

1162d. Anubis comes, meeting thee,

1163a. Geb gives thee his arm, father N.

1163b. Guardian of the earth, leader of spirits————

1163c. he mourns him, who was mourned, his father————,

1164a. O, raise thyself up, N.;

1164b. receive these thy four *nmś.wt*-jars and *ꝫb.wt*-jars;

1164c. purify thyself in the Lake of the jackal; purify thyself by incense in the Lake of the *Dꝫ.t*;

1164d. purify thyself before thy *śꝫb.t*-bush in the Marsh of Reeds.

1165a. Thou voyagest over the sky;

1165b. thou makest thy abode in the Marsh of Offerings, among the gods who are gone to their *kas*.

1165c. Seat thyself upon thy firm throne;

1166a. take thy mace and thy sceptre,

1166b. that thou mayest lead those who are in Nun, that thou mayest command the gods,

1166c. and that thou mayest put a spirit in his spirit.

1167a. Take thy walk; voyage over thy *ḥnti*-ocean,

1167b. like Rç' on the shores (or, lands) of the sky.

1107c. N. lift thyself up; hasten to thy spirit.

Utterance 513.

1168a. To say: When father N. ascends to heaven among the gods who are in heaven;

1168b. and when he stands by the great *w'r.t*;

1168c. he hears the words of the blessed dead

1169a. Rç' finds thee on the shores (or, lands) of the sky, in the *ḥnti*-ocean, in Nut.

1169b. "He comes, who should come," say the gods.

1170a. He gives thee his arm on (at) the *'iskn* of the sky.

1170b. "He comes who knows his place," say the gods.

1171a. Pure one, assume thy throne in the boat of Rç',

1171b. that thou mayest sail the sky, that thou mayest mount above the ways (or, the far-off ways);

1171c. that thou mayest sail with the imperishable stars;

1171d. and that thou mayest voyage with the indefatigable (stars).

1172a. Thou receivest the tribute of the evening boat;

1172b. thou becomest a spirit in the *D3.t*;

1172c. thou livest in this sweet life in which the lord of the horizon lives.

1173a. "Great Flood dwelling in Nut, who indeed has done this for thee?",

1173b. say the gods who follow Atum.

1174a. A greater than he hath done that for him, he who is north of the *ḥnti*-ocean of Nut.

1174b. He has heard his appeal; 'he has done for him what he said.

1174c. He has received his, body in the court of the prince of Nun,

1174d. before the Great Ennead.

Utterance 514.

1175a. To say: *Nḥi*————*Nḥi*, serpent————

1175b.————who is before Letopolis; his living ones are at his neck.

1175c. Thy place is for thy son; thy (?) place is for thy (?) son.

1175d. Geb has called————

Utterance 515.

1176a. To say: Two legs of Horus, two wings of Thot,

1176b. ferry N. over; leave him not without a boat!

1177a. Give thou bread to N.; give thou beer to N.,

1177b. from thy eternal bread, this thy everlasting beer.

1178a. N. is by these two obelisks of Rç', which are on earth;

1178b. N. is by these two holy signs of Rç', which are in heaven;

1179a. N. goes on these two reed-floats of the sky which are before Rç';

1179b. he brings this jar of the libation of Rç',

1179c. which purifies the land of the south before Rç', when he ascends in his horizon.

1180a. (When) N. comes to the field of life, to the birthplace of Rç' in ḳbḥ.w,

1180b. N. finds Ḳbḥ.wt, daughter of Anubis;

1180c. she approaches him with these her four nmś.t-jars,

1180d. with which she refreshes the heart of the Great God, on the day of awakening.

1181a. She (also) refreshes the heart of N. therewith to life,

1181b. she purifies N., she censes N.

1182a. N. receives his provision from that which is in the granary of the Great God;

1182b. N. is clothed with imperishable stars;

1182c. N. presides over the two 'itr.t-palaces,

1182d. he sits at the place of him equipped with the form (of a man).

Utterance 516.

1183a. Further, to say: O Nwrw, ferryman of the marsh of Pȝ'ṯ,

1183b. N. is the herdsman of thy cattle, who is over thy Birthplace;

1184a. N. is thy potter who is on earth,

1184b. who will break the jar, the child of Nut.

1185a. N. is come; he brought to thee this thy house here which he made for thee

1185b. on the night of thy birth, on the day of thy Mśḥn.t;

1185c. it is a jar.

1186a. Thou art Bes who knows not his father; thou knowest not thy mother.

1186b. Let him not announce thee to those who do not know thee that they may know thee.

1187a. Ferry him over rapidly

1187b. to the land of smȝ, to this field where the gods were be gotten,

1187c. over which the gods rejoice on these their New Year's days.

Utterance 517.

1188a. Further, to say: O thou who ferriest over the just, who is without a boat,

1188b. ferryman of the Marsh of Reeds,

1188c. N. is just before heaven, before the earth;

1188d. N. is just before this isle of the earth,

1188e. to which he has been swimming, and has arrived there,

1188f. and which is between the two thighs of Nut.

1189a. It is N., a pygmy, a dancer of the god,

1189b. who makes glad the heart of the god, before his great throne.

1189c. This is what thou hast heard in the houses,

1189d. and what thou hast learned in the streets,

1189e. that day when N. was summoned to life,

1189f. to hear the sentence.

1190a. Behold, the two who are on the throne of the Great God,

1190b. they summon N. to life and joy for ever,

1190c. they are prosperity and health.

1191a. (So) ferry N. over to the field, the beautiful seat of the Great God,

1191b. where he does the things to be done among the 'im3ḫw.w (venerable ones),

1191c. appoints them to food and assigns them to fowling.

1192a. It is N.,

1192b. whom he appoints to food and assigns to fowling.

Utterance 518.

1193a. Further, to say: O *Iw*, ferryman of the Marsh of Offerings,

1193b. bring for N. this (boat); N. goes, N. should come,

1194a. the son of the Morning Boat whom she bore before the earth, his happy birth,

1194b. whereby the Two Lands live, on the right side of Osiris.

1195a. N. is the annual messenger of Osiris.

1195b. Behold, he is come with a message from thy father Geb:

1195c. "If the year's yield is welcome, how welcome is the year's yield; the year's yield is good, how good is the year's yield!"

1196a. N. has descended with the Two Enneads in $ḳbḥ.w$,

1196b. N. is the measuring line of the Two Enneads,

1196c. by which the Marsh of Offerings is established.

1197a. N. found the gods standing,

1197b. wrapped in their garments,

1197c. their white sandals on their feet.

1197d. Then they threw their white sandals on the ground,

1197e. they cast off their garments.

1198a. "Our heart was not joyful until thou didst descend," say they;

1198b. "may that which was said of you be that which you now are."

11199a. Stand up, Osiris,

1199b. commend N. to those who are on "$Šḫm$ is joyous" north of the Marsh of Offerings,

1199c. like as thou didst commend Horus to Isis the day that thou didst impregnate her,

1200a. that they may give food to N. in the fields,

1200b. and that he may drink at the sources

1200c. in the Marsh of Offerings.

Utterance 519.

1201a. Further, to say: O $Ḥr.f-ḥȝ.f$, doorkeeper of Osiris,

1201b. Osiris has said: "Let this thy boat be brought for N.,

1201c. in which thy pure ones ferry,

1201d. that thou mayest receive a libation in this eastern (?) quarter of the imperishable stars

1202a. that N. may ferry in it

1202b. with that band of green tissue,

1202c. woven, as an eye of Horus,

1202d. to bandage with it that finger of Osiris which became affected."

1203a. N. arrives, *šśw*, *šśw*.

1203b. The shoals of the great sea protect him.

1203c. The double doors with windows (of heaven) are open; the double doors of the lower region are open.

1203d. Ye Two Enneads, take N. with you

1203e. to the Marsh of Offerings, in accordance with the dignity (quality) of N., (of the) lord of the '*im3ḥw.w*.

1204a. N. strikes with the '*b3*-sceptre; N. directs with the '*i33-t*-sceptre;

1204b. N. conducts the servants of Rç'.

1204c. The earth has been refreshed; Geb has been censed

1204d. the Two Enneads have been *ndśdś* (?);

1205a. N. is a *ba* which passes among you, O gods.

1205b. The *p3'ḥ*-pool (?) has been opened up; the *p3'ḥ*-pool has been filled with water;

1205c. the Marsh of Reeds has been inundated;

1205d. the Marsh of Offerings has been filled with water.

1206a. They come to these four long-haired youths,

1206b. who stand on the eastern side of the sky,

1206c. and who prepare the two reed-floats for Rç',

1206d. that Rç' may go thereby to his horizon.

1206e. They prepare the two reed-floats for N.,

1206f. that N. may go thereby to the horizon, to Rç'.

1207a. O morning star, Horus of the *D3.t*, the divine falcon, the great green (?),

1207b. children of heaven, greetings to thee in these thy four faces, which are satisfied

1207c. when they see those who are in *Kns.t*,

1207d. who drive away the storm from those who are satisfied.

1208a. Give thou these thy two fingers to N.,

1208b. which-thou gavest to the beautiful one (*Nfr.t*), daughter of the Great God,

1208c. when the sky was separated from the earth, and when the gods ascended to heaven,

1209a. whilst thou was a soul appearing in the bow of thy boat of 770 cubits (long),

1209b. which the gods of Buto constructed for thee, which the eastern gods shaped for thee.

1210a. N. is son of Khepri, born from the vulva,

1210b. under the curls of *Ṯw.ś-'ȝ.ś*, north of Heliopolis, out of the forehead of Geb.

1211a. N. is he who was between the legs of *Mḫnti-'irti*,

1211b. that night when be made the bread plain,

1211c. that day when the heads of the mottled serpents were cut off.

1212a. Take thou to thyself thy favourite *m'bȝ*-harpoon,

1212b. thy spear which seizes the canals,

1212c. whose two points are the rays of the sun,

1212d. whose two barbs are the claws of *Mȝfd.t*,

1212e. with which N. cuts off the heads

1212f. of the adversaries, who are in the Marsh of Offerings,

1213a. when he descended to the ocean (great green).

1214b. Bow thy head, decline thine arms (bow in humility), great green.

1213c. The children of Nut are those who descend to thee,

1213d. their garlands on their heads,

1213e. their garlands of leaves on their necks;

1214a. (those) who cause to flourish the crowns (of the North) of the canals of the Marsh of Offerings

1214b. for the great Isis, who fastened on the girdle in Chemmis,

1214c. when she brought her garment and burned incense before her son, Horus, the young child,

1215a. when he was journeying through the land in his two white sandals,

1215b. and went to see his father, Osiris.

1215c. N. opened his way like fowlers;

1215d. N. exchanged greetings with the lords of *kas*;

1216a. N. went to the great island in the midst of the Marsh of Offerings,

1216b. on which the gods cause the swallows to alight.

1216c. The swallows are the imperishable stars.

1216d. They give to N. the tree of life whereof they live,

1216e. that N. may, at the same time, live thereof.

1217a. (Morning Star), cause thou N. to ferry over with thee,

1217b. to this thy great field, which thou didst subdue with the aid of the gods,

1217c. (where) thou eatest at evening and at dawn, which is full of food.

1218a. N. eats of that which thou eatest;

12 18b. N. drinks of that which thou drinkest.

1218c. Put thou the back of N.

1218d. against the post, against it who is before its sisters.

1219a. Thou (Morning Star) makest N. to sit down because of his truth

1219b. (and) to stand up because of his venerableness.

1219c. N. stands; he has taken (his) venerableness in thy presence,

1219d. like Horus who took the house (heritage) of his father from the brother of his father, Set, in the presence of Geb.

1220a. Put thou N. as a prince among the spirits,

1220b. the imperishable stars of the north of the sky,

1220c. who direct the offerings and protect the gifts,

1220d. who cause to come those things (offerings and gifts) for those who preside over the *kas* in heaven.

Utterance 520.

1221a. Further, to say: O ye four who are in possession of curls,

1221b. your curls are in front of you (or, on your forehead),

1221c. your curls are at your temples,

1221d. your curls are at the back of your head,

1221e. (and that which is) in the middle of your head are braids.

1222a. Bring this boat to N.; bring this boat to N.

1222b. It is *Ḥkrr* and Sees-behind-him who will ferry N. over,

1222c. (when) N. ferries over to that side where the imperishable stars are,

1222d. that N. may be with them.

1223a. If you do not at once ferry over in the ferry-boat of N.,

1223b. then N. will tell this your name to the people whom he knows,

1223c. to the "wicked-men";

1223d. so then N. will pluck out those braids, which are in the middle of your head,

1223e. like lotus flowers in-the lotus pond.

Utterance 521.

1224a. To say: He who journeys over the sea, the messenger; he who journeys over the sea, the messenger

1224b. it is a *śr*-gander, who brings himself; it is a *s₃t*-goose, who brings herself;

1224c. it is a *ng*-bull, who brings himself.

1225a. N. flies, as a cloud, like a heron;

1225b. thou fliest low (?) like the father of a *ḥ₃*-heron.

1225c. N. goes off

1225d. to these his fathers, who are over (chief of) *Pdw-š*;

1226a. N. brings his bread which cannot mould,

1226b. his beer which cannot sour.

1226c. N. eats this his one bread alone;

1226d. N. gives it not to one at his back;

1226e. he rescues it from the *knm.t*-bird.

1227a. To say: Sees-behind-him, His-face-behind-him,

1227b. behold thou, N. is come to life.

1227c. He has brought to thee this eye of Horus, bound in the field of wrestlers.

1227d, Bring it to N., namely, the "work of Khnum."

1228a. O *Ḥpi, 'Imś.ti, Dwȝ-mut.f, Ḳbḥ-śn.w.f,*

1228b. bring it to N., namely, the "work of Khnum,"

1228c. which is in the Winding Watercourse.

1229a. O devourer, open the way to N.;

1229b. O *ḳrr*-serpent, open the way to N.;

1229c. O Nekhbet, open the way to N.

1230a. Greetings to thee, good one, (come) in peace.

1230b. Love N. as N. loves thee.

1230c. Unwanted (?) art thou, evil one;

1230d. if thou avoidest N., N. will avoid thee.

25.

MISCELLANEOUS TEXTS CHIEFLY ABOUT THE DECEASED KING'S RECEPTION AND LIFE IN HEAVEN, UTTERANCES 523-533.

Utterance 523.

1231a. To say: The sky has strengthened the radiance for N.,

1231b. that N. may lift himself to heaven as the eye of Rç',

1231c. and that N. may stand at this left eye of Horus

1231d. where the word of the gods is heard.

1232a. Thou shalt stand in the presence of the spirits,

1232b. as Horus stood in the presence of the living.

1232c. N. shall stand in the presence of the spirits, the imperishable stars,

1232d. as Osiris stands in the presence of the spirits.

Utterance 524.

1233a. To say: N. is pure with the purification which Horus did to his eye.

1233b. N. is Thot who avenges thee (the eye); N. is not Set who seizes it.

1233c. Rejoice, O gods; rejoice, O Two Enneads.

1234a. Let Horus approach N.

1234b. N. is crowned with the white crown, the eye of Horus wherewith he is powerful.

1234c. The gods rejoice for him who ascends.

1235a. The face of N. is as that of a jackal; the two arms of N. are as those of a falcon;

1235b. the extremities of the wings of N. are as those of Thot.

1235c. May Geb let N. fly to heaven,

1235d. that this N. may take the eye of Horus, to himself!

1236a. N. has penetrated your frontier, ye dead;

1236b. N. has overturned your boundary stones, ye who are before and with Osiris;

1236c. N. has conjured the paths of Set;

1236d. N. has passed by the messengers of Osiris.

1237a. No god can hold N.;

1237b. no opponent stands in the way of N.

1237c. N. is Thot, the strongest of the gods;

1237d. Atum calls N. to heaven for life.

1237e. N. has taken the eye of Horus to himself!

1238a. N. is the son of Khnum; there is nothing evil which N. has done.

1238b. Weighty is this word before thee, O Rç'.

1238c. Hear it, bull of the Ennead.

1239a. Open the way of N.; enlarge the place of N. before the gods.

1239b. N. has taken the eye of Horus to himself; N. has attached to himself that which went forth from his head.

1240a. N. has caused him to see with both his eyes complete,

1240b. that he may punish his enemies therewith.

1240c. Horus has taken his eye and has given it to N.

1241a. His odour is the odour of a god; the odour of the eye of Horus appertains to the flesh of N.

1241b. N. is in front with it; N. sits upon your great throne, O gods;

1241c. N. is side by side with Atum, between the two sceptres.

1242a. N. is the *ḥwnnw* (messenger?) of the gods in search of the eye of Horus;

1242b. N. searched for it at Buto; he found it at Heliopolis;

1242c. N. snatched it from the head of Set, at the place where they fought.

1243a. Horus, give thine arm to N.; Horus take to thyself thine eye;

1243b. it mounts up to thee; it ascends to thee; it comes to thee, N., for life;

1243c. the eye of Horus comes to thee with N., before N., for ever.

Utterance 525.

1244a. To say: Rꞔ' purified himself for thee; Horus adorned himself for thee,

1244b. so that blindness (?) might cease and that sleeplessness might be repelled,

1244c. before there existed a god, a son of god, a messenger of god.

1245a. N. descends in the lake of *Kns.t*;

1245b. N. purifies himself in the Marsh of Reeds;

1245c. N. is purified by the Followers of Horus,

1245d. who recite for N. "the chapter of those who ascend,"

1245e. who recite for N. "the chapter of those who raise themselves up."

1246a. Descend, N., into this thy boat of Rꞔ' which the gods row.

1246b. When N. rises they (the gods) rejoice at the approach of N.,

1246c. as they rejoice at the approach of Rꞔ',

1246d. when he comes forth in the East, mounting, mounting.

Utterance 526.

1247a. To say: N. has purified himself in the Lake of Reeds,

1247b. wherein Rꞔ' was purified.

1247c. Horus dries the back of N., the back of Thot, the legs of N., the legs of Shu.

1247d. Shu, take N. to heaven; Nut, give thine arm to N.

1248a. To say: Atum created by his masturbation in Heliopolis.
1248b. He put his phallus in his fist,
1248c. to excite desire thereby.
1248d. The twins were born, Shu and Tefnut.
1249a. They put N. between them;
1249b. they put N. among the gods in the Marsh of Offerings.
1249c. To say four times: N. mounts to heaven;
1249d. N. descends to the earth; for life everlasting.

Utterance 528.

1250a. Further, to say: O *Swnt*, who traverses the sky nine times in the night,
1250b. lay hold of the arm of N. for life;
1250c. ferry him on this sea.
1250d. (So) N. descends into this boat of the god,
1250e. in which the corporation of the Ennead rows,
1250f. to row N. in it.
1251a. "The chapter of *Bdw*" is recited for thee;
1251b. "the chapter of natron" is recited for thee.
1251c. Incense stands (as chief) before the Great Ennead,
1251d. while *Bdw* is seated before (or, in) the great *'itr.t*-palace.

Utterance 529.

1252a. Further, to say: O this Doorkeeper of heaven,
1252b. pay attention to this messenger of a god, ascending.
1252c. When he goes forth by the western portal of the sky,

1252d. bring him to the southern portal of the sky;
1252e. when he ascends by the eastern portal of the sky,
1252f. bring him to the northern portal of the sky.

Utterance 530.

1253a. To say: Greetings to thee, Ladder, which the Souls of Buto and
   the Souls, of Nekhen have set up and built:
1253b. Give thou thine arm to N.;
1253c. that N. may sit between the two great gods;
1253d. that the places of N. be in front; and that his arm be held as far
   as the Marsh of Offerings,
1253e. so that he may sit among the stars which are in the sky.

Utterance 531.

1254a. To say: O ye two Kites who are on the wing of Thot,
1254b. who are *Whnnw.ti* and *Dndnw.ti*,
1254c. bring this (message) to N.; put him on that side.
1254d. N. comes for life as messenger of Horus, the rapid one (or, in
   (his) service).

Utterance 532.

1255a. To say: O Mooring-post of the morning-boat of its lord;
1255b. O Mooring-post of the morning-boat of him who is in it,
1255c. Isis comes, Nephthys comes, one of them on the right, one of
   them on the left,
1255d. one of them as a *ḥ3.t*-bird, one of them (Nephthys) as a kite.
1256a. They found Osiris,
1256b. after his brother Set had felled him to the earth in *Ndi.t*,

1256c. when Osiris (N.) said, "come to me," hence comes his name as "Seker."

1257a. They prevent thee from rotting, in accordance with this thy name of "Anubis";

1257b. they prevent thy putrefaction from flowing to the ground,

1257c. in accordance with this thy name of "jackal of the South";

1257d. they prevent the smell of thy corpse from being bad, in accordance with this thy name of "Ḥr-ḫꜣ.tï."

1258a. They prevent Horus of the East from rotting; they prevent Horus, lord of men, from rotting;

125 8b. they prevent Horus of the *Dꜣ.t* from rotting; they prevent Horus, lord of the Two Lands from rotting.

1258c. And Set will not ever free himself from carrying thee, Osiris N.

1259a. Wake up for Horus; stand up against Set;

1259b. raise thyself up, Osiris N., son of Geb, his first (-born),

1259c. before whom the Two Enneads tremble.

1260a. The keeper (*min.w*) stands up before thee, so that (the feast) of the New Moon may be celebrated for thee; thou appearest for (the feast of) the month;

1260b. thou advancest to the sea (of N.); thou traversest to the Great Green;

1261a. for thou art "he who stands without being tired" in Abydos;

1261b. thou art spiritualized on the horizon; thou endurest in *Dd.t* (Mendes);

1261c. thine arm is taken by the Souls of Heliopolis; thine arm is seized by Rꜥ.

1262a. Thy head, N., is raised up by the Two Enneads;

1262b. they have put thee, Osiris N., as chief of the double *'itr.t*-palace of the Souls of Heliopolis.

1262c. Thou livest, thou livest, raise thyself up.

1263a. To say:————

1263b.————which goes forth————

1263c. N. is the blood, which goes forth from Rç'; the sweat which goes forth from Isis.

26.

FOR THE PROTECTION OF THE PYRAMID ENCLOSURE AGAINST OSIRIS AND HIS CYCLE, UTTERANCE 534.

Utterance 534.

1264a. To say by Horus: May Geb make an offering.

1264b. Be gone, flee (thou) whom Horus guards, whom Set protects;

1264c. be gone, flee, (thou) whom Osiris guards, whom *Hrti* protects;

1265a. be gone, flee, (thou) whom Isis guards, whom Nephthys protects;

1265b. flee, chief, (thou) whom *Mḫnti-'irti* guards, whom Thot protects;

1265c. be gone, flee (thou) whom the *ḫз.tiw* guard, whom the *'imi.w-'iзw. w* protect.

1266a. I have come; I have dedicated this house to N.;

1266b. purer is this broad-hall than *ḳbḥ.w*;

12 66c. at its door (or, entrance) is an obelisk; the door is double (i.e. with two leaves), and is sealed with two evil eyes.

1267a. Let not Osiris come in this his evil coming;

1267b. do not open to him thine arms.

1267c. Let him be gone; let (him) go to *Ndi.t*; at once; let him be gone to *'dз*.

1268a. Let not Horus come in this his evil coming;

1268b. do not open to him thine arms; that which is said to him is his name of *Šp-'iri—————ś33.w*.

1268c. Let him go to *'np.t*; at once; let him go to *Ntr*.

1269a. Let not Set come in this his evil coming;

1269b. do not open to him thine arms; that which is said to him is his name of *šš*.

1269c. Let him go to *dw.t*; at once; let him go to *Ḥn.t*.

1270a. If *Mḫnti-'irti* comes in this his evil coming;

1270b. do not open to him thine arms; that which is said to him is his name of *nš* (driveller).

1270c. Let him go to *Ddnw*-(him whom) they found in (the condition of) quaking;

1270d. at once; let him go to *Ḥm*.

1271a. If Thot comes in this his evil coming;

1271b. do not open to him thine arms; that which is said to him is his name of "thou hast no mother."

1271c. Let him go; let him be gone to his (?) two *'int.wi*; let him go to Buto, to *Ḥri-Dḥwti*.

1272a. If Isis comes in this her evil coming;

1272b. do not open to her thine arms; that which is said to her is her name (of) "wide of *ḥwʒ-t* (evil-smelling)."

1272c. Let her (lit. him) be gone; let her go to the houses of *Mʒnw*;

1272d. at once; let her go to *Ḥdb.t*, to the place where thou hast (she has) been struck.

1273a. If Nephthys comes in this her evil coming;

1273b. that which. is said to her is this her name of "substitute without vulva."

1273c. Go thou to the house of *Šerḳet*, to the place where thou didst strike thy two *'nn.twi* (thighs?).

1274a. If enemies come with those who are among the elders

1274b. that which is said to them (lit. her) is this their (lit. her) name of *Šp-šʒ.w*.

1274c. Go to———*tw.t*.

1275a. If N. comes with his *ka*;

1275b. the mouth of his gods opens: "(If) he desires to descend to the [underworld, let him descend]

1275c. to the place where there are gods."

1276a. If N. comes with his *ka*, open thou thine arms to him;

1276b. the mouth of his gods opens: "(If) he desires to ascend to heaven, let him ascend."

1277a. I am come as judge; may Geb make offerings, and Atum.

1277b. I consecrate this pyramid, this temple, to N. and to his *ka*;

1277c. that which this pyramid, this temple, contains is for N. and for his *ka*;

1277d. pure is this eye (pyramid enclosure) of Horus,

1278a. O may it be pleasing to thee. He who puts his finger against this pyramid, this temple of N. and of his *ka*;

1278b. he who will put his finger against the house of Horus in *ḳbḥ.w*,

1278c. may Nephthys and Isis go against him———Geb.

1279a. His case will be heard by the Ennead,

1279b. he will be without support, his house will be without support;

1279c. he is accursed; he is one who eats his (own) body.

27.
TEXTS OF MISCELLANEOUS CONTENTS, UTTERANCES 535-538.

Utterance 535.

1280a. To say by Isis and Nephthys:

1280b. The *ḥȝ.t*-bird comes, the kite comes; they are Isis and Nephthys.

1280c. They are come in search of their brother Osiris;

1280d. (They are come) in search of their brother N.

1281a. Thou who art (here), thou who art (there), weep for thy brother; Isis, weep for thy brother; Nephthys, weep for thy brother.

1281b. Isis sits, her hands upon her head;

1282a. Nephthys has indeed seized the tip of (her) two breasts because of her brother, N.;

1282b. Anubis being on his belly; Osiris being wounded; Anubis being before the fist (?).

1283a. Thy putrefaction, N., is not; thy sweat, N., is not;

12 83b. thy outflowing, N., is not; thy dust, N., is not.

1284a. *Ḥȝ.ti* son of *Ḥȝ.ti* (is) at *Mnii*, coming as *Mn.ti*,

1284b. to divide in three these your four days and your eight nights.

1285a. The stars follow thy beloved *Ḳbḥ.wt*,

1285b. who is chief of thy *nmḥ* (attendants); thou art chief of those who are chief of the *nmḥ.w* (attendants); thou hast made *nmḥ* the *nmḥ.w*.

1285c. Loose Horus from his bonds, that he may punish the Followers of Set;

1286a. that he may seize them; that he may remove their heads; that he may take off their legs.

1286b. Cut thou them up, take thou out their hearts;

1286c. drink thou of their blood;

1287a. count their hearts, in this thy name of "Anubis counter of hearts."

1287b. Thy two eyes have been given to thee as thy two uraeus-serpents,

1287c. for thou art like Wepwawet on his standard, Anubis who presides in *sḥ-ntr*.

1288a. O N., the houses of the great who are in Heliopolis make thee "first";

1288b. the spirits and even the imperishable stars fear thee.

1288c. The dead fall on their face before thee; the blessed dead(?) care for thee.

1289a. "Eldest (son), *Imȝḥ* is for N.," say the Souls of Heliopolis,

1289b. who furnish thee with life and satisfaction.

1289c. He lives with the living as Seker lives with the living;

1289d. he lives with the living as N. lives with the living.

1290a. O N., come, live thy life there, in thy name, in thy time,

1290b. in these years, which are to be peaceful, according to (?) thy wish.

Utterance 536.

1291a. To say: Thy water belongs to thee, thine abundance belongs to thee, thine efflux comes out of Osiris to thee.

1291b. The double doors of heaven are open for thee; the double doors of Nut are open for thee;

1291c. the double doors of heaven are open for thee; the double doors of *ḳbḥ.w* are open for thee.

1292a. "Welcome," says Isis; "(come) in peace," says Nephthys, when they see their brother.

1292b. Raise thyself up;

1292c. untie thy bandages; shake off thy dust.

1293a. Sit thou upon this thy firm throne.

1293b. Thou art pure with thy four *nmś.t*-jars and thy four *ȝḥ.t*-jars,

1293c. which come for thee out of thy chapel of natron, which were filled for thee in the natron lake,

1293d. and which Horus of Nekhen has given thee.

1294a. He has given to thee his spirits, the jackals,

1294b. like (to) Horus who is in his house, like (to) Ḫnti (Osiris) chief of the mighty.

1294c. A durable offering is made for thee.

1295a. Anubis, chief of the *sḥ-ntr*, has commanded that thou come in as a star, as god of the morning (or, as god of the morning star),

1295b. that thou pass through the region of Horus of the South and that thou pass through the region of Horus of the North.

1296a. (And) men will construct with their arms a stairway to thy throne.

1296b. He comes to thee his father; he comes to thee Geb.

1297a. Do for him that which thou hast done for his brother, Osiris,

1297b. on this day of thy feast, the water being full (i. e. at inundation),

1297c. when (his) bones are counted, when (his) sandals are repaired,

1297d. when his nails, upper and lower, are cleaned for him,

1297e. There will come to him (people of) the Upper Egyptian *'itr.t*-palace and of the northern *'itr.t*-palace, bowing———.

Utterance 537.

11298a. To say: O N., arise, sit thou on the throne of Osiris;

1298b. thy flesh is complete like (that of) Atum; thy face like (that of) a jackal.

1299a. Give thou thy mouth to Rç'.

1299b. He congratulates thee on what thou hast said; he praises thy words.

1299c. Arise; thou ceasest not to be; thou perishest not.

1300a. Live, N., thy mother Nut lays hold of thee, she unites her. self with thee;

1300b. Geb seizes thine arm. "Thou comest in peace," say thy fathers.

1300c. Thou art possessed of thy body; thou art clothed in thy body.

1301a. Thou ascendest like Horus of the *D3.t*, chief of the imperishable stars;

1301b. thou sittest upon thy firm throne at the head of thy canal of *ḳbḥ. w*;

1301c. thou livest as the coleoptera (lives); thou endurest as the *dd*, eternally.

Utterance 538.

1302a. To say: Back, thou lowing ox.

1302b. Thy head is in the hand of Horus; thy tail is in the hand of Isis;

1302c. the fingers of Atum are at thy horns.

28.
A LITANY OF ASCENSION,
UTTERANCE 539.

Utterance 539.

1303a. To say: The head of N. is like that of the vulture,

1303b. when he ascends and lifts himself to the sky.

1303c. The skull of N. is like that of divine stars,

1303d. when it ascends and [lifts itself to the sky].

1304a. [The forehead of N. is like that of]————and Nu,

1304b. when it ascends and lifts itself to the sky.

1304c. The face of N. is like that of Wepwawet,

1304d. when he ascends and lifts himself to the sky.

1305a. The eyes of N. (are like those of) the Great One who is chief of
the Souls of Heliopolis,

1305b. when he ascends and lifts himself to the sky.

1305c. The nose of N. is like that of Thot,

1305d. when he ascends [and lifts himself to the sky].

1306a. [The mouth of] N. is like that of him who traverses the great
lake,

1306b. when he ascends and lifts himself to the sky.

1306c. The tongue of N. is like that of truth in the boat of truth,

1306d. when he ascends and lifts himself to the sky.

1307a. The teeth of N. are (like those of) spirits,

1307b. when he ascends and lifts, himself to the sky.

1307c. The lips of N. are like those of————)

1307d. [when he ascends and lifts] himself to the sky.

1308a. The chin of N. is like that of *Hrti-ḫnti-Ḥm*,

1308b. when he ascends and lifts himself to the sky.

1308c. The back of N. is like that of the wild-bull,

1308d. when he ascends, and lifts himself to the sky.

1309a. The arms of N. are like those of Set,

1309b. when he ascends and lifts himself [to the sky].

1309c.————

1309d. [when he ascends and lifts himself to the sky].

1310a.————like————*Bʒibw*,

1310b. when he ascends and lifts himself to the sky.

1310c. The heart of N. is like that of Bastet,

1310d. when he ascends and lifts himself to the sky.

1311a. The belly of N. is like that of Nut,

1311b. when he ascends and lifts himself [to the sky].

1311c.————

1311d. [when he ascends and lifts himself to the sky].

1312a.————of N.————like————of the Two Enneads,

1312b. when he ascends and lifts himself to the sky.

1312 C. The seat of N. is like that of *Ḥeket*,

1312d. when he ascends and lifts himself to the sky.

1313a. The buttocks of N. are like those of the boat of the evening, and the boat of the morning,

1313b. when he ascends and lifts, himself to the sky.

1313c. The phallus of N. is like that of *Ḥapi*,

1313d. when he ascends and lifts himself to the sky.

1314a. The thighs of N. are like those of Neit and *Serḳet*,

1314b. when he ascends and lifts himself to the sky.

1314c. The legs of N. are like those of the two souls who are before the field *dr*,

1314d. when he ascends and lifts himself to the sky.

1315a. The feet of N. are like those of the two morning boats of the sun,

1315b. when he ascends and lifts himself to the sky.

1315c. The toes of N. are like those of the Souls of Heliopolis,

1315d. when he ascends and lifts himself to the sky.

1316a. N. is he who belongs to a god, the son of a god,

1316b. when he ascends and lifts himself to the sky.

1316c. N. is the son of Rç', his beloved,

1316d. when he ascends and lifts himself to the sky.

1317a. N. is begotten of Rç',

1317b. when he ascends and lifts himself to the sky.

1317c. N. is conceived of Rç',

1317d. when he ascends and lifts himself to the sky.

131 8a. N. is born of Rç',

1318b. when he ascends, and lifts himself to the sky.

1318c. This magic is in the body of N.,

1318d. when he ascends and lifts himself to the sky.

1319a. N. is the great sceptre in the great court in Heliopolis,

1319b. when he ascends and lifts himself to the sky.

1320a. (He is) *Hnnw*,

1320b. when he ascends and lifts himself to the sky.

1320c. (He is) Horus, the child, the youth,

1320d. when this N. ascends and lifts himself to the sky.

1321a. Nut (is) she who cannot be fertilized without putting (down) her arms,

1321b. when he ascends and lifts himself to the sky.

1321c. Geb is not diverted from his way,

1321d. when N. ascends and lifts himself to the sky.

1322a. Each god who constructs not a stairway for N.,

1322b. when he ascends and lifts himself to the sky,

1322c. he shall have no *pḳ*-cake, he shall have no shade,

1323a. he shall not wash himself in the *ḥȝw*-bowl,

1323b. he shall not smell (taste) a leg (of meat); he shall not pass a cutlet (over the mouth) (i.e., he shall not taste a cutlet),

1323c. the earth shall not be hoed for him; the *wdn.t*-offerings shall not be made for him,

1323d. when this N. ascends and lifts himself to the sky.

1324a. It is certainly not N. who says that against you, O gods;

1324b. it is magic which says that against you, O gods.

1324c. N. belongs to a region under magic.

1325a. Each god who constructs stairs (or, stairway) for N.,

1325b. when N. ascends and lifts himself to the sky;

1325c. each god who vacates his throne in his boat, 1325d. when this N. ascends, and lifts himself to the sky,

1326a. the earth shall be hoed for him, the *wdn.t*-offering shall be made for him,

1326b. a *nmt.t*-bowl shall be made for him,

1326c. he shall smell a leg (of meat), he shall pass a cutlet (over the mouth),

1326d. when this N. ascends and lifts himself to the sky.

1327a. Each god who takes the arm of N. to the sky, 1327b. when he comes to the house of Horus which is in *ḳbḥ.w*,

1327c. his *ka* shall be justified before Geb.

29

TEXTS OF MISCELLANEOUS CONTENTS, UTTERANCES 540-552.

Utterance 540.

1328a. To say: N. comes to thee, his father; he comes to thee, Osiris.

1328b. He has brought to thee this thy *ka*; how wonderful it is!

1328c. His mother Nut has punished him who shines on her forehead.

1329a. *Ḥtmw.t* has raised thee up;

1329b. thy mouth is opened by *Šś3*, chief of the city of *Šn'.t*;

1329c. thy mouth is opened by *Dw3-wr* in the house of gold;

1329d. [thy mouth] is opened by the *tt.wi* which are before the house of natron;

1330a. thy mouth is opened by Horus with his little finger,

1330b. with which he opened the mouth of his father, with which he opened the mouth of Osiris.

1331a. N. is thy son; N. is Horus;

1331b. N. is the beloved son of his father, in this his name of "Son whom he loves."

1332a. Thou art purified: thou art dried. Thy clothing is given (to thee),

1332b. thy thousand of alabaster (vessels), thy thousand of garments,

1332c. which N. has brought to thee, that he might clothe thee therewith.

1333a. To say: Children of Horus,

1333b. Ḥ3pi, Dw3-mu.t.f, 'Imś.ti, Ḳbḥ-śn.w.f,

1333c. protect life for your father, Osiris N.

1333d. from the time that he is given his endurance (or, that he endure) among the gods.

1334a. Smite Set, protect this Osiris N. from him before the earth is brightened.

1334b. Horus is powerful; he himself will avenge this his father, Osiris N.

1334c. The father has caused that you honour him.

Utterance 542.

1335a. To say: It is Horus; he is come to reclaim his father, Osiris N.;

1335b. he has proclaimed a royal (death) decree in the places of Anubis——
———everyone recognizing it, he shall not live.

1336a. Thot, spare not any among those who wronged the king;

1336b. Thot, hasten that thou mayest see (grasp) this; O father (Thot), announce to him his (death) decree.

Utterance 543.

1337a. To say: Bring (him) to this Osiris N.

1337b. Osiris N., he who killed thee is brought to thee; let him not escape from thee.

1337c. Osiris N., he who killed thee is brought to thee; perform his execution.

1337d. Osiris N., he who killed thee is brought to thee, cut (him) in three.

Utterance 544.

1338a. To say: Children of Horus, go to this Osiris N.;
1338b. Children of Horus, hurry, put yourselves under this Osiris N.; let
there be none among you who shall withdraw.
1338c. Carry him.

Utterance 545.

1339a. To say: Osiris N., he who killed thee is brought to thee; cut (him)
up; perform his execution.
1339b. Children of Horus,
1339c. Ḥȝpi, Dwȝ-mu.t.f, 'Imś.ti, Ḳbḥ-śn.w.f,
1340a. carry your father, this Osiris N.; lead him.
1340b. Osiris, N., make thy endurance; open thy mouth; stand up.

Utterance 546.

1341a. To say: I am Nut; bring to (me) Osiris N.,
1341b. give him to (me), that I may embrace him.

Utterance 547.

1342a. To say: O father, Osiris N., I betake myself to thee;
1342b. Osiris N., approach thyself to (me).

Utterance 548.

1343a. To say: The mouth of the earth opens for Osiris N.; Geb said to
him:
1343b. "N. is great like a king, mighty like Rç'."
1343c. "Come in peace," say the Two Enneads to N.

1343d. The eastern door of heaven is open for him, to the abode of *kas*.

1344a. The great Nut gives her arms to him, she of the long horn, she of the protruding breast.

1344b. She will nurse N.; she will not wean him.

1345a. She takes him to herself to heaven, she does not cast him down to the earth.

1345b. She makes this N. remain as chief of the two '*itr.t*-palaces.

1345c. He descends into the boat like Rç', on the shores of the Winding Watercourse.

1346a. N. rows in the *ḥnbw*-boat,

1346b. where he takes the helm, towards the field of the two lower heavens,

1346c. to the beginning of this land of the Marsh of Reeds.

1347a. His arm is taken by Rç'; his head is raised up by Atum;

1347b. his forward cable is taken by Isis; his stern cable is seized by Nephthys.

1348a. Ḳbḥ.w.t places him at her side, and puts him among the *ḥnti.w-š*,

1348b. as the herdsmen of (his) calves.

Utterance 549.

1349a. To say: Back, *B3bwi*, red-eared, with coloured hind-quarters,

1349b. pass thou the cutlet, from thy chapel (or, of thy lady), over thy mouth.

Utterance 550.

1350a. To say: Back, *Km-wr*,

1350b. glide away in Babylon (*Hri-'ḥ3*), in the place where they glided (i.e. fell).

Utterance 551.

1351a. To say: Open, Frontier (?), open———as its (?) barrier inclines;
1351b. back, *Rw-ḫȝ.t*; retreat *Pḥ.wi*,
1351c. let thou (me) pass by, the passing by of a god.

Utterance 552.

1352. To say: I am alive, says N., for ever.

30.

RESURRECTION, MEAL, AND ASCENSION OF THE DECEASED KING, UTTERANCE 553.

Utterance 553.

1353a. To say: Geb has raised thee up; this thy spirit has been guarded for thee.

1353b. Thy *mns*-jar remains; thy *mns*-jar is caused to remain.

1353c. Thou art more exalted than Shu and Tefnut in the house of H̱*tmw.t* (the destroyer), N.,

1354a. for thou art verily a spirit who wast nursed by Nephthys with her left breast.

1354b. Osiris has given to thee the spirits; take the eye of Horus to thee.

1355a. These thy four ways which are before the grave of Horus

1355b. are those whereon one goes (lit. goes a going) to the god as soon as the sun sets (or, as far as the setting of the sun).

1356a. He takes hold of thine arm, after Seker, chief of *Pdw-š* purified thee,

1356b. (and he conducted thee) to thy throne which is in ḳbḥ.w.

1357a. Raise thyself up, spirit of N.; sit, eat thou;

1357b. let thy *ka* be seated, that he may eat bread and beer with thee without ceasing for ever and ever.

1358a. Thy going is as a representative of Osiris;

1358b. thy feet hit thine arms;

1358c. they bring thee to thy feasts,

1358d. to thy white teeth, (to) thy fingernails, (to) the *Dw.f*-nome.

1359a. Thou ferriest over as the great bull to the green fields,

1359b. to the pure places of Rç'.

1360a. Raise thyself up, spirit of N.; thy water belongs to thee, thine abundance belongs to thee;

1360b. thine efflux belongs to thee, which issued from the secretion of Osiris.

1361a. The double doors of heaven are open for thee; the double doors of *ḳbḥ.w* are undone for thee;

1361b. the double doors of the tomb are open for thee; the double doors of Nut are unfastened for thee.

1362a. "Greeting," says Isis; "ferry on in peace," says Nephthys,

1362b. after she had seen thy father, Osiris, on the day of the *mm.t*-feast (or, of feasting him who is in need ?).

1362c. Elevated is the *ddb.t*-chapel of the double *'itr.t*-palace of the North, thy *Grg.w-b3*.

1363a. Raise thyself up; shake off thy dust;

1363b. remove the dirt which is on thy face; loose thy bandages.

1363c. They are indeed not bandages; they are the locks of Nephthys.

13 64a. Travel over the southern regions; travel over the northern regions;

1364b. be seated on thy firm throne.

1364c. Anubis, who is chief of the *sḥ-nṯr*, commands that thy spirit be behind thee, that thy might be in thy body,

1364d. that thou remain Chief of the mighty ones (or, spirits).

1365a. Thou purifiest thyself with these thy four *nmś.t*-jars,

1365b. (with) the *špn.t* and *3t*-jar, which come from the *sḥ-nṯr* for thee, that thou mayest become divine.

1365c. The sky weeps for thee; the earth trembles for thee;

1366a. the *śmnt.t*-woman laments for thee; the great *min.t* mourns for thee;

1366b. the feet agitate for thee; the hands wave for thee,

1366c. when thou ascendest to heaven as a star, as the morning star.

1367a. N. is come to thee, his father; he is come to thee, Geb;

1367b. he is united with your dead, O gods.

1367c. Let him sit on the great throne, on the lap of his father *Mḫnti-'irti*;

1368a. let him purify his mouth with incense and natron; let him purify his nails upper and lower.

1368b. Let one do for him what was done for his father, Osiris, on the day of assembling the bones,

1368c. of making firm (or, adjusting) the sandals, of crossing the feet (i.e. when ferrying over).

1369a. To thee come the wise and the understanding;

1369b. to thee comes the southern *'itr.t*-palace,

1369c. to thee comes the northern *'itr.t*-palace, with a salutation,

1369d. (thou) who endurest eternally at the head of the mighty ones.

31.

TEXTS OF MISCELLANEOUS CONTENTS, UTTERANCES 554-562.

Utterance 554.

1370a. To say: N. is verily a son of the great wild-cow; she conceived him and gave him birth;

1370b. they place him in the interior of her wing;

1370c. she ferries over the lake with thee (i.e. him); she traverses the ~iw-canal with thee (i.e. him).

1371a. Thy fillet as chief of the house is at thy back;

1371b. thy '*ḅ3-mnḥi*-sceptre is, in thy hand,

1371c. that thou mayest strike, that thou mayest rule, in accordance with thy dignity, which appertains to lords of the '*im3ḥ*,

1372a. for indeed thou art of the Followers of Rç', who are behind the morning star (*Dw3*).

1372b. Let no evil be to thee; let no evil be to thy name, the first on earth.

Utterance 555.

1373a. To say: N. is come forth from Buto, to the gods of Buto;

1373b. N. is adorned as a falcon, bedecked as the Two Enneads.

1374a. N. dawns as king (of Upper Egypt); he is elevated as Wepwawet,

1374b. (after) he has taken the white crown and the green crown,

1374c. his *ḥd*-mace on his arm, his sceptre in his hand.

1375a. The mother of N. is Isis; his nurse is Nephthys;

1375b. she who suckles N. is *Šḥз.t-ḥr*.

1375c. Neit is behind him; *Srkt-ḥtw* is before him.

1376a. The ropes are knotted; the boats of N. are tied together

1376b. for the son of Atum————hungry and thirsty, thirsty and hungry————

1376c. on the southern shore of the Winding Watercourse.

1377a. Thot, who is in the shade of his bush,

1377b. put N. upon the tip of thy wing.,

1377c. on the northern shore of the Winding Watercourse.

1378a. N. is well, his flesh is sound; N. is well, his garments are sound,

1378b. (as) he ascends to heaven like Montu,

1378c. (as) he descends as *Bз-'ibt.f*, as *Bз-'šm.f*.

Utterance 556.

1379a. To say: He hastens, who hastens————

1379b.————the great to the places of the gods.

1379c. Elevated is father, Osiris N., like Wepwawet.

1380a.————father, Osiris N.

1380b. Let him raise himself up, Anubis, he who is in the *mnwi*-shrine.

1380c. Thy feet are like those of a jackal; stand up.

1380d. Thine arms are like those of a jackal; stand up.

1381a.————

1381b.————to row before him; he brings to thee alone the double crown,

1381c. that he may fer[ry thee over]————

1382a. father, Osiris N., the Winding Watercourse is inundated.

1382b. Father Osiris N. calls to *Ḥm*;

1382c. father N. calls to *Šmti*,

1382d. that they may [certainly] ferry over father Osiris. N.

1382e. to yonder eastern side of heaven, [to the birthplace of the gods],

320

1382f. [when this hour of the morrow comes————this hour of the third day (comes)],

1383a. where [father Osiris N.] will be born, [at the place] where the gods are born;

1383b. when this hour of the morrow comes,————this hour of the third day,

1384a. [when father Osiris N. stands. there] like this star which is on the under (side) of the body of the sky

1384b.————like Horus of the horizon.

1385a. [O ye four gods, who stand upon the *d'm*-sceptres] of heaven,

1385b. father Osiris N. verily has not died the death (i.e. really died);

1385c. but father Osiris N. has become a spirit (*ȝḫw*) a glorified one.

1386a. [Father Osiris N.] has come to you

1386b.————

Utterance 557.

1387a.————

1387b. Return thou to thy house; return thou.

1388a. Thine heir is on thy throne; he [tills the barley for thee]

1388b.————

1389.————

Utterance 558.

1390a. To say: O N., greetings to thee, Ḥḥ.

1390b. *Km-wr* sets the course for thee;

1390c. thou alightest an alighting of the eldest god;

1390d. he of the long curls offers incense in Heliopolis for thee.

1391. Thou livest, thou livest; thou art satisfied, thou art satisfied, pouring out life as thou goest (lit. behind thee); thou livest.

1392a. To say: "Come in peace," says Osiris; "come in peace," says Osiris to thee.

1392b. The marshes are filled for thee; the river-banks are inundated for thee,

1392c. on account of the royal offering.

1393a. The chief of the west lays hold of thy arm at the border of mount *ḥb.t.*

1393b. Let Osiris be recompensed, for he gives thee (to be) in the presence of princes, as supports.

Utterance 560.

1394a. To say: The earth is hacked by the hoe;

1394b. the *wdn.t*-offering is made; the earth of *Tbi* is broken up;

1394c. the two nomes of the god shout before [the king] as he descends into the earth.

1395a. Further, to say: Geb, open thy mouth for thy son, Osiris;

1395b. that which is behind him belongs to (i.e. has to do with) food; that which is before him belongs to snared fowl (or, the snaring of fowl).

Utterance 561.

1396a.————

1396b. command————

1397.————

1398a.————of the boat of the evening————

1398b.————

1399.————

1400. Thy face is like————

1401.————

1402.————
1403.————
1404.————

Utterance 562.

1405a. To say: The earth is high under the sky by (means of) thine arms, Tefnut.

1405b. Lay hold of the two hands of N., lay not hold of the arm of N., for life, satisfaction, eternity.

1405c. Put him in————as a distinguished one.

1405d. N. is seated as chief of the Two Enneads;

1406a. he judges the gods

1406b. as a king, (and) as deputy of Horus, who avenges his father, Osiris.

1406c. Thy body, N., is as that of a god; as your body, O gods, is like that of N.

1407a. N. is come in peace to thee, Horus.

1407b. The eye of Horus is young with you; it is not given over to the anger of Set.

32.
A PURIFICATION LITANY,
UTTERANCE 563.

Utterance 563.

1408a. To say: The double doors of heaven are open, the double doors
of *k̭bḥ.w* are open for Horus of the Gods,

1408b. that he may ascend and purify himself in the Marsh of Reeds.

1408c. The double doors of heaven are open for N., the double doors of
k̭bḥ.w are open for N.,

1408d. that he may ascend and purify himself in the Marsh of Reeds.

1409a. The double doors of heaven are open, the double doors of *k̭bḥ.w*
are open for Horus *Šsm.t*-land,

1409b. that he may ascend and purify himself in the Marsh of Reeds.

1409c. The double doors of heaven are open for N., the double doors of
k̭bḥ.w are open for N.,

1409d. that he may ascend and purify himself in the Marsh of Reeds.

1410a. The double doors of heaven are open, the double doors of *k̭bḥ.w*
are open for Horus of the East,

1410b. that he may ascend and purify himself in the Marsh of Reeds.

1410c. The double doors of heaven are open for N., the double doors of
k̭bḥ.w are open for N.,

1410d. that he may ascend and purify himself in the Marsh of Reeds.

1411a. The double doors of heaven are open, the double doors of *k̭bḥ.w*
are open for Horus of the Horizon,

1411b. that he may ascend and purify himself in the Marsh of Reeds.

1411c. The double doors of heaven are open, the double doors of $k\underline{b}h$. w are open for N.,

1411d. that he may ascend and purify himself in the Marsh of Reeds.

1412a. He who ascended, ascended, Horus of the Gods, that he might purify himself in the Marsh of Reeds.

1412b. He who ascended, ascended, N., that he might purify himself in the Marsh of Reeds.

1413a. He who ascended, ascended, Horus, of the *Šsm.t*-land, that he might purify himself in the Marsh of Reeds.

1413b. He who ascended, ascended, N., that he might purify himself in the Marsh of Reeds.

1414a. He who ascended, ascended, Horus of the East, that he might purify himself in the Marsh of Reeds.

1414b. He who ascended, ascended, N., that he might purify himself in the Marsh of Reeds.

1415a. He who ascended, ascended, Horus of the Horizon, that he might purify himself in the Marsh of Reeds.

1415b. He who ascended, ascended, N., that he might purify himself in the Marsh of Reeds.

1416a. N. is purified; N. has taken the *św$\underline{h}$*-vestment.

1416b. N. truly ascends to heaven, permanent like the earth.

1416c. It is grievous (?) for thy body, O Nut, because of the divine seed, which shall be in thee (or, in thy mother).

1417a. N., this one, he is the divine seed, which shall be in thy mother, Nut.

1417b. Receive him, this N., as thou didst receive thy divine son.

1418a. *Hp3t, Hp3t, Hnni, Hnni,*

1418b. take him with you; let N. be established among you.

1419a. *Hftn.t,* mother of the gods,

1419b. give thy hand to N.; take his hand (or, take to thee the hand of N.), for life;

1419c. draw him to heaven, like as, thou hast drawn this one, Osiris, to heaven.

1420a. *Hnni, Hnni, Hpꜣt, Hpꜣt,*

1420b. take N. with you; let N. be established among you.

33.
TEXTS OF MISCELLANEOUS CONTENTS, UTTERANCES 564-569.

Utterance 564.

1421a. To say: He is pure who purifies himself in the sea of reeds;

1421b. Rç' purifies himself in the sea of reeds;

1421c. N. himself purifies himself in the sea of reeds.

1421d. Shu purifies, himself in the sea of reeds;

1421e. N. himself purifies himself in the sea of reeds.

1422a. Shu, Shu, lift N. up to heaven;

1422b. Nut, give thine arms to N.;

1422c. let him fly, let him fly, rejoicing, rejoicing, rejoicing, let him fly, let him fly.

Utterance 565.

1423a. To say: N. be thou purified, (when) thou comest to heaven.

1423b. N. lasts longer than men; he dawns for the gods.

1423c. N. dawned with Rç' at his dawning.

1424a. Their third is he who is with him;

1424b. one is behind N.; the other is before N.;

1424c. one gives, water; the other gives sand.

1425a. N. leans upon thy two arms, Shu, just as Rç' leans upon thine arm.

142 5b. N. found them, sitting, at his approach

1425c. the two spirits, mistresses of this land.

1426a. Let Nut rejoice at the approach of N.;

1426b. *Npnp.t* has received him;

1426c. she who is in her k, for life and joy, and she who wears her *Ntśtn*-garment.

1427a. they gave birth, for themselves, to N.

1427b. N. is loosed from the evil which (was) in him.

1427c. Nephthys gave her arms to N.;

1427d. she passed her breast over the mouth of N.

1428a. *Dw3-wr* shaved N.;

1428b. Sothis washed the hands of N.,

1428c. at his birth, on that day, O gods.

1428d. N. knows (remembers?) not his first mother whom he knew;

1428e. it is Nut who has borne N., with Osiris.

Utterance 566.

1429a. To say: Take N. away with thee, Horus;

1429b. transport him, Thot, on the tip of thy wing,

1429c. like Seker who is in the *m3'.t*-boat.

1429d. Horus does not pass the night (lit. go to bed) behind the canal; nor is Thot without a boat (lit. boatless);

1429e. and N. is not without a boat, for he has the eye of Horus.

Utterance 567.

1430a. To say: Rç' is purified in the Marsh of Reeds;

1430b. Horus is purified in the Marsh of Reeds;

1430c. N. is purified in the Marsh of Reeds,

1430d. that he may arise with him. Nut give him thine arm.

1430e. Rejoice, rejoice, he flies, he flies!

Utterance 568.

1431a. To say: He is gone who went to his *ka*; M*ḫnti-'irti* is gone to his *ka*;

1431b. N. is gone to his *ka*, to heaven.

1431c. A ladder is made for him, upon which he mounts, in its name of "That which mounts to heaven."

1432a. His boat is brought to him by the *d'm*-sceptres of the imperishable stars.

1432b. The bull (or, ox) of heaven lowers its horn, so that he may pass thereon to the lakes of *D3.t*.

1433a. O N., thou dost not fall to the ground.

1433b. N. lays hold of the two sycamores, which are in the middle of yonder side of the sky,

1433c. which ferry him over, and they set him on the eastern side of the sky.

Utterance 569.

1434a. To say: N. knows thy name; N. forgets not thy name.

1434b. "Limitless" is thy name. The name of thy father is "Thou art great."

1434c. Thy mother is "Satisfaction," who bears thee morning by morning.

1435a. The birth of "Limitless" in the horizon shall be prevented,

1435b. if thou preventest N. from coming to the place where thou art.

1435c. The birth of *Śerḳet* shall be prevented,

1435d. if thou preventest N. from coming to the place where thou art.

1436a. The two regions shall be forbidden to Horus,

1436b. if thou preventest N. from coming to the place where thou art.

1436c. The birth of *Ś3ḥ* shall be prevented,

436d. if thou preventest N. from coming to the place where thou art.

1437a. The birth of Sothis shall be prevented,

1437b. if thou preventest N. from coming to the place where thou art.

1437c. The (coming of) the two apes (*bnt.wi*) to Rç', his two beloved sons, shall be prevented,

1437d. if thou preventest N. from coming to the place where thou art.

1438a. The birth of Wepwawet in the *pr-nw*-palace shall be prevented,

1438b. if thou preventest N. from coming to the place where thou art.

1438c. The (coming of) men to the king, son of a god, shall be prevented,

1438d. if thou prevents N. from coming to the place where thou art.

1439a. The (coming of) thy crew of the imperishable stars to row thee over shall be prevented,

1439b. if thou preventest them from letting N. descend into thy boat.

1439c. The (coming of) men to death shall be prevented,

1439d. if thou preventest N. from descending into thy boat.

1440a. Men's eating of bread shall be prevented,

1440b. if thou preventest N. from descending into thy boat.

1440c. N. is *Śkśn*, the messenger of Rç';

1440d. N. shall not be prevented from (entering) heaven.

1440e. The *mȝt.t*-tree, which is at the door of heaven, has stretched out its arms to N.

1441a. His-face-behind-him, the ferryman of the Winding Watercourse, is united to him.

1441b. N. is not prevented; an obstacle is not opposed to N.,

1441c. for N. is one of you, O gods.

1442a. N. is come to thee, O Rç';

1442b. N. is come to thee, "Limitless,"

1442c. that he may row thee over, that he may do service of a courtier to thee.

1442d. N. loves thee in his body; N. loves thee in his heart.

34.

NEW-BIRTH OF THE DECEASED KING AS A GOD IN HEAVEN, UTTERANCE 570.

Utterance 570.

1443a. To say: The face of heaven is washed; the vault of heaven is bright;

1443b. a god is brought to birth by the sky upon the arms of Shu and Tefnut, upon the arms of N.

1444a. "Great *wbn*," say the gods;

1444b. "hear it, this word which N. says to thee;

1444c. let thy heart be glad for this N., for this N. is a Great One, the son of a Great One;

1444d. N. is with thee; take this N. for life, joy, and eternity, with thee."

1445a. "Khepri, hear it, this word, which is spoken to thee by N.;

1445b. let thy heart be glad for N., for N. is a Great One, the son of a Great One;

1445c. N. is with thee; take him with thee."

1446a. "Nun, hear it, this word, which is spoken to thee by N.;

1446b. let thy heart be glad for N., for N. is a Great One, the son of a Great One;

1446c. N. is with thee; take him with thee."

1447a. "Atum, hear it, this word, which is spoken to thee by N.;

1447b. let thy heart be glad for N., for N. is a Great One, the son of a Great One;

1447c. N. is with thee; take him with thee."

1448a. "W₃š, son of Geb; Šḥm, son of Osiris,

1448b. hear it, this word is spoken to thee by N.;

1448c. let thy heart be glad for N., for N. is a Great One, the son of a Great One;

1448d. N. is with thee; take him with thee."

1449a. Mayest thou be near to N., in thy name of "Rꜥ"'; drive thou away the garments (darkness) of the sky.

1449b. May Horus of the Horizon cause him to hear his glory and his praise

1449c. out of the mouth of the Two Enneads.

1450a. "How beautiful art thou," said his mother; "(mine) heir," said Osiris.

1450b. N. has not swallowed the eye of Horus,

1450c. so that men might say, "he will die for that."

1450d. N. has not swallowed a limb of Osiris,

1450e. so that the gods might say, "he will die for that."

1451a. N. lives on the 'iṣnw (bread of offering) of his father Atum; protect him, Nḫb.t;

1451b. thou hast protected N., Nḫb.t, in the princely house which is in Heliopolis.

1452a. Thou hast commended him to him who is within his ḥn.ti (two limits),

1452b. that N. may be expedited.

1452c. He who is within his ḥn.ti (two limits) has recommended N. to him who is on his carrying litter,

1452d. that N. may be expedited.

1453a. N. has escaped his day of death,

1453b. even as Set escaped his day of death;

1453c. N. has escaped the half-months of death,

1453d. even as Set escaped his half-months of death;

1453e. N. has escaped his months of death,

1453f. even as Set escaped his months of death;

14539. N. has escaped the year of death,

1453h. even as Set escaped his year of death,

1454a. by ploughing the earth. The hands of N. support Nut, like Shu,

1454b. even the bones of N. which are firm (or, iron; or, copper), and his imperishable limbs;

1455a. for N. is a star, the light-scatterer of the sky.

1455b. Let N. ascend to the god; let N. be avenged,

1455c. so that heaven may not be void of N., so that earth (lit. this land, i.e. Egypt) may not be void of N., for ever.

1456a. N. lives a life in accordance with your rule,

1456b. O gods of the lower sky, imperishable stars,

1456c. which traverse the land of Libya, which are supported by their *d'm*-sceptres;

1456d. just as N. is supported, with you, by a *w3ś*-sceptre and a *d'm*-sceptre.

1457a. N. is your fourth,

1457b. O gods of the lower sky, imperishable stars,

1457c. which traverse the land of Libya, which are supported by their dm-sceptres;

1457d. just as N. is supported, with you, by a *w3ś*-sceptre and a *d'm*-sceptre.

1458a. N. is your fourth,

1458b. O gods of the lower sky, imperishable stars,

11458c. which traverse the land of Libya, which are supported by their d'm-sceptres;

1458d. just as N. is supported, with you, by a *w3ś*-sceptre and a *d'm*-sceptre,

1458e. by command of Horus, hereditary prince and king of the gods.

1459a. N. seizes the white crown; that upon which is the wire of the green crown.

11459b. N. is the *'iʾr.t*-serpent, which comes forth from Set, which was robbed, but which was returned.

1459c. N. was robbed; he is returned; he is made alive.

1460a. N. is this (kind of) colour which comes out of Nun.

1460b. N. is the eye of Horus, which was not chewed, nor spit out;

1460c. he is not chewed nor spit out.

1461a. Hear it, this word, O Rç', said by N. to thee:

1461b. "Thy body is in N., O Rç'; let thy body live in N., O Rç'."

11462a. "The baboon is a wild-ox," so said *knm.wt*;

1462b. "*knm.wt* is a wild-ox," so said the baboon.

11462c. O that castrated one! O this man! O he who hurries him who hurries (?), among you two!

11462d. These-this first corporation of the company of the justified

11463a. was born before there was any anger;

11463b. was born before there was any clamour (lit. voice);

1463c. was born before there was any strife.,

11463d. was born before there was any conflict;

1463e. was born before the eye of Horus was plucked out; before the testicles of Set were torn away.

1464a. N. is blood' which came from Isis; N. is red blood which came from Nephthys.

1464b. N. does *dḥ'w3* against his *bnw*; there is nothing which the gods can do against N.;

1464c. N. is the deputy of Rç'; N. shall not die.

1465a. Hear, O Geb, hereditary prince of all the gods, endue him with his form.

1465b. Hear, O Thot, who art among the peaceful ones of the gods,

1465c. let a door for N. be opened by Horus; let N. be protected by Set.

1465d. N. appears in the eastern side of the sky,

1465e. like Rç' who shines in the eastern side of the sky.

35.
TEXTS OF MISCELLANEOUS CONTENTS, UTTERANCES 571-575.

Utterance 571.

1466a. To say: The mother of N., dweller in the lower sky, became pregnant with him;

1466b. N. was given birth by his father Atum,

1466c. before the sky came into being, before the earth came into being,

1466d. before men came into being, before the gods were born, before death came into being.

1467a. N. escapes the day of death, as Set escaped his day of death.

1467b. N. belongs to your company (?), O gods of the lower sky,

1468a. who cannot perish for their enemies.

1468b. N. perishes not for his enemies.

1468c. O ye who die not for a king————N. does not die for a king.

1468d. O ye who die not for any death————N. does not die for any death.

1469a. N. is an imperishable star, the great————of heaven in the house of *Śerkset.*

1469b. Rç' has taken N. to heaven, that N. may live,

1469c. as he lives who enters into the west of the sky and goes forth at the east of the sky.

1470a. He who is within his *ḥn.ti* (two limits) has commended N. to him who is in his carrying-litter;

1470b. they acclaim N., for N. is a star,

1470c. The protection of Rç' is upon N. Rç' will not abandon the protection of N.

1471a. Horus has set N. on his shoulders;

1471b. he has assigned N. to Shu (who says): "My arms are exalted under Nut."

1471c. Rç', give thine arm to N.; Great God, give thy staff to N.,

1471d. that he may live for ever.

Utterance 572.

1472a. To say: "How beautiful indeed is the sight, how pleasant indeed is the view," says Isis,

1472b. "that this god ascends to heaven, his renown over him,

1472c. his terror on both sides of him, his magic before him!"

1473a. It was done for him, for N., by Atum, like that which one did for him (Atum).

1473b. He brought to N. the gods belonging to heaven;

1473c. he assembled to him the gods belonging to the earth.

1474a. They put their arms under him.

1474b. They made a ladder for N., that he might ascend to heaven on it.

1474c. The double doors of heaven are open for N.; the double doors of *śḥd.w* are open for him.

1475a. Atum united the nomes for N.;

1475b. Geb gave him the cities, that is to say (lit. in speaking of it),

1475c. the regions, the regions of Horus; the regions of Set,

1475d. the Marsh of Reeds.

1476a. N. is *Ἰʒḥś*, chief of the land of Upper Egypt;

1476b. N. is *Ddwn*, chief of the land of Nubia;

1476c. N. is Sopdu, (who lives) under his *kśb.t*-trees.

1477a. Have you acted against him? Have you said that he would die?

1477b. He will not die. N. will live a life for ever.

1477c. N. is become in spite of them as the surviving bull of the wild-bulls;

1477d. N. is at their head; he will live and last for ever.

Utterance 573.

1478a. To say: Awake in peace, *Ḥsmnw*, in peace.

1478b. Awake in peace, Eastern Horus, in peace.

1478c. Awake in peace, Eastern Soul, in peace.

1478d. Awake in peace, Harachte, in peace.

1479a. Thou sleepest in the evening boat; thou wakest in the morning boat,

1479b. for thou art as he who oversees the gods; no god oversees thee.

1479c. Father of N., Rç', take N. with thee, for life, to thy mother, Nut.

1480a. The double doors of heaven shall be open for N.; the double doors of *ḳbḥ.w* shall be open for N.

1480b. When N. comes to thee, that thou mayest make him live,

1480c. command N. to sit by thy side,

1480d. near the *dw3*-canal on the horizon.

1481a. Father of N., Rç', commend N. to *Msḫ33.t*, she who is at thy side,

1481b. to cause to designate a place for N. near the *Rd-wr*-lake under *ḳbḥ.w*.

1482a. Commend N. to Ni-'nh, son of Sothis, to speak for N.,

1482b. to establish a throne for N. in heaven.

1482c. Commend N. to *Wr-špś.f*, the beloved Ptah, the son of Ptah,

1482d. to speak for N.,

1482e. to cause food to grow for his dining pavillion on earth,

1483a. for N. is one of those four gods,

1483b. *'Imś.ti, Ḥ3pi, Dw3-mw.t.f, Ḳbḥ-śn.w.f,*

1483c. who live on truth, who lean upon their d'm-sceptres,

1483d. who guard the land of Upper Egypt.

1484a. He flies, he flies from you, O men, as birds;

1484b. he takes his flight from you (lit., he takes his arms from you) like a falcon;

1484c. he takes his body from you like a kite;

1484d. he is delivered from that which shackles his feet on earth,

1484e. he is freed from that which ties his hands.

Utterance 574.

1485a. To say: Greetings to thee, Sycamore, who protects the god, under which the gods of the underworld stand,

1485b. whose tips are seared, whose inside is burned, (whose) suffering is real.

1486a. Assemble those who dwell in Nun; collect those who are among the bows.

1486b. Thy forehead is upon thine arm (in mourning) for Osiris, O Great Mooring-post,

1486c. who art like her who is chief of the offering (to), and of the worship (?) of the lord of the East.

1487a. Thou art standing, Osiris; thy shadow is over thee, Osiris;

1487b. thy diadem repels Set,

1487c. the generous damsel who acted for this spirit of *Ghś.ti* is

1487d. thy shadow, Osiris.

1488a. Thy dread is among those in heaven; thy fear among those on earth.

1488b. Thou hast hurled thy terror into the heart of the wings of Lower Egypt, dwelling in Buto.

1489a. N. is come [to thee], Horus, heir of Geb, of whom Atum speaks;

1489b. "all belongs to thee," say the Two Enneads; "all belongs to thee," thou sayest.

1490a. It is even N. among them-the gods who are in heaven.

1490b. Collect those who are among the bows; assemble those who are among the imperishable stars.

1491a. N. rejoices; N. rejoices, O, 0.

1491b. Day is day; night is night; Rç' is Rç';

1491c.————he is for ever.

Utterance 979.

1492a. To say: "Behold, he comes; behold, he comes," says *Shpw*;

1492b. "behold, the son of Rç' comes; the beloved of Rç' comes," says *Shpw*;

1492c. "I caused him to come; I caused him to come," says Horus.

1493a. "Behold, he comes; behold, he comes," says *Shpw*;

1493b. "behold, the son of Rç' comes; the beloved of Re, comes," says *Shpw*.

1493c. "I caused him to come; I caused him to come," says Set.

1494a. "Behold, he comes; behold, he comes," says *Shpw*;

1494b. "behold, the son of Rç' comes; the beloved of Rç' comes," says *Shpw*;

1494c. "I caused him to come; I caused him to come," says Geb.

1495a. "Behold, he comes; behold, he comes," says *Shpw*;

1495b. "behold, the son of Rç' comes; the beloved of Rç' comes," says *Shpw*;

1495c. "I caused him to come; I caused him to come," say the Souls of Heliopolis and the Souls of Buto.

1496a. "O Rç'," say men, when they stand by the side of N. on the earth,

1496b. while thou dawnest on the east of the sky, "give thy hand to N.;

1496c. take him with thee to the eastern side of the sky."

1497a. "O Re," say men, when they stand by the side of N. on the earth,

1497b. while thou dawnest on the southern side of the sky, "give thy hand to N.;

1497c. take him with thee to the southern side of the sky."

1498a. "O Rç'," say men, when they stand by the side of N. on the earth,

1498b. while thou dawnest at the centre of the sky, "give thy hand to N.,

1498c. take him with thee to the centre of the sky."

1499. One hastens with thy message; the runners are before thee.

36.

THE RESURRECTION AND ASCENSION OF THE DECEASED KING, UTTERANCE 576.

Utterance 576.

1500a. To say: Osiris was placed upon his side by his brother Set;

1500b. he who is in *Ndi.t* stirs; his head is raised up by Rç';

1500c. his abomination is to sleep; he hates to be tired;

1501a. N. rots not; he stinks not;

1501b. N. is not bound (bewitched) by your wrath, O gods.

1502a. Awake thou in peace;

1502b. Osiris awakes in peace; he who is in *Ndi.t* awakes in peace.

1503a. His head is lifted up by Rç'; his odour is [as] that of the *Ih̬.t-wt.t-* serpent.

1503b. The head of N. also is lifted up by Rç'; the odour of N. is as that of *Ih̬.t-wt.t-*serpent.

1504a. He rots not; he stinks not,

1504b. N. is not bound (bewitched) by your wrath, O gods.

1505a. N. is thy seed, Osiris, the pointed,

1505b. in his name of "Horus in the great green"; "Horus chief of spirits."

1506a. N. rots not; he stinks not;

1506b. he is not bound (bewitched) by your wrath, O gods.

1507a. N. goes forth from his house, adorned like Horus, bedecked like Thot;

1507b. the mother of N. is thy Heliopolitan, O god; the father of N. is a Heliopolitan;

1507c. N. himself is thy Heliopolitan, O god.

1508a. N. is conceived by Rç'; he is born of Rç'.

1508b. N. is thy seed, O Rç', the pointed,

1508c. in his name of "Horus, chief of spirits, star which ferries over the "great green."

1509a. N. rots not; he stinks not;

1509b. he is not bound (bewitched) by your wrath, O gods.

1510a. N. is one of those four gods, born of Geb,

1510b. who travelled over the South, who travelled over the land of [the North],

1510c. who leaned upon their dm-sceptres,

1511a. anointed with the best ointment, clothed in [purple],

1511b. living on figs, drinking wine.

1512 a. N. anoints himself with that with which you anoint yourselves;

1512b. N. clothes himself with that with which you clothe yourselves;

1512c. N. lives on that on which you live;

1512d. N. drinks that of which you [drink].

1513a. N. is safe with you, he lives on that on which you live.

1513b. May you give him of those possessions which your father Geb gave you,

1513c. (so that) because of which none of you may hunger, because of which none of you may rot.

1514a. Lay hold of the arm of N. for life before the sweet-smelling ones,

1514b. unite the bones of N., assemble his limbs,

1514c. that N. may sit upon his throne.

1515a. He rots not; he stinks not;

1515b. N. is not bound (bewitched) by your wrath, O gods.

1516a. N. is come to thee, mother of N.; he is come to Nut.

150b. Make the sky mount for N.; place the stars upside down for him.

1516c. Let his odour be like the odour of thy son, who is come forth from thee;

1516d. let the odour of N. be like that of Osiris, thy son, who is come forth from thee.

1517a. Nun, lift up the arm of N. towards the sky, that he may support himself (on) the earth which he has given to thee,

151 7b. that he may ascend, that he may rise to the sky,

1517c. that he may do service of a courtier to Rç'.

1518a. Horus chief of the spirits, who is before the sweet-smelling ones,

1518b. awake thou in peace, as Rç' awakes, in peace;

1518c. awake in peace, as *Mdi* awakes in peace.

1519. Let him put the writing of N. in his register before the sweet-smelling ones.

37.

THE RESURRECTION OF OSIRIS WITH WHOM THE GODS ARE SATISFIED, UTTERANCE 577.

Utterance 577.

1520a. To say: Osiris dawns, pure, mighty; high, lord of truth

1520b. on the first of the year; lord of the year.

1521a. Atum father of the gods is satisfied; Shu and Tefnut are satisfied; Geb and Nut are satisfied;

1521b. Osiris and [Isis] are satisfied; Set and [Neit] (Nephthys?) are satisfied;

1522a. all the gods who are in heaven are satisfied; all the gods who are on earth and in the lands are satisfied;

1522b. all the southern and northern gods are satisfied; all the western and eastern gods are satisfied;

1522c. all the nome gods are satisfied; all the city gods are satisfied

1523a. with the great and mighty word, which comes forth from the mouth of Thot, concerning Osiris,

1523b. the seal of life, the seal of the gods.

1523c. Anubis, the counter of hearts, deducts Osiris N. from the gods who belong to the earth, (and assigns him) to the gods who are in heaven,

1524a. lord of wine at the inundation.

1524b. His year is calculated for him; his hour knows him.

1524c. N. is known by his year which is with him;

1524d. his hour which is with him knows him.

1525. "Come, my child," says Atum, "come to us," say they, say the gods to thee, Osiris.

1526a. ("Our) brother is come to us, the eldest, the first (begotten) of his father, the first (born) of his mother,"

152 6b. say they, say the gods.

1527a. Heaven conceived him: *Dw3.t* gave him birth;

152 7b. N. was conceived with him by heaven;

1527c. N. was given birth with him by *D3.t*.

152 8a. Thou supported the sky on thy right side, having life;

1528b. thou livest, because the gods ordained that thou live.

1528c. N. supports the sky on his right side, having life;

1528d. he lives, his life, because the gods have ordained that he live.

1529a. Thou leanest on the earth on thy left side, having joy;

1529b. thou livest thy life, because the gods have ordained that thou live.

1529c. N. leans on the [earth] on his left side, having life (or joy?);

1529d. he lives his life, because (the gods) have ordained that he live.

1530a. N. ascended on the eastern side of the sky;

1530b. he descends as a green bird;

1530c. he descends————lord of the *D3.t*-lakes.

1530d. N. is purified in the lakes of the *śmn*-goose.

38.
TEXTS OF MISCELLANEOUS CONTENTS, UTTERANCES 578-586.

Utterance 578.

1531a. To say: Osiris N., thou shalt not hasten to those lands of the East;

1531b. thou shalt hasten to these lands of the West by the way of the Followers of Rç'.

1532a. Thy messengers hasten; thy runners go;

1532b. those who are before thee rush on,

1532c. that they may announce thee to Rç', to him who lifts up (his) arm in the East.

1533a. Thou dost not know them; thou art astonished at them;

1533b. thou hast laid them in thine arms like herdsmen of thy calves.

1534a. Thou art as he who prevents them from slipping out from thine arms.

1534b. Thou goest forth to them; thou art glorified, by birth; preeminent, by birth,

534c. in thy name of *"śpd.w"*;

1535a. A (thy?) whip in thy hand; and thy sceptre on thine arm.

1535b. Enemies fall on their face before thee;

1535c. the imperishable stars kneel before thee.

1536a. Thou art as he who prevents them from falling out of thine arms,

1536b. and (who prevents) that thou be sick because of them, in thy
name of "*mḥi.t.*"

1537a. They recognize thee, in thy name of "Anubis."

1537b. The gods do not descend to thee, in thy name of *'i̯.t*.

1538a. Thou standest as chief of the gods, eldest son,

1538b. as heir on the throne of Geb.

Utterance 579.

1539a. To say: Thy going from thy house, Osiris N.,

1539b. is the going of Horus in search of thee, Osiris N.

1539c. Thy messengers hasten; thy runners run; thine envoys hurry.

1540a. They announce to Rç',

1540b. that thou, N., art come, as son of Geb, from upon the throne of
Amŭn;

1541a. that thou hast ferried over the Winding Watercourse; that thou
hast traversed the canal of [*Knsi.t̯*].

1541b. Thou settlest down on the eastern side of the sky; thou sittest in
the double *'itr.t*-palace of the horizon;

1541c. thou givest to them thine arm; thou givest thine arm to the gods.

1542a. They praise thee; they come to thee with salutations,

1542b. as they do homage to Rç', as they come to him with salutations.

Utterance 580.

1543a. To say: Thou who hast smitten (my) father; he who has killed
(one) greater than he;

1543b. thou hast smitten (my) father, thou hast killed one greater than
thou.

1544a. Father Osiris N. I have smitten for thee him who smote thee as
an ox;

1544b. I have killed for thee him who killed thee as a wild-bull.

1544c. I have overpowered for thee him who overpowered thee as an ox;

1544d. thou art upon his back as he who is upon the back of an ox.

1545a. He who stretched thee out as the stretched out ox; he who slaughtered thee as the slaughtered ox;

1545b. he who stunned thee as the stunned ox————

1545c. I have cut off his head; I have cut off his tail;

1545d. I have cut off his two hands; I have cut off his two feet.

1546a. His upper fore-legs including (lit. "being to") his lower forelegs belong t[o Atum], father of the gods;

1546b. his two thighs belong to Shu and Tefnut;

1546c. his two sides belong to Geb and Nut;

1547a. his two shoulder blades belong to Isis and Nephthys;

1547b. his two shoulders belong to *Mḫnti-'irti* and *Hrti*,————

1547c. his spinal column belongs to Neit and Śerḳet; his heart belongs to Sekhmet, the great;

1548a. that which is in the back part of his body belongs to those four gods, the sons of Horus, his beloved,

1548b. *Ḥȝpi, 'Imś.ti, Dwȝ-mw.t.f, Ḳbḥ-śn.w.f.*

1549a. His head, his tail, his two hands, his two feet

1549b. belong to Anubis, who is upon his mountain; to Osiris who is chief of his department (or, thigh-offering).

1549c. That which the gods leave belongs to the Souls of Nekhen and the Souls of Buto.

1550a. Eat, eat the red ox, for the voyage by sea,

1550b. which Horus did for his father, Osiris N.

Utterance 581.

1551a. To say: This thy cavern there is the broad-hall of Osiris N.

1551b. which brings the wind. The north wind refreshes;

1551c. it raises thee as Osiris N.

1552a. Šsm.w comes to thee, bearing water and wine;

1552b. Ḫnti-mnwt.f (comes) bearing the vases which are before the two 'itr.

t-palaces.

1552c. Thou standest, thou sittest like Anubis, chief of the necropolis.

1553a. Aker stands up for thee; Shu dries (lit. something like. "lies down,"

Wb. V 366) for thee.

1553b. They tremble who see the inundation (when) it tosses;

1554a. (but) the marshes laugh; the shores are become green;

1554b. the divine offerings descend; the face of men brightens; the heart

of the gods rejoices.

1555a. "Deliver N. from his bandages, which restrain (?) the living, O

gods,"

1555b. (is) in the mouth of those who run to them on the good day of

running (while running is good).

1556a. "Set is guilty; Osiris is justified,"

1556b. (is) in the mouth of the gods, on the good day of the going upon

the mountain.

1557a. (When) inundations are upon the land,

1557b. he who hastens with his soul goes to his cave;

1557c. (but) thou marchest behind thy spirit towards Knm-'iwnw,

1557d. like the successor of Ḥrti, chief of [Nš]з.t.

Utterance 582.

1558a. To say: N. is come to thee, Horus,

1558b. that thou mayest recite for him this great and good word, which

thou didst recite for Osiris,

1558c. by which N. may be great; by which he may be powerful.

1559a. His šḥm is within him; his ba is behind him;

1559b. his špd is upon him, which Horus gave to Osiris,

1559c. that N. may rest in heaven, as a mountain, as a support.

1560a. He shall fly as a cloud to heaven, like a heron;

1560b. he shall pass by the side-locks of the sky;

1560c. the feathers on the two arms of N. shall be like knives.

1561a. *Šзḥ* shall give him his arm,

1561b. Sothis shall take his hand;

1561c. the ground shall be hoed for N.; an offering shall be made for N.;

1561d. the two nomes of the god shall shout for N.

1562a. He will be more at the head than he who is at the head of the Two Enneads;

1562b. he sits upon his firm throne,

1562c. his sceptre glittering in his hand.

1563a. If N. raises his hand towards the children of their fathers,

1563b. they stand up for N.;

1563c. if N. lowers his hand towards them, they sit down.

1564a. The face of N. is like that of a jackal; the middle (of his body) is like that of *ḳbḥ.wt*;

1564b. N. judges like Sebek in Crocodilopolis,

1564c. like Anubis in *Tзb.t* (Hypselis?).

1565a. When N. calls for a thousand,

1565b. there come to him the blessed dead (?) with salutations,

1565c. while they say to him: "Who is it who has done this to thee?"

1566a. It is the mother of N., the great wild cow, she with the two long feathers,

1566b. with the brilliant head-dress, with the two hanging breasts,

1566c. who has lifted N. up to heaven————she did not leave N. on the earth————

1566d. among the glorious gods,

1567a. that N. may see their spirit and that he may be a spirit likewise.

1567b. N. [is protected] by his, father Osiris (just as) the blessed dead (?) protect N.

Utterance 583.

1568a. To say: Rç', turn thou, that N. may see

1568b. ———N. Thy red (crown) is that of N.

1568c. ———N. of Rç', the uraeus-serpent, which is on the forehead of Rç'.

1569a. Thou art Shu; thou art height, O father;

1569b. thou art the *nšs*; thou art the *nšss.t*;

1569c. thou art———

1570a. ———

1570b. The arm of Horus is behind thee; the arm of Thot [is before thee].

1571a. The two Great Gods support thee;

1571b. they prepare thy place which is in [heaven]———

1572a. ———

1572b. ———

1572c. Arisen, arisen, on thy feet———

Utterance 584.

1573a. To say: N. [has occupied] his seat;

1573b. [N. has taken] his helm (oar);

1573c. [N. seats himself in the bow] of the boat of the Two Enneads.

15 74a. [N. rows Rç' to the west. He writes (the name) of N. over the living];

1574b. he establishes the seat of N. [over the lords of the *kas*]

1574c. [he puts N. on the shores of the Winding Watercourse];

1574d. he puts N. over the *nḥḥ.w* (-stars).

1575a. [The double doors of the *bȝ-kȝ*, which are in *ḳbḥ.w* are open for N.];

1575b. [the double doors of] *bïȝ*, which are in *šḥd.w* [are open for N].

1575c. ———

1575d. [N. is pleased] with his name.

1575e. ———

Utterance 585.

1576a.————[star] s

1576b. they [prepare]————

1577.————upon the forehead (or, to judge)————

1578a.————lakes

1578b. great————

1579. It is N————

1580.————truth

1581.————this

Utterance 586.

1582a (Nt. Jéquier, VIII 14). To say: N. shines like Rç', expelling the dawn, establishing Truth behind Rç',

1582b (Nt. VIII 14). shining every day for all of those who are on the horizon of the sky.

1583a (Nt. VIII 15). The upper gates of heaven (?) are open.

1583b (Nt. VIII 15). To say: Great is Atum; the son of a great one is Atum; N. is the *śḥd*-star in the sky among the gods.

1584a (Nt. VIII 16). Thy mother says to thee that *Śśȝ*, like N., weeps for thee;

1584b (Nt. VIII 16). like N. he mourns for thee.

1585a (Nt. VIII 16). To say————wash, give thou (thine) arm to N. while thou causest her to come.

1585b (Nt. VIII 16). Ho! His-back-behind-him, bring the [*ḳd-ḥtp*]-ladder to N.,

1586 (Nt. VIII 17). made by Khnum, that N. may ascend to heaven upon it, to do service of a courtier to Rç' in heaven.

39.
AN EARLY HYMN TO THE SUN,
UTTERANCE 587.

Utterance 587.

1587a. To say: Greetings to thee, Atum.

1587b. Greetings to thee, Khepri, who created himself.

1587c. Thou art high, in this thy name of "Ḳꜣ."

1587d. Thou comest into being, in thy name of "Khepri."

1588a. Greetings to thee, eye of Horus, which he adorned with his two hands completely.

1588b. He does not make thee hearken to the West;

1588c. he does not make thee hearken to the East;

1588d. he does not make thee hearken to the South;

1588e. he does not make thee hearken to the North;

1588f. he does not make thee hearken to those who are in the middle of the land;

1589a. (but) thou harkenest to Horus.

1589b. It is he who adorned thee; it is he who built thee; it is he who settled thee;

1590a. thou doest for him everything which he says unto thee, in every place whither he goes.

1590b. Thou carriest to him the fowl-bearing waters which are in thee;

1590c. thou carriest to him the fowl-bearing waters which are to be in thee;

1591a. thou carriest to him the gifts which are in thee;

1591b. thou carriest to him every tree which is to be in thee;

1591c. thou carriest to him the food which is in thee;

1591d. thou carriest to him the food (in thee) which is to be in thee;

1592a. thou carriest to him the gifts which are in thee;

1592b. thou carriest to him the gifts which are to be in thee;

1592c. thou carriest to him everything which is in thee;

1592d. thou carriest to him everything which is to be in thee;

1592e. thou carriest (it) to him to every place wherein his heart desires to be.

1593a. The doors stand fast upon thee like Inmutef;

1593b. they open not to the West; they open not to the East;

1593c. they open not to the North; they open not to the South;

1593d. they open not to those who are in the middle of the land;

1594a. (but) they are open to Horus. It was, he who made them; it was he who made them stand fast;

1594b. it was he who rescued them from every evil which Set did to them;

1595a. it was he who settled thee, in this thy name of "Settlements" ("Colonies");

1595b. it was he who went, doing obeisance; after thee, in this thy name of "City";

1595c. it was he who rescued thee from every evil which Set did to thee.

1596a. Go, go, Nut.

1596b. Geb commanded that thou go, in thy name of "City."

1596c. N. is Horus, who adorned his eye with his two hands completely.

1597a. N. adorned thee with an adornment;

1597b. N. settled for thee these his settlements;

1597c. N. built thee (as) a city of N.,

1597d. that thou mayest do for N. every good thing which the heart of N. loves,

1597e. that thou mayest do (it) for N., in every place where he goes.

1598a. Thou shalt not hearken to the West; thou shalt not hearken to the East;

1598b. thou shalt not hearken to the North; thou shalt not hearken to the South;

1598c. thou shalt not hearken to those who are in the middle of the land;

1599a. (but) thou shalt hearken to N.; it is N. who adorned thee;

1599b. it is N. who built thee; it is he who settled thee.

1600a. Thou doest for him everything which he says unto thee in every place whither N. goes.

1600b. Thou carriest to him the fowl-bearing waters which are in thee;

1600c. thou carriest to him the fowl-bearing waters which are to be in thee;

1601a. thou carriest to him every tree which is in thee;

1601b. thou carriest to him every tree which is to be in thee;

1601c. thou carriest to him the food which is in thee;

1601d. thou carriest to him all food which is to be in thee;

1602a. thou carriest to N. the gifts which are in thee;

1602b. thou carriest to N. the gifts which are to be in thee;

1602c. thou carriest to him everything which is in thee;

1602d. thou carriest (it) to N. to the place wherein the heart of N. desires to be.

1603a. The doors stand fast upon thee like Inmutef;

1603b. they open not to the West; they open not to the East;

1603c. they open not to the North; they open not to the South;

1603d. they open not to those who are in the middle of the land;

1604a. (but) [they are open to] N.

1604b. It was he who made them; it was he who made them fast;

1604c. it was he who rescued them from all the evil which men did to them;

1605a. it was N. who [settled thee], in this thy name of "Settlements" ("Colonies");

1605b. it was N. who went, doing obeisance, after thee, in this thy name of "City";

1605c. it was N. who rescued thee from all the [evil which men did] to thee.

1606a. Hearken to N. alone; it is N. who made thee.

1606b. Thou shalt not hearken to the malefactor.

40.
TEXTS OF MISCELLANEOUS CONTENTS,
UTTERANCES 588-600.

Utterance 588.

1607a. To say: Osiris N., thy mother Nut has spread herself over thee, in her name of "She of *Št-p.t*";

1607b. she has caused thee to be as a god, in spite of thee, in thy name of "God";

1608a. she has protected thee against all evil things, in her name of "Great Sieve" (protectress).

1608b. Thou art the greatest among her children.

Utterance 589.

1609a. To say: Osiris N., thou art the *ka* of all the gods;

1609b. Horus has avenged thee; thou art become his *ka*.

Utterance 590.

1610a. To say: Osiris N., behold, thou art avenged; thou livest;

1610b. thou movest daily, without anything being disordered in thee (or, there is no disorder in thee).

1611a. Thou hast settled for (thy) father, so (thy) father did the same for thee,

1611b. like the vulture which places herself over her son.

1612a. To say: Horus adorns himself with his *šsmt*-apron, (when he) moves (about) on his land like *tiwti*;

1612b. Set adorns himself with his *šsmt*-apron, (when he) moves (about) on his land like *tiwti*;

1613a. Thot adorns himself with his *šsmt*-apron, (when he) moves (about) on his land like *tiwti*;

1613b. the god adorns himself with his *šsmt*-apron, (when he) moves (about) on his land like *tiwti*;

1614a. N. also adorns himself with his *šsmt*-apron, (when he) moves, (about) on his land like *tiwti*.

1614b. Horus, take to thyself thine eye, which was recognized as thine in the house of the prince of Heliopolis.

1614c. O N., thy *ka* has recognized thee in spite of thine enemies.

Utterance 592.

1615a. To say: Geb, son of Shu, this is Osiris N.;

1615b. the heart of thy mother trembles for thee, in thy name of "Geb."

1615c. Thou art the eldest son of Shu, his primogeniture.

1616a. O Geb, Osiris N. is this one here;

1616b. heal him, that [what is the matter with him] may cease;

1616c. thou art the Great God, the only one.

1617a. Atum has given thee his heritage; he has given thee the whole Ennead;

1617b. even Atum himself together with them. The son of his eldest son (Shu) is united with thee (Geb),

1618a. (when) he sees thee, that thou art glorified, that thy heart is great (proud).

1618b. Thou art *p'n*, in thy name of "wise mouth," "Hereditary prince of the gods."

1619a. Thou art standing on the earth; thou judgest at the head of the Ennead;

1619b. thy fathers and thy mothers are at their head; thou art More powerful than any god;

1619c. thou art come to Osiris N., that thou mayest protect him against his enemy.

1620a. O Geb, wise-mouth, hereditary prince of the gods, it is thy son, Osiris N.

1620b. Thou causest thy son to live with him; make thy son prosperous with him;

1621a. Thou art lord of the entire earth;

1621b. thou art powerful over the Ennead and even (over) every god.

1622a. Thou art mighty; thou turnest away every evil from Osiris N.;

1622b. thou shalt not cause it to return to him, in thy name of "Horus who repeats not his work."

1623a. Thou art the *ka* of all the gods;

1623b. thou hast brought them; thou nourishest them; thou causest them to live.

1623c. Make Osiris N. live.

1624a. Thou art a god; thou art powerful over all gods.

1624b. An eye goes forth from thy head, like the one Great-in-charms, the Upper Egyptian white crown;

1624c. an eye goes forth from thy head, like the one Great-in-charms, the Lower Egyptian red crown.

1625. Horus has followed thee for he loves thee;

1626. thou dawnest as king of Lower Egypt; thou art powerful over all the gods together with their *kas*.

1627a. To say: Stand up, give thine arm to Horus; he causes thee to stand up.

1627b. Geb has wiped thy mouth for thee.

1628a. The Great Ennead avenged thee;

1628b. they placed Set under thee, that he may serve under thee;

1628c. they prevented his spittle from spilling on thee.

1629a. Nut throws herself upon her son, who is in thee; she protects thee;

1629b. she defends thee; she embraces thee; she raises thee up,

162 91c. for thou art the greatest among her children.

1630a. Two sisters, Isis and Nephthys, come to thee;

1630b. they hasten to the place in which thou art.

1630c. Thy sister Isis laid hold of thee, when she found thee

1630d. complete and great, in thy name of "Great black."

1631a. Encircle all things in thine arms, in thy name of "Circle which encircles the *nb.wt*";

1631b. thou art great, in thy name of "Great circle which sets."

1632a. Horus has brought Set to thee; he has given him to thee; he bends (him) under thee;

1632b. thy strength is greater than his.

1632c. Horus has caused thee to encircle all the gods, in thine arms.

1633a. Horus has loved his father, in thee; Horus has not suffered thee to go away;

1633b. Horus has not gone away from thee; Horus has avenged his father, in thee.

1633c. Thou livest as the coleoptera (lives); thou endures, in Mendes.

1634a. Isis and Nephthys protected thee in Siût,

1634b. even their lord in thee, in thy name of "Lord of Siût";

1634c. even their god in thee, in thy name of "Divine canal";

1635a. they adored thee, so that thou shalt not (again) withdraw from them.
1635b. Isis comes to thee rejoicing for love of thee;
1636a. thy semen goes into her, while it is pointed like Sothis.
1636b. Horus the pointed has come forth from thee, in his name of "Horus who was in Sothis."
1637a. Thou art pleased with him, in his name of "Spirit who was in the *dndr.w*-boat";
1637b. Horus has avenged thee, in his name of "Horus, the son, who avenges his father."

Utterance 594.

1638a. To say: N. has ascended to the portal,
1638b. dawning as king, and being high as Wepwawet;
1638c. he supports himself, he is not tired.

Utterance 595.

1639a. To say: Greetings to thee, N.,
1639b. I am come to thee on thy day, since night,
1639c. I have given to thee *Nwtknw*.
1640a. I have brought to thee thy heart and have put it in thy body,
1640b. as Horus brought the heart to his mother Isis,
1640c. as (she) brought the heart to her son Horus.

Utterance 596.

1641a. To say: They have raised themselves up, those who reside in graves,
1641b. in secret places;
1641c. Awake, raise thyself up; thine arms are to thy good.

1642. To say: O N., come, clothe thyself with the sound eye of Horus, which was in *T3i.t.*

1643a. To say: This is this eye of Horus which he gave to Osiris,

1643b. thou hast given it (back) to him, that he may equip his face with it;

1643c. but this is this (eye) of sweet odour————concerning which Horus spoke in the presence of Geb————

1643d. of incense and flame.

1644a. One pellet of incense;

1644b. three pellets of incense;

1644c. a bow.

1645a. To say: N. is Geb, the wise-mouth, hereditary prince of the gods,

1645b. whom Atum has placed at the head of the Ennead, with whose words the gods, are satisfied;

1645c. and all the gods are satisfied with all which N. has said———— everything wherewith it goes well with him for ever and ever.

1646a. Atum said to N.: "Behold, the wise-mouth, who is among us;

1646b. he greets us; let us unite for him."

1647a. O all ye gods, come, assemble; come, unite,

1647b. as ye assembled and united for Atum in Heliopolis,

1648a. that N. might greet you. Come ye,

1648b. do everything wherewith it might go well with N. for ever and ever.

362

1649a. May Geb give an offering; may he give an offering of these joints of meat, an offering of bread, drink, cakes, fowl,

1649b. to all the gods, who will cause every good thing to happen to N.;

1649c. who will cause this pyramid of N. to endure,

1649d. who will cause this temple to endure

1649e. just as (in the condition in which) N. loved it to be, for ever and ever.

1650a. All gods, who shall cause this pyramid and this temple of N. to be good and to endure

1650b. they shall be pre-eminent, they shall be in honour,

1650c. they shall become *ḫ3* (spiritually strong), they shall become *šḥm* (physically strong);

1651a. to them shall be given royal offerings of bread, drink, cakes, meat, fowl, linen, oil;

1651b. they shall receive their divine offerings;

1651c. to them their joints of meat shall be presented;

1651d. to them oblations shall be made;

1651e. they shall bear off the white crown;

1651f. among the Two Enneads.

Utterance 600.

1652a. To say: O Atum-Khepri, when thou didst mount as a hill,

1652b. and didst shine as *bnw* of the *ben* (or, benben) in the temple of the "phoenix" in Heliopolis,

1652c. and didst spew out as Shu, and did spit out as Tefnut,

1653a. (then) thou didst put thine arms about them, as the arm(s) of a *ka*, that thy *ka* might be in them.

1653b. Atum, so put thine arms about N.,

1653c. about this temple, about this pyramid, as the arm (s) of a *ka*,

1653d. that the *ka* of N. may be in it, enduring for ever and ever.

1654a. O Atum, put thy protection upon N.,

1654b. upon this his pyramid, (upon) this temple of N.;

1654c. prevent any evil thing happening to him for ever and ever;

1654d. just as thy protection was put upon Shu and Tefnut.

1655a. O Great Ennead who are in Heliopolis,

1655b. Atum, Shu, Tefnut, Geb, Nut, Osiris, Isis, Set, Nephthys,

1655c. children of Atum————his heart is broad (glad) because of his children, in your name of *"Nine [Bows]."*

1656a. no one among you separates himself from Atum, (when) he protects N.,

1656b. (when) he protects this pyramid of N., (when) he protects this his temple,

1656c. against all the gods, against all the dead.

1656d. He prevents any evil thing from happening to him for ever and ever.

1657a. O Horus, this N. is Osiris;

1657b. this pyramid of N. is Osiris; this his temple is Osiris;

1657c. approach thyself to N.;

1657d. be not far from him, in his name of "Pyramid."

1658a. Thou wast complete, thou wast great, in thy name of "House of the Great black."

1658b. Thot has put the gods under thee, because they are intact and just,

1658c. in the *ddȝ*-fortress, in the *dmȝ'*-fortress.

1658d. O Horus, like thy father, Osiris, in his name of, "He of the royal castle,"

1659a. Horus has given the gods to thee; he has caused them to ascend to thee, as (reed)-pens,

1659b. that they may illuminate thy face (cheer thee) as temples.

41.

A LITANY-LIKE INCANTATION FOR THE ENDURANCE OF A PYRAMID AND TEMPLE, UTTERANCE 601.

Utterance 601.

1660a. To say: O Great Ennead, who are in Heliopolis, make N. endure;

1660b. make this pyramid of N. endure, and this his temple, for ever and ever,

1660c. as the name of Atum, chief of the Great Ennead, endures.

1661a. As the name of Shu, lord of the upper *mnś.t* in Heliopolis, endures,

1661b. so may the name of N. endure,

1661c. so may this his pyramid endure, and this his temple, likewise, for ever and ever.

1662a. As the name of Tefnut, lady of the lower *mnś.t* in Heliopolis, is established,

1662b. so may the name of N. be established,

1662c. so may this pyramid be established, likewise, for ever and ever.

1663a. As the name of Geb, even the soul of the earth, endures,

1663b. so may the name of N. endure,

1663c. so may this pyramid of N. endure,

1663d. so may this his temple endure, likewise, even for ever and ever.

1664a. As the name of Nut, in the encircled mansion in Heliopolis, endures,

1664b. so may the name of N. endure,

1664c. so may this his pyramid endure,

1664d. so may this his temple endure, likewise, for ever and ever.

1665a. As the name of Osiris, in Abydos, endures,

1665b. so may the name of N. endure,

1665c. so may this pyramid of N. endure,

1665d. so may this his temple endure, likewise, even for ever and ever.

1666a. As the name of Osiris, as First of the Westerners, endures,

1666b. so may the name of N. endure,

1666c. so may this pyramid of N. endure,

1666d. so may this his temple endure, likewise, for ever and ever.

1667a. As the name of Set, in Ombos, endures,

1667b. so may the name of N. endure,

1667c. so may this pyramid of N. endure,

1667d. so may this his temple endure, likewise, for ever and ever.

1668a. As the name of Horus endures, in Buto,

1668b. so may the name of N. endure,

1668c. so may this pyramid of N. endure,

1668d. so may this his temple endure, likewise, for ever and ever.

1669a. As the name of Rç', on the horizon, endures,

1669b. so may the name of N. endure,

1669c. so may this pyramid of N. endure,

1669d. so may this his temple endure, likewise, for ever and ever.

1670a. As the name of *Mḥnti-'irti*, of Letopolis, is established,

1670b. so may the name of N. endure,

1670c. so may this his pyramid endure,

1670d. so may this temple of N. endure, likewise, for ever and ever.

1671a. As the name of *Wȝd.t*, in Buto, endures,

1671b. so may the name of N. endure,

1671c. so may this pyramid of N. endure,

1671d. so may this his temple endure, likewise, for ever and ever.

42.
TEXTS OF MISCELLANEOUS CONTENTS, UTTERANCES 602-605.

Utterance 602.

1672a. To say by the Earth, by Geb, by Osiris, by Anubis, by *Wr-ḥb*:

1672b. Make N. festive at the Feast of Horus.

1672c. Let him who is among the falcons hasten to the *ka* of N., who is *Ḥmmi*.

1673a. Open for N. his eyes, open for him his nose;

1673b. open for N. his mouth, open for him his ears;

1673c. make prosperous for N. his two plumes.

1674a. Let N. be allowed to pass, by the god,

1674b. filled with the force of the winds.

1674c. After you have eaten this, N. will find what is left by you.

1674d. Give the remainder to N.; behold, he is come.

Utterance 603.

1675a. (N. Jéquier, VII 709 + 40). To say: Lift thyself up, father N.; fasten to thee thy head; take to thee thy limbs;

1675b. (N. VII 709 + 40). lift thyself up upon thy feet; follow thy heart.

1675c. Thy runners hasten; thy messengers rush on behind;

1676a. thy herald of the horizon comes; Anubis approaches thee;

1676b. *Ḥtp* gives his arm to thee; the gods desire (or, rejoice)———

1676c (N. VII 709 + 40: Thot comes in his dignity of spirit to the Two Enneads.

1676c + 1 (N. VII 709 + 42). He ferried over the lake; h[e] avoided the *Dꝫ.t*

1677a.————

1677b.————with this mighty one who endures each day.

1678a. He comes that he may govern the cities, that he may rule over the settlements,

1678b. that he may command those who are in Nun

1678c. sitting, to him————

1679a.————

1679b.————he rests alive in the West (or, he is satisfied in living in the West),

1679c. among the Followers of Rꜥ', who make the way ,of twilight mount up.

Utterance 604.

1680a. To say: Raise thyself up, father, N., the great; sit before them;

1680b. the apertures of the (heavenly) windows are open for thee;

1680c. broad are thy steps of light;

1680d. this is said to thee, father N. To say: O! Ho!'

Utterance 605.

1681a. To say: Father N., I am come; I bring to thee the green cosmetic;

1681b. I am come; I bring to thee the green cosmetic, which Horus put on Osiris.

1682a. I put thee on my father N., as Horus put thee on his father Osiris,

1682b. when (or, as) Horus filled his empty eye with his full eye.

368

43.

THE RESURRECTION, ASCENSION, AND RECEPTION OF THE DECEASED KING IN HEAVEN, UTTERANCE 606.

Utterance 606.

1683a. To say: Arise for me, father; stand up for me, Osiris N.

1683b. It is I; I am thy son; I am Horus.

1684a. I have come to thee, that I may purify thee, that I may cleanse thee,

1684b. that I may revivify thee, that I may assemble for thee thy bones,

1684c. that I may collect for thee thy flesh, that I may assemble for thee thy dismembered limbs,

1685a. for I am as Horus his avenger, I have smitten for thee him who smote thee;

1685b. I have avenged thee, father Osiris N., on him who did thee evil.

1686a. I have come to thee by order of Ḥrw,

1686b. (for) he has appointed thee, father Osiris N., (to be) upon the throne of Rç'-Atum,

1686c. that thou mayest lead the blessed dead(?).

1687a. Thou shalt embark into the boat of Rç', in which the gods love to ascend,

1687b. in which the gods love to descend, in which Rç' is rowed to the horizon;

1687c. N. shall embark into it, like Rç'.

1688a. Thou shalt seat thyself upon this throne of Rç', that thou mayest command the gods,

1688b. for thou art indeed Rç', who comes forth from Nut, who gives birth to Rç' every day.

1688c. N. is born every day like Rç'.

1689a. Take to thyself the heritage of thy father Geb before the corporation of the Ennead in Heliopolis.

1689b. "Who is equal to him?",

1689c. say the Two great and mighty Enneads who are at the head of the Souls of Heliopolis.

1690a. These two great and mighty gods have appointed thee

1690b.————those who are chiefs of the Marsh of Reeds————upon the throne of *Ḥrw*,

1690c. as their eldest son;

1691a. they placed Shu at thy left (east side), Tefnut at thy right (west side),

1691b. Nun before thee (at thy south side), *Nnt* behind thee (at thy north side);

1692a. they lead thee to these their places, beautiful and pure,

1692b. which they made for Rç' when they placed him upon their thrones (his throne).

1693a. N., they make thee live,

1693b. so that thou mayest surpass the years of Horus of the horizon,

1693c. when they make thy (for "his") name, "Withdraw not thyself from the gods."

1694a. They recite for thee this chapter, which they recited for Rç'-Atum who shines every day;

1694b. they have appointed N. to their thrones (his throne)

1694c. at the head of every Ennead, as Rç' and as his deputy.

1695a. They cause N. to come into being as Rç', in this, his name of "Khepri."

1695b. Thou mountest to them as Rç', in this his name of "Rç'";

1695c. thou turnest back again from their face as Rç', in this his name of
"Atum."

1696a. The Two Enneads shall rejoice, O father;

1696b. when thou approachest, O father, Osiris N., they say:

1696c. "Our; brother is come to us."

1696d. The Two Enneads say to Osiris N.: "King, Osiris N.,

1697a. one of us is come to us."

1697b. The Two Enneads say to thee: "King, Osiris N.,

1698a. the eldest son of his father is come to us."

1698b. The Two Enneads say to thee: "King, Osiris N.,

1698c. he is the eldest son of his mother."

1698d. The Two Enneads say to thee: "King, Osiris N.,

1699a. he to whom evil was done by his brother Set comes to us."

1699b. The Two Enneads say:

1699c. "And we shall not permit that Set be delivered from carrying thee
for ever, king, Osiris N."

1699d. The Two Enneads say to thee: "King, Osiris N.,

1700. raise thyself up, king, Osiris N.; thou livest."

44.

TEXTS OF MISCELLANEOUS CONTENTS, UTTERANCES 607-609.

1701a. To say: Nun has begotten N. on his left hand
1701b. a child; the intelligence of N. is not.
1701c. N. is freed from the evil gods;
1701d. N. is not given to the evil gods.

Utterance 608.

1702a. To say: N., stand up for thy father, the Great One; be seated for thy mother, Nut.
1702b. Give thy hand to thy son, Horus; behold, he is come; he approaches thee.

Utterance 609.

1703a. To say: N., thy mother Nut has given birth to thee in the West;
1703b. thou hast descended in the West in company with the lord of veneration (?);
1703c. thy mother Isis has given birth to thee at Chemmis;
1703d. thy hand which is (full of) the north wind takes (Possession) of thee
1703e. overflowing thee, behind the north wind, father N.

1704a. The Lake of Reeds is full; the Winding Watercourse is inundated;

1704b. the *mn'*-canal of N. is open,

1704c. whereby he may ferry over to the horizon, to the place where the gods will be born,

1704d. and where thou wilt be born with them.

1705a. The two reed-floats of heaven are placed for Rç',

1705b. that he may ferry over therewith to the horizon to the place where the gods will be born,

1705c. and where he will be born with them.

1706a. The two reed-floats of heaven are placed for N.,

1706b. that he may ferry over therewith to the horizon to the place where they will be born,

1706c. and where he will be born with them.

1707a. Thy sister is Sothis; thy mother (bearer) is the morning star;

1707b. thou sittest between them on the great throne,

1707c. which is at the side of the Two Enneads.

1708a. Behold, let these four dwellers of the region (or, height) be brought,

1708b. who sit upon their *d'b*-sceptres, who come forth on (or, from) the eastern side of the sky,

1708c. that they may proclaim this thy goodly utterance to *Nḥb-k3.w*,

1708d. which thy daughter, (*Ḥm.t*), said to thee, and

1708e. *Nḥb-k3.w* shall proclaim this thy goodly utterance

1708f. to the Two Enneads.

1709a. It is *Hpnti*, he who lays hold of thy hand when thou descendest into the boat of Rç',

1709b. descending into the boat with an offering which the king gives; descending and ferrying over.

45.
THE DECEASED KING ON EARTH AND IN HEAVEN UTTERANCE 610.

Utterance 610.

1710a. To say: Wake up for Horus; stand up before Set;

1710b. raise thyself up, eldest son of Geb,

1710c. before whom the Two Enneads tremble.

1711a. (The keeper) of the palace stands up before thee, so that the three beginnings (of the divisions of the year) may be celebrated for thee.

1711b. Thou dawnest on the (first of the) month; thou purifiest thyself on the day of the new-moon.

1711c. The great *mni.t* (-stake) mourns for him,

1711d. as for "Thee who standest without being tired," who resides in Abydos.

1712a. Earth, hear that which the gods have spoken, what Horus says as he spiritualizes his father,

1712b. like Horus-*Ḫ3* and like Min (or, Amún),

1712c. like Seker who is at the head of *Pdw-š.*

1713a. The earth speaks to thee: "The door of Aker is open for thee; the double doors of Geb are open for thee.

1713b. Thou goest forth at the voice (of Anubis), for he has spiritualized thee,

1713c. like Thot, (or) like Anubis, prince of the court of justice (or, divine court),

1714a. that thou mayest judge, that thou mayest lean upon the Two Enneads,

1714b. who are between the two sceptres, in this thy dignity of spirit, commanded by the gods to be in thee.

1715a. If thou goest, Horus goes; if thou speakest, Set speaks;

1715b. if thy step be hindered, the step of the gods will be hindered.

1716a. Thou approachest the lake; thou advancest to the *t3 wr*, the Thinite nome;

1716b. thou passest through Abydos, in this thy dignity of spirit., commanded by the gods to be in thee.

1717a. A ramp is trodden for thee to the *D3.t* to the place where *Š3ḥ* is.

1717b. The ox of heaven seizes thine arm;

1717c. thou nourishest thyself with the food of the gods.

1718a. The odour of *Ddwn* is on thee, the Upper Egyptian Youth, who is come from Nubia;

1718b. he gives thee the incense wherewith the gods cense themselves.

1719a. The two children (twins?) of the king of Lower Egypt have given birth to thee————

1719b. (they) who are on (his) head, (he) the lord of the great crown.

1719c. Rç' calls to thee out of the *'iskn* of heaven,

1719d. as the jackal (god), nome-governor (of the Bows), the Two Enneads,

1719e. as Horus who presides over his, abode (or thigh-offering).

1719f. He appoints thee as the morning star (lit. god of the morning) in the midst of the Marsh of Reeds.

1720a. The portal of heaven is open for thee towards the horizon;

1720b. the heart of the gods rejoice at thy approach,

1720c. as a star which ferries over the ocean which is under the underpart of Nut,

1720d. in this, thy dignity issuing from the mouth of Rç'.

1721a. Thou sittest upon this thy firm throne, like the Great One who is in Heliopolis;

1721b. thou leadest the spirits (spiritualized ones); thou satisfiest the imperishable stars.

1722a. Thine abundance is in that herb in which the gods, abound,

1722b. and on which the spirits nourish themselves;

1722c. thine eyes are opened by the earth, thy limbs are gathered up by the lord of (*Śbw.t*) the rebel city.

1723a. Raise thyself up (like) Ḫnti-Ḫm (chief of Letopolis),

1723b. when the great bread and this wine-like water were given to him.

1723c. The '*im3*-trees serve thee, the *nbś*-tree, bows its head to thee;

1723d. a royal offering will be given to thee, such as Anubis will do for thee.

46.
TEXTS OF MISCELLANEOUS CONTENTS, UTTERANCES 611-626.

Utterance 611.

1724a. To say: Thou who livest art living, father, in this thy name of "With the gods";

1724b. thou shalt dawn as Wepwawet, a soul at the head of the living,

1724c. that mighty one at the head of the spirits.

1725a. The king N. is a *ḥd-wr*, who is at your head, spirits;

1725b. the king N. is the great mighty-one, who is at your head, spirits;

1725c. the king N. is a Thot among you, gods.

1726a. The bolt is drawn for thee,

1726b. (the bolt) to the two ram-portals, which hold people back.

1726c. Thou countest enemies; thou takest the hand of the imperishable stars.

1727a. Thine eyes are open; thine ears are open;

1727b. enter into the house of the guardian; let thy father Geb guard thee.

1728a. The water-holes are united for thee; the lakes are brought together for thee,

1728b. for Horus who will avenge his father, for king N. who will avenge his body.

1729a. A vulture greater than thou (does) triple homage to thee.

1729b. It is agreeable to thy nose on account of the smell of the *'iḥ.t-wt.t-* crown.

1730a. Further, to say: Let this thy going, king N., be like the going of Horus to his father, Osiris,

1730b. that he may be a spiritualized one thereby, that he may be a soul thereby, that he may be an honoured one thereby, that he may be a mighty one thereby.

1731a. Thy spirit is behind thee———

1731b.———king N.

1732a. Collect thy bones; take to thee thy limbs;

1732b. shake off this earth (dust of the earth) from thy flesh;

1733a. take to thee these thy four *nmś.t*-jars [filled at the divine-lake in *Ntr.w*],

1733b. (and) [the wind of the great Isis, together with (which) the great Isis dried (him)] like Horus.

1734a. Raise thyself towards the eye of Rç'; and according to this thy name so will the gods do

1734b. to Horus of the *Dʒ.t*, even to Horus-*Śkśn*,

1734c. to Horus———

1734d.———

1735a. Raise thyself up, be seated on thy firm throne;

1735b. thy finger-nails scratch the castle (-door?).

1735c. Thou travellest over the regions of Horus; thou travellest over the regions of Set.

1735d.———

1736a.———

1736b.———

1736c.———N., father———

1736d. *Hdhd*———

1736e———
1736f———to the Marsh of Offerings.
1737a. *Hdhd*, the ferryman of the Winding Watercourse, comes
1737b.———
1738a.———
173 8b. [Osiris] N. [comes] on the right side of the Marsh of Offerings, behind the two Great Gods,
1738c. that N. may hear what they say———
1739a.———coming forth (?) like Osiris to wash thy hands———
1739a + 1 (N. Jéquier, XXIV 1350 + 74-75). ear———Tefnut.
1739b. If Tefnut seizes thee; if Shu grasps thee,
1739c. then the majesty of Rç' will shine no more (?) in the horizon, that every god may see him.

Utterance 614.

1740a. To say:———
1740b. Thou [goest] to the portal of the house of *Bɜ*;
1740c. thou givest thy hand to them, when they come to thee with salutations;
1741a. but thou smitest them with———
1741b.———in accordance with thy dignity which appertains to the lords of the *'imɜh*.

Utterance 615.

1742a. To say: The eye of Horus is mounted (or, is placed upon) the wing of his brother Set.
1742b. The ropes are tied, the boats are assembled,
1742c. so that the son of Atum be not without a boat.
1742 d. N. is with the son of Atum who is not without a boat.

Utterance 616.

1743a. To say: O thou who art in the fist of the ferryman of the Marsh of Reeds,

1743b. bring this (boat) to N.; ferry N. over.

Utterance 617.

1744a. To say: Hasten, hasten———

1744b.———

1744c.———unite thyself with the gods in Heliopolis.

1745a. May the king make an offering: "in all thy places"; may the king make an offering: "in all thy dignities."

1745b (N. Jéquier, XX 1315). Thou goest in thy sandals; [thou slaughterest an ox]

1745c.———

Utterance 618.

1746a. To say: Now be still, men, hear———

1746b.———

1746c.———

1746d.———with the First of the Westerners.

Utterance 619.

1747a. To say: Raise thyself up, N.; raise thyself up, great *nw3*;

1747b. raise thyself up from (lit. on) thy left side, place thyself on thy right side.

1748a. Wash thy hands with this fresh water which I have given thee, my (lit. thy) father Osiris.

1748b. I have tilled the barley; I have reaped the spelt,

1748c. with which I made (an offering) for thy feasts, which the First of the Westerners offered for thee.

1749a. Thy face is like that of a jackal; thy heart is like that of, K̲bḥ.t, thy seat is like that of a broad-hall.

1749b. A stairway to heaven is built (for thee), that thou mayest ascend.

1750a. Thou judgest between the two great gods,

1750b. who support the Two Enneads.

1750c. Isis weeps for thee; Nephthys calls thee;

1751a. as for 'Imt.t she sits at the feet of thy throne.

1751b. Thou seizest thy two oars

1751c. of which one is of pine, the other of id;

1752a. thou ferriest over the lake of thy house, the sea;

1752b. and thou avengest thyself against him who did this against thee.

1752c. O, Ho, may the great lake protect thee!

Utterance 620.

1753a. To say: I am Horus, Osiris N., I will not let thee sicken.

1753b. Come forth, awake, I will avenge thee.

Utterance 621.

1754. To say: Osiris N., take to thyself the odour of the eye of Horus, like the eye of Horus, which he traced by its odour.

Utterance 622.

1755a. To say: Osiris N., I have adorned thee with the eye of Horus,

1755b. (which is) that *Rnn-wt.t* of whom the gods have fear.

1755c. The gods fear thee, as they have fear of the eye of Horus.

Utterance 623.

1756. Osiris N., take to thyself the eye of Horus, which made its *śtnf.*

Utterance 624.

1757 (Nt. Jéquier, VIII 1). To say: N. has gone forth on the sea of *Iw* (the ferryman); N. has ascended with the help of the wing of Khepri.

1758a. It is Nut who takes the hand of N.; it is Nut who prepares the way for N.

1758b. (Nt. VIII 1). The falcon defends thee against these,

1759a. who are in this boat of Rç', who transport the boat of Rç' to the east.

1759b. Carry N.; lift him up.

1760a. Set this N. among these gods, the imperishable stars; fallen among them.

1760b. He does not perish; he is not destroyed.

1761a. N. is——————among the great gods; he is judge among the gods.

1761b. He who supplies (or, fills) N., supplies N., for his brother

1761c (Nt. VIII 4).——————this N., *Iri.f* ascends like Rç'.

1761d. N. is Osiris, who is come forth out of the night.

Utterance 625.

1762a. To say: N. is the *d'm*-sceptre which is in *Grg.w-b3* (*.f*).

1762b. N. has descended upon the perch; N. has ascended among the great ones.

1763a (Nt. XXXI 806). I have descended into the field of royal women;

1763b. N. has ascended upon the ladder,

1763c. his foot on *S3ḥ* the arm of N. in its.

1764a. I took hold of the reins of him who is chief of his department, (and)

1764b. he takes the arm of N. to the great place,

1764c. (where) N. has seized his throne in the divine boat.

1765a.————

1765b. N. as prince of heaven;

1765c. the house of N. is there among the lords of names.

1766a.————

1766b.————the men and his two boats.

1766c. The name of N. is in the horizon; the 'ḥm.w fear him

1767a.————

1767b.————the great game-board, at the side of him who is with Nḥdf.

1768a. Every god who gives to N. his power to carry off————

1768b.————N. truth.

1768c. He causes those to live who ceased in the fight at the side of Dbḥś.

1769a. N————

1769b. [Ho!] He-who-sees-behind-him, bring to N. the ḳd-ḥtp, made by Khmun,

1769c. that N. may ascend to heaven upon it; that N. may do service of a courtier to Rç' in heaven.

Utterance 626.

1770a. To say: N. has ascended like a swallow; N. has alighted like a falcon.

1770b. The face of N————

1770c. That fortress of his, every one, all of them [have been given to him]; the two nomes of the god have been given to him.

47.

THE ASCENDED KING, HIS WORKS, AND IDENTIFICATIONS, UTTERANCE 627.

Utterance 627.

1771a. To say: N. is a well-equipped spirit, who asks to be;

1771b. heaven is agitated; the earth quakes

1771c.————

1772a. N. was born on (the day of the feast) of the month; N. was conceived on (the day of the feast) of the half-month;

1772b. (for) he came forth with the dorsal carapace of a grasshopper,

1772c. as among that (of) which the wasp bore.

1773a. The two wings————

1773b.————two uraeuses. N. was conceived in the night and ascends to Rç' each day.

1773c. The chapel is open for him (when) Rç' appears.

1774a. N. has ascended on the rain-cloud; he has descended————

1774b.————truth is before Rç'

1774c. on the day of (the feast) of each first-of-the-year.

1775a. Heaven was in satisfaction; the earth was, in joy,

1775b. (after) they heard that N. had put truth [in the place of error].

1776a.————protect (or, avenge)————N. in his divine court

1776b. with the true decision, which comes forth from his mouth,

1776c. demanded his installation as chief: Two acres

1776d.————

1777a. N. is the great falcon who asks to be;

1777b. N. ferries over the sky on four geese (?).

1777c. N. has ascended on the rain-cloud; he has descended————

1777d.————

1778a. N: is the great falcon, who is upon the battlements (or, cornice blocks) of the house of "him of the hidden name,"

1778b. who will seize the (possessions, or) provisions of Atum for him who separates the sky from the earth and Nun

1778c.————this N. in all (?)————shines.

1779a. His two lips are like those of the male of the divine falcons;

1779b. his neck is like that of the mistress of the *nbi*-flame;

1779c. his claws are like those of the bull of the evening;

1780a. his wings are like those of him who presides over (his) abode within the lake of his chapel.

1780b. The *ḥw* (taste) of N. is like the *swnw-ḥr.f-wr*, who is at the side of him who is, in Nun.

1780c. N. was born at (or, on) the hand of eternity.

1781a.————

1781b. N. [went?] to the field of the glorified;

1781c. his hands fell upon *Dbn-wp.wt* (him of the twisted horns), north of the island of Elephantiné (*3bw*);

1781d. he has illuminated the earth with his first divine being.

1782a (N. I 168). To the side————

1782b.————the [urae]us, the gu[ide], in his first birth.

1782c. He is busying himself with *špd.w nw3.t*;

1782d. It goes well with N. because of his *ba*.

1783a.————

1783b.————*wš 'irmn.wt nfr.š*

1783c. The name of N. is made like that of a divine falcon, through which he who passes by it fears;

1784a. because like N. *Šmšw* is older than *nḥd*————

1784b.————

1784c. N. goes to his seat (place?) of (in) the *Šsm.t*-land;

1784d. that which N. eats comes from the Marshes, of Offerings
1784e. and from the lakes of malachite————
1785a (N. I 171). He————a *ka* in the body of a hundred thousand—

————

1785b. N. conducts Rç' into his two boats of *mȝ'.t*
1785c. on the day (of the feast) of the end of the year,

48.
TEXTS OF MISCELLANEOUS CONTENTS, UTTERANCES 628-658.

Utterance 628.

1786a. To say: O thou N.; O thou N.,

1786b. I am Nephthys; I am come, I lay hold of thee; I have put thy heart into thy body for thee.

Utterance 629.

1787. To say: Osiris N., I am come, rejoicing for love of thee, N.

Utterance 630.

1788a. To say: Osiris N., this source is in thee;

1788b. I am the water-hole; I am the flowing (or, overflowing).

Utterance 631.

1789. To say: I have assembled my brother; I have united his limbs.

Utterance 632.

1790a. To say: My heart is full of the place where thou art;

1790b. how harmful is thine odour, how bad is thine odour, how great is thine odour!

Utterance 633.

1791. To say: Thou art she who weeps for him.

Utterance 634.

1792 (N. V 474). To say: Osiris N., I have brought to thee————
1793a (N. 474-475)————thee, in which are spirits.
1793a + 1 (N. 475). Osiris N., I have brought to thee————
1793b (N. 475-476). thou livest in————thy, with her.

Utterance 635.

1794a. To say: Osiris N., I have brought thee the eye of Horus which was in *Tȝi.t,*
1794b. this *Rn(n)-wt.t,* of whom the gods have fear.
1794c. The gods fear thee as they have fear of Horus.
1795a. Osiris N., Horus has put his eye in thy forehead, in its name of "Great-in-charms," (and so),
1795b. Osiris N., thou shalt dawn as king of Upper and Lower Egypt.

Utterance 636.

796. To say: Great Watcher, give me thine arm that I may cause thee to stand.
1797a. I have come [to seek thee]; I have come to protect thee;
1797b. I have avenged thee; I have not delayed to avenge thee.
1797c. Thou art alive; thou livest a life,
1798a. for thou art————thou art healthier than they.
1798b. The father of Osiris N. lives. Thou hast put the eye of Horus to thyself.

Utterance 637.

1799a. To say: Horus comes; filled [with ointment], he sought his father, Osiris;

1799b. he found him on his side in *Gḥś.ti*.

1800a. Osiris filled himself with the eye of him whom he begat.

1800b. O N., I have come to thee also,

1800c. that I may fill thee with the ointment that came forth from the eye of Horus.

1801a. Fill thyself with it.

1801b. It will assemble thy bones; it will unite thy limbs;

1801c. it will collect thy flesh; it will let thy evil sweat flow to the ground.

1802a. Take its odour to thee, that thy odour may be sweet like that of Rç',

1802b. when he ascends in the horizon, and the gods of the horizon delight in him.

1803a. O N., the odour of the eye of Horus is upon thee;

1803b. the gods who follow Osiris delight in thee.

1804a. Thou hast borne off their white crown, while thou art endued with the form of Osiris,

1804b. whereby thou art a spirit, more than the spirits, as Horus himself, lord of men, commanded.

Utterance 638.

1805a. To say: Osiris N., the gods have bound thy face to thee;

1805b. Horus has given his eye to thee, that thou mayest see [with it].

1806a. Osiris N., Horus has opened thine eye for thee, that thou mayest see with it,

1806b. in its name of "She who opens the ways of god."

1807a. To say [Osiris N.], take the eye of Horus, being alive, that thou mayest see with it.

1807b. Osiris N., thy face is opened by the light.

1807c. Osiris N., thy [face is illuminated] as the earth is illuminated.

1808a. Osiris N., I have given the eye of Horus to thee, as Rç' gives it (the light).

1808b. Osiris N., [put the eye] of Horus to thyself, that thou mayest see with it.

1809a. Osiris N., I have opened thine eye that thou mayest see with it.

1809b. Osiris N. [I have given to thee] the ointment.

Utterance 640.

1810a. To say: O Geb, thy son is Osiris N.;

1810b. make thy son live in himself; make thy son well in himself,

1810c. that he may not die, that he may not die.

1811a. If he lives, thou livest; if he is well, thou art well.

181b. Geb, be pre-eminent for thyself; Geb, be honoured for thyself.

1811c. Geb, [be a soul for thyself]; Geb, be mighty for thyself.

1812a. Thou art mighty; thou drivest out every evil thing which pertains to Osiris N.;

1812b. thou [doest service of courtier] for life for (or, behind) Osiris N.,

1812c. that he may not die, that he may not perish.

Utterance 641.

1813a. To say: Osiris N., I have come with————I am Horus.

1813b. I have come, that I may speak for thee; I am thy son.

1814a. Osiris N., thou art the eldest son of Geb,

1814b. his primogeniture, his heir.
1814c. Osiris N., thou art he who dawnest after him;
1815a. the inheritance was given to thee by the Ennead;
1815b. thou art powerful over the Ennead, and even (over) every god.
1816a.———
1816b.———[an eye which goes] forth from thy head
1816c.———

Utterance 642.

1817a. To say: Shu, thou envelopest all things within thine arms.
1817b.———Osiris N., thou preventest that he escape [from thee]
1818a.———of Atum who masturbated for thee.
1818b. Thou art———his *ka.*
1818c. Protect him from———

Utterance 643.

1819a. To say: Osiris N———
1819b.———he lives. Thou art a god; [thou art powerful over the gods].
1820a. [An eye has gone forth from thy head, like] the Great-in-charms, the Upper Egyptian white crown.
1820b.———great
1820c. *śšȝȝ*———a thing gone out from him.
1821a.———thy
1821b. Thy *ka* stands among the gods———thy———on earth.
1822a. O N———
1822b. draw the *ka* after thee; [draw life after thee]
1822c. draw joy after thee; Osiris N———

1823a. [To say: Children of] Horus, put yourselves under N.;
1823b. carry him lest he escape from you;
1823c. carry him [like Horus in the *ḥnw*-boat].

1824a. To say: Osiris, N., Horus has carried thee in the *ḥnw*-boat;
1824b. he carries thee as a god, in thy name of "Seker,"
1824c. as he carries his father.
1824d. Osiris N., [he unites himself with thee];
1824e (Nt. XIII 361). thou shalt be powerful over Upper Egypt as Horus, over whom thou art powerful;
1824f (Nt. XIII 361-362). thou shalt be powerful over Lower Egypt as Horus, over whom thou art powerful;
1824g. thou shalt be powerful, thou shalt be protected (in) thy body from thine enemy.

1825a-1 (Nt. 358). The Ennead has put thine enemy under thee,
1825a-2 (Nt. 358-359). as he spoke to (thee) in thy name of "Osiris N."
1825a (Nt. 359). Horus has made (thee) great in thy charms in thy name of "Great-in-charms."

1826a. To say: Osiris N., Horus has carried thee;
1826b. [he lifts thee up into] the *ḥnw*-boat, in thy name of "Seker."
1827a.————thou art equipped with him;
1827b. thou shalt be powerful [over Lower Egypt as Horus], over whom [thou art powerful].

Utterance 648.

1828a. To say: Osiris N., Horus has given thee these four children of his,

1828b. that thou mayest be powerful over them.

1829a. [He said to them: "Put yourselves] under N.;

1829b. carry [him; not one of you shall escape]."

1829c. They came to thee;

1829d. they carried [thee; not one of them escaped].

Utterance 649.

1830a. To say: Osiris N., Geb has given thee all the gods,

1830b. that they may unite with thee. Thou hast power over them;

1830c. and they fraternize with thee, in their name of "*Śn.wt*";

1830d. they have not rejected thee in their name of ["The two *'itr.t*-palaces"].

1831a. Osiris N., Horus has assigned them to thee, united (them).

1831a + 1. He has encircled for thee all the gods in the embrace of thy two arms,

1831a + 2. together with their lands, together with all their possessions,

1831a + 3. that they may do service of courtier, as thy "bodyguard."

1831a + 4. O N., thou art a great god;

1831a + 5. thou art great, thou art bent around like the "Circle which encircles the *nb.wt*."

1831b. Osiris N., behold, thou art avenged, thou livest; thou movest daily.

1831c. Osiris N., there is no discord in thee.

1831 d. Osiris, N., thou art the *ka* of all the gods.

1832a. Horus has avenged thee; thou art become his *ka*.

1832a + 1. O Osiris N., thou art a god, the power of all the gods.

1832b. An eye has gone forth from thy head like the "Great-in-charms" of Upper Egypt.

1832b + 1. He has given to thee as his eye in thy forehead as the "Great-in-charms" of Upper Egypt.

1832b + 2. An eye has gone forth from thy head (in) Lower Egypt.

1832b + 3. Thou dawnest as Horus, king of Lower Egypt; they are fraternizing with thee,

1832b + 4. in alliance with Horus, king of Lower Egypt.

1832b + 5. Thou dawnest as king of Upper and Lower Egypt.

1832b + 6. Thou art powerful over the gods, also their *kas*.

1832b + 7. O Osiris N., thou art the two souls, thou shalt not die;

1832b + 8. Osiris N., thou hast spoken; thou hast rejoiced, Osiris N.

1832b + 9. Thou hast a *ba*, Osiris N.; thou hast life, Osiris N.;

1832b + 10. thou art powerful; thou destroyest thine enemies, Osiris N.

1832b + 11. Horus, thou hast made peace (to be) with Osiris N.-

1832b + 12. peace be upon her.

1832b + 13. Thou hast put thy regard upon her.

1832b + 14. May peace be to thee, which he gives to thee, (to) thy head.

Utterance 650.

1833a. [To say]:————it is Osiris N., son of [Nut].

1833b. She caused him to appear as king of Upper and Lower Egypt in all his dignity.

1833c. [She caused him to appear as] Anubis, First of the Westerners, as Osiris son of Geb.

1833d.————gods, as *'nd.ti*, chief of the eastern nomes.

1834a. The earth [produces] N.; he shall be chief of the gods who are in heaven,

1834b. as Geb, chief of the Ennead.

1835a. His mother, heaven, bears him, living, each day, beloved of Rç',

1835b. with whom he dawns in the east, with whom he sets in the west.

394

1835c. His mother Nut is not void of him, daily.

1836a. He equips N. with life;

1836b. he makes his heart rejoice; he makes his heart sweet.

1837a. He settles for him the South; he settles for him the land of the North;

1837b. he destroys for him the fortresses of Asia;

1837c. he quells for him all the people, rebels, under his fingers.

Utterance 651.

1838. To say: Osiris N., take to thyself the eye of Horus, [to thy forehead]————

Utterance 652.

1839a. To say: Osiris N., take to thyself the eye of Horus, which I have taken from Set, (after) he had ravaged it.

1839b.————

Utterance 653.

1840. To say: Osiris N., take to thyself the eye of Horus————[a libation].

Utterance 654.

1841a. [To s]ay: O N————

1841b.————braids of hair,

1841c. that he may pass when he comes.

Utterance 655.

1842a. To say: N————

1842b.————thighs of the gods————

1843-1.————N.

1843a (N. pl. 1575). Says *Šsmtt*, N. as a falcon comes forth as the eye of Horus;

1843b. (N. pl. 1575). an '*iʼr.t*-serpent is coming forth like a falcon————

1844.————

1845a. birds to the sky; birds to the earth, a feather of (?) N. a bird (?)————

1945b. he reaches heaven like divine falcons————[Marsh of Reed],

1845c. the great uninjured star.

1846a (N. 577). To [slay————

1846b (N. 577). *gšp* of N., *gšp* of the boat of Seker,

1847a (N. 577). going (?)————[in] the [lakes] of the jackal;

1847b (N. 577). N. makes (his) way towards you.

Utterance 656.

1848. To say: N————

1849.————to a message of the Ennead.

Utterance 657.

1850. To say: N. came————

1851.————N————[First of the West]erners, upon his throne.

1852. N————

Utterance 658.

1853. [To say]:————

1854a. The gods [caused] thee to prosper; they love thee.

1854b (N. VII 580). The gods wish these things for thee in thy name of "Ceaseless."

1854c. thou hast done————

1855a. [He quakes under thee] as the quaking of the earth; he does not escape thee.

1855b. O, thou art more exalted I than he, in thy name of "He of the exalted land"].

1855c (N. 581). Spring thou upon him————[life?]————*bḥḥ n.k*———— —

1856a (N. 582)————lifted up————

1856b.————[without thy separating] from him, without his getting away from thee.

1857a. Horus has placed for thee thine enemies under thee; health and wealth he has accounted for thee.

1857b.————he has cast down————

1857c.————this his eye————

1858. Horus has filled thee with his eye in its name of "The enduring one."

1859 (N. 583). Horus delivered his eye from Set; he gave————

1859 + 1————

1859 + 2————in thy name of "Inundation."

1859+ 3————like————

1859 + 4.————in thee————

1859+ 5————thou art powerful over————

1859 + 6————to thee————

1859 + 7————

1859 + 8————

1859 + 9. To say: Osiris N————in thee

1859 + 10————

1859 + 1,. in (or, with) the eye————

49.

THE DEATH OF THE KING AND HIS ARRIVAL IN HEAVEN, UTTERANCE 659.

Utterance 659.

1860a. To say: He is assembled: This thy going;

1860b. He is assembled: These thy goings,

1860c. are the goings of Horus in search of his father, Osiris.

1861a. His messengers go; his runners hasten,

1861b. his envoys rush on.

1862a. Hasten to Rç'; say to Rç, to him who lifts up his arm in the East,

1862b. that he is coming as a god, that N. stands in the double *'itr.t*-palace of the horizon.

1863a. Thou hearest the words of Rç', as a god, as Horus *mśti*:

1863b. "I am thy brother, like Sopdu."

1864a. Behold, he comes; behold, he comes;

1864b. behold, thy brother comes; behold, *Mḫnti-n-'irti* comes.

1865a. Thou recognizest him not, though thou spendest the night in his arms———

1865b. thy putrefaction being avoided-

1865c. like thy calf, like thy herdsman.

1866a. Thou hast taken these thy white teeth of this *mḥn*;

1866b. they go around like an arrow, in their name of "Arrow;"

1867a. thy leg of beef is in the nome of Abydos, thy (lit. his) piece of meat is in the land of Nubia;

1867b. thou hast descended like the jackal of the South, like Anubis who
   is over (i.e. protects) the (southern) *'itr.t*-palace;
1868a. thou standest before the *Rd-wr*-lake,
1868b. like Geb, at the head of his Ennead.
1869a. Thou hast thy heart; thou hast thy *ka*, N.;
1869b. thou furnishest thy house, N.; thou fastenest thy door, N.

50.
TEXTS OF MISCELLANEOUS CONTENTS, UTTERANCES 660-669.

Utterance 660.

1870a. [To say]: Shu. son of Atum is Osiris N.

1870b. Thou art the great son of Atum, his eldest son.

1871a. Atum has spit thee out of his mouth, in thy name of "Shu."

1871b. He said: "Count my children, in thy name of 'Upper *Mnś.t*'"

1872a. O Shu, this is Osiris N. whom thou hast made to endure and to live.

1872b. If thou livest, he lives; thou art lord of the entire earth.

Utterance 661.

1873a. To say: O father N., take to thyself this thy liquid, the protected (?) (milk),

1873b. which is in the breasts of thy mother, Isis.

1873c. Nephthys, give him thy hand.

Utterance 662.

1874a. O brilliant, brilliant; Khepri, Khepri,

1874b. thou art on the way to N.; N. is on the way to thee;

1874c. thy life is on the way to N.; the life of N. is on the way to thee.

1875a. O papyrus, going forth from *Wȝd.t,*

1875b. thou art gone forth as N.; N. is gone forth as thou.

1875c. N. is strong through thine appearance.

1876a. Appetite belongs to the breakfast of N.;

1876b. plenty belongs to the supper of N.

1876c. Hunger is not powerful in the life of N.;

1876d. fire is far from N.

1877a. N. lives from thy plenty;

1877b. N. abounds in the abundance of thy food, O Rç', every day.

1877c. Father N., arise,

1877d. take this thy first libation, coming out of Chemmis.

1878a. Let them who are in their graves, arise; let them undo their bandages.

1878b. Shake off the sand from thy face;

1878c. raise thyself up (from) on thy left side, support thyself on thy right side (upright).

1879a. Raise thy face, that thou mayest see that which I have done for thee.

1879b. I am thy son, I am thine heir.

1880a. I have hoed wheat (or spelt) for thee; I have tilled barley for thee-

1880b. barley for thy *w3g*-feast, wheat for thy yearly feast.

1881a. The eye of Horus is offered to thee; it is young with thee; it is large with thee,

1881b. O lord of the house; thy hand is upon thy property.

Utterance 663.

1882a-1.————

1882a-2. Thy bread is for every day, I said to thee it is.

1822a. I have said to thee, build————thine arm before thee, Osiris.

1882b. Thine ox————red;

1882c. thy thousand of figs; thy thousand of (jars?) of wine;

1882d. thy thousand of *nbś*-fruit bread; thy thousand of ḥ [*b*]————;

1883a. thy thousand of ground corn. Geb was begotten for thee. The name to thee————

1883b.————Hail, to thee, father N.;

1883c. thy water is to thee; thine inundation is to thee;

1883d. thy milk is to thee, in the bre[asts] of thy mother Isis.

Utterance 664.

1884. To say: O thou N., greetings to thee N., to thee Osiris,

1885. I have come to take thee; I give thy heart to thee; I am thy servant.

1886a. To say: Osiris N., I am Isis; I have come, the beloved of the earth, to the place where thou dwellest;

1886b. I have come to set thy name in thee.

1887a. To say:————in thine arms; he avenges thee.

1887b. He has shone beautifully upon thee, in thy name of "Horizon whence Rç' goes forth."

1887c. Thine arms have embraced him; he does not withdraw himself from thee.

1888. To s[a]y: Osiris N., joi[ned]?————

1889. 1 have united thy limbs for thee; I have put thy heart in its place.

1890. Osiris N., in (?), or, as (?)————

1891. [Osiris] N. I have brought thy heart for thee into thy body; I have put it for thee [in] its place.

1892. He has need of thee *m sʒ*————

1893. Osiris N., I am Horus; I have come to thee————for (or, concerning) that which he has done for thee.

1894. Osiris N., thou hast commanded————she [rai]se thee up.

1895. Osiris N., Nut comes, protecting thee; [she] ha[s] embraced [thee].

1896. Nut [has,] raised [thee] up————

1897. To say: Osiris N., I am Nut, born of this *šnw.t*-palace, like thee. Chapter of Osiris N.

Utterance 665.

1898a. To say: Awake, awake, N., for me, thy son;

1898b. awake for me, Horus; aw[ake thou].

1899a. He lives, who lives, Osiris N., in this thy name of "He who is with the spirits."

1899b. Thou dawnest as *Wpi.w*;

1899c (N. Jéquier, IX 719 + 20). as Spirit, chief of the living; as powerful, chief of the spirits;

1899d (Nt. Jéquier, XXV 559). as the first star, he ate with him.

1899e (N. 719 + 21). [0. N.], thou art Thot in his palace,

1899f (Nt. Jéquier, XXV 660). in thy name of "*Ḥr-wśir-'-Dḥwti.*"

1900a (N. Jéquier, IX 719 + 21). [I am] in thy hand like mud; I am [like?] thousands.

1900b (Nt. Jéquier, XXV 660). Thy hand carries thee to the imperishable stars.

1901a. O. N., rise up [from] sleep, distant one, transfigured, Horus-*nḥ*'.

1901b (N. Jéquier, IX 719 + 21). The great stand for thee; watchmen sit for thee,

1902a (Nt. Jéquier, XXV 661-662). like Horus, avenger of his father. The smell of the *'im₃*-tree is to thee, (thy) nose.

1902b (Nt. Jéquier, XXV 662). The perfume, N., is (that of) the 'im3-tree to thee, (thy) nose.

1902c (N. Jéquier, IX 719 + 22). Raise thyself up, N.; take to thyself these thy four *nmś'.t*-pitchers,

1902d (N. IX 719 + 22). which have been filled for thee in the divine lake; take to thyself this thy *nḥb.t*-sceptre,

1902e (N. IX 719 + 22). which thy mother Nekhbet has given thee; it shall not be taken away from its sheath (?).

1903a (=: 1908a in Sethe's order). Raise thyself up, N.

1903b (Nt. Jéquier, XXV 663-664). Thou seest thy regions, the Horite, also their great houses;

1903c (Nt. XXV 664) thou seest thy regions, the Setite, also their great houses.

1904a (Nt. XV 664). Thou hast released thy bands, like Horus who is in his house;

1904b (Nt. 664-665). thou hast drawn thy bonds, like Set who is in *Ḥn.t.*

1905a (Nt. 66S). I have freed thee from *Ḥr.ti*; he lives on the hearts of men;

1905b (Nt. 665). 1 have not given (permitted) thee to return to the desert.

1906a (Nt. 665-666). Thou hast said, "Hail, this my protector, like Isis;

1906b (Nt. 666). greetings to thee, *Śmnd.t.t*, like Nephthys;

1906c (Nt. 666). thou hast shaken the earth; thou hast brought an offering;

1906d (Nt. 666). thou hast certainly escaped (evil)."

1906e (Nt. 666-667). Thot comes to thee like a knife; he comes like Set.

1906f (N. IX 719 + 24). He finds thee sitting upon thy throne of ebony,

1906g (N. IX 719 + 24). like Rç', chief of the Ennead.

1907a (N. Jéquier, IX 719 + 24). Thou speakest to the spirits; thou hast united their heads.

1907b (Nt. Jéquier, XXV 668). Thou hast brought their runners; thou livest in their hearts;

1907c (Nt. 668). thou standest upon————foot————sea;

1907d (Nt. 668). thou hast given thy name to the jackal; thou hast taken thy name to *Wpi.w.*

1907e (Nt. 668). O N., thy great name is "*Ḥnti-Ḥr.k.*"

1908a (N. Jéquier, IX 7 19 + 25). To say: Raise thyself up, N.

1908b (N. IX 719 + 25). Thy bones have been collected for thee; thy limbs have been assembled for thee;

1908c (N. IX 719 + 25). thy water comes forth from Elephantiné;

1908d (N. IX 7 19 + 2 5). thy natron is in the temple; thou standest as chief of the *'itr.t*-palaces,

1908e (Nt. Jéquier, XXVIII 730). as chief of the gods, lord of the jackals.

1909a (Nt. XXVIII 730). Thy hand smites thine enemies, whom Anubis, chief of the temple, gave to thee.

1909b. (Nt. XXVIII 730). Thou art in his hand, N., as Horus, First of the Westerners.

1909c (Nt. 731). The Serḳet-temple is open for thee; the double doors of the necropolis are open for thee.

1909d (N. 719 + 26). Thou findest thine abundance, which approaches thee.

1910a (N. IX 719 + 26). Raise thyself up, N.,

1910b (N. 719 + 26). for thy thousand of bread, thy thousand of beer, thy thousand of cattle, thy thousand of fowl,

1910c (Nt. XXVIII 732). thy thousand of clothes, thy thousand of every (kind of) bag.

1911-1 (Nt. XXVIII 732). Thou hast come to the house of this N.; thou inheritest the leadership as lord of the gods,

1911-2 (Nt. 732). Thou givest commands (lit., "commands words") to the Horus-gods of the West, likewise to thee, great and mighty spirit.

1911 (N. IX 719 + 27). Thou hast united with the dead in every place in which thou desirest to be.

1912a (N. 719 + 27). N. thou art powerful there.

1912b (N. 719 + 27). The gods command that thou protect thyself against the words of thine enemy.

1912c (Nt. 733). This N., like thee, sacrifices to Osiris on his throne.

1912d (Nt. 733-734). Thou followest the Horus-gods of the West, thy spirit (being) chief of the gods.

1913-1 (Nt. 734). To say: O N., he lives, who lives; he lives, who lives,

1913a (N. 719 + 28). in thy name of *Ḥri-ntr.w*.

1913b (N. 719 + 28). Thou dawnest as *Wpi.w*,

1913C (N. 719 + 28). as a soul, chief of the living; as powerful, chief of the spirits.

1914a (N. 7 19 + 28). Thot is this N.

(1914a (N. VI 709 + 2).————together with you, O gods);

1914b (Nt. 735). unite ye, O gods, who are in the temple,

(1914b (N. 709 + 2). offer a sacrifice with thy hand).

1914c (Nt. 735). This is this N. (for whom) thou, Osiris, shalt open the six doors.

(1914c (N. 709 + 2). Thou openest doors),

1914d (Nt. 735-736). which hold Libya back.

1914e (Nt. 736). Offer a sacrifice with thy hand;

1914f (Nt. 736). take a thousand *Mw.w*; lead the Nine Bows;

1915a (Nt. 736). grasp the hand of the imperishable stars.

1915b (Nt. 7,36-737). The great unite for thee; the watchers stand for thee;

1915c (N. 719 + 29). also Horus avenges his father.

1916-1 (N. 719 + 29). O N., great is sleep; it is great to sleep.

1916-2 (N. 709 + 4). This great one sleeps, he sleeps; wake up, raise thyself up.

1916-3 (Nt. 738). Great is thine odour, pleasant to the nose, the odour of *Ṯḥ.t-wt.t*.

1916a (Nt. 738). O N., thou hast collected thy bones; thou hast collected thy limbs;

1916b (Nt. 738-739). Thou hast assigned (left in legacy) thy teeth; thou hast taken thy heart to thy body;

1917 (Nt. 739). thou hast shaken the dust (lit. earth) from thy flesh;

1918 (N. 719 + 30). thou hast received this thy purification, these thy four *ȝb.t*-jars.

1919a (Nt. 739). Draw fully from the divine lake, the lake in which [they] purify thee, as a god.

1919b (N. 709 + 6). Thou comest with them as an eye, thou dawnest; thou [comest] (as) chief of the imperishable stars,

1919c (Nt. 740). like Geb, chief of the corporation of the Ennead of Heliopolis.

1920a (Nt. 740). He gives commands to the gods;

1920b (N. 720). he gives commands while sitting as a living god.

1921-1 (Nt. 741). Thou hast carried off the *wrr.t*-crown, like a star, the unique;

1921-2 (Nt. 741). its enemies are no more. Thy death is gone (from) thee,

1921-3 (Nt. 741). N. says to Horus, to his father, Osiris.

1921 (Nt. 741). O N., thine Endurance says to thee, "thy death is gone (from) thee."

1921 + 1 (Nt. 742). Thy spirit consists in thy greatness, in thy respect,

1921 + 2 (Nt. 742). in thy power (as a digger?), in thy might.

1921 + 3 (Nt. 742). O N., thou hast thy spirit in thy body;

1921 + 4 (Nt. 742-743). thy spirit is behind thee; thy heart is in thy body;

1921 + 5 (Nt. 743). thy judgment is thy protection, like Horus who is in his house;

1921 + 6 Wt. 743). thine evil is in thy wickedness, like Set who is in his *Ḥnb.t*-city.

1922 (Nt. 743). Thou enterest when thy father Geb is protecting thee.

1922 + 1 (Nt. 744). If (thy) father does not know thee, he is not alive;

1922 + 2 (Nt. 744). if (thy) father calls thee "*Ḥ.t*," retreat, such is not thy name.

1922 + 3 (Nt. 744). O N., take the eye of Horus; thy hand is upon thy bread;

1922 + 4 (Nt. 744). O N., present thyself as thy bread,

1922 + 5 (Nt. XXIX 745). like as Horus presents it as his, eye.

1922 + 6 (Nt. 745). Thy name is that of an offering.

1922 + 7 (Nt. 745). Thy *w3g*-feast is as this thy bread,

1923 (Nt. 745). just as the *w3g*-feast is king Horus with his eye.

1924 (Nt. 745). Thy name is that of thy *w3g*-offering.

1924 + 1 (Nt. 746). Raise thyself up to heaven together with the stars which are in heaven;

1924 + 2 (Nt. 746). throw down those who are before thee; protect thyself from those who are behind thee,

1924 + 3 (Nt. 746). because of this thy name, which thy father Osiris made for thee, of "Horus of the *D3.t*."

1924 + 4 (Nt. 747).]Because they smite their *'ḥš*-star, and because they destroy (him),

1925 (Nt. 747). thou shalt smite them, because of their *'ḥš*-star, and thou shalt destroy them at the lake, at the sea ("great green").

1926 (Nt. 747). Thou standest before the imperishable stars;

1926a + 1 (Nt. 747). thou sittest upon thy firm throne, keeping the dead far from him————

1926a + 2 (Nt. 748). thou who seest the hacking up of the house (by)

1926a + 3 (N. VI 709 + 16). [N]*wtknw*.

1927a-1 (Nt. 749). O N., behold that which was done to thee,

1927a-2 (N. 709 + 16). king N., and not only to thee, but, behold, against thy foot;

192 7a-3 (Nt. 750). it is not done on account of thee, nor on account of thy hand.

1927a (Nt. 750-751). Protect thyself against *Nwtknw*.

1927b (Nt. XXIX 751). Behold the evil (?) which is done to thee, sleeper.

1927c (Nt. 752). The double doors of heaven are open for thee; the double! doors of $ḳbḥ.w$ are open for thee.

192 7c + 1 (Nt. 752). Thou goest forth through them like $Wpi.w$;

192 7c + 2 (Nt. 753). the white crown upon thine arms like Thot.

1927C + 3 (Nt. 753). Behold, their evil (?) goes forth like Set.

1927c + 4 (Nt. 753-754). He did thee damage, in thine eyes.

192 7c + 5 (Nt. 754). The *min.t* (-stake) mourns (lit. calls) thee like Isis;

192 7c + 6 (N. 709 + 18). the *min.t* (-stake) mentions it to thee like Nephthys.

192 7c + 7 (N. 709 + 18). [Thou] dawnest on the *Rd-wr*-lake.

1928a (Nt. 755-756). Thou journeyest through thy regions of Horus;

1928b (Nt. 756). thou journeyest through thy regions of Set,

1928c (Nt. 757). like Min before the corporation of the Ennead.

1929 (Nt. 757). Thou hast opened the door of the house of him who is chief of his department (or, thigh-offering).

1930-1 (Nt. 758). O N., behold that which was done to thee;

1930-2 (Nt. 758). thou has been transfigured; thou hast not decayed.

1930-3 (Nt. XXIX 759). Guard thyself; it is thou who art strong as chief of thy door;

1930-4 (Nt. 759). thy bread, thy bread is for its year, thy morning bread is for its year;

1930-5 (Nt. 760). thy bread, it is likewise for N. every day.

1930 (Nt. 760). O N., thou knowest that also, without (i.e. not) being ignorant, that one may voyage from the boundary to thee.

1930 + 1 (Nt. 761). Whether not speaking, or speaking————thy shoulder before thee, Osiris!

Utterance 666.

1931-1(Nt. Jéquier, XXIX 761). To say: O N. [pass?] the great lake (?), even this, to the spirits,

1931-2 (Nt. 762). this water (*ḥnš*) to the dead.

1931-3 (Nt. 762). Guard thyself against these its people, whose house (home) is that bush,

1931a (Nt. 762). the heavenly (?) *ḏз.t*, in its name of "*Dзt.t*,"

1931b (Nt. 762). where they take not thy hand to that house (home) of the bush.

1932 (Nt. 763). He, he is a pyramid, he protects;

1932 + 1 (Nt. 763). he is the east, he is thy protector, he protects; a father, thy east, he is the Easterner.

1933a (Nt. 763). Go to *Dз.w-'ib*, brother of Seker, whom he loves;

1933b (Nt. 764). he will make a way for thee with them,

1933b + 1 (Nt. 764). where thou mayest eat bread with them,

1933b + 2 (Nt. 764). where thou mayest row the *wзd* with them,

1933b + 3 (Nt. 764). where the sky trembles for thee, the earth quakes for thee,

1933b + 4 (Nt. 764-765). and the imperishable stars come to thee.

1934a (Nt. 763). And so, behold, he seized thy hand (at) the *Nḥb-kз.w*-feast, at (in) the Marsh of Reeds (or, at inundation time?),

1934b (Nt. 765). (while thou) sittest upon thy firm throne,

1934c (Nt. 765). and judgest with the Two Enneads.

Utterance 667.

1934 + 1 (Nt. Jéquier, XXX 766). O N., take to thee thy head,

1934 + 2 (Nt. 766). to thee thy teeth, to thee thy hair;

1934 + 3 (Nt. 766). thou has opened the neighbouring doors of the people, enduring for ever and ever.

1935-1 (Nt. 766). O N., thou goest forth, thy face towards the sea;

1935-2 (Nt. 766). thou sittest chief of the great ones, with thee;

1935 (Nt. 767). thou hast preserved the sky, thou hast caused the earth to tremble, thou hast protected the imperishable stars.

1936a (N. IX 730). I am come to thee (in) secret places, seeking thee (even) to heaven,

11936b (Nt. 768). but (in) the secret (place) there is no spirit there,

1936b + 1 (Nt. 768). from the peace of heaven to, the peace of earth,

1936b + 2 (Nt. 768). the peace of the two lords (Horus and Set), the peace of high (heaven), the peace of peace.

11936b + 3 (Nt. 768). The mowing of corn (is) for thy *w3g*-feast,

11936b + 4 (Nt. 768). the *nri*-corn (?) for thy years (livelihood, cf. 1950b); thy white bread, Anubis, for (thy) flat-cakes, and this its dough,

1936b + 5 (Nt. 768-769). thy drink, First of the Westerners, thy warm bread,

1937 (Nt. 769). N., (are) before the gods.

1938a (Nt. 769). O N., raise thyself up,

1938b (Nt. 769). raise thyself from thy left side, put thyself (lit. sit) on thy right side,

1938b + 1 (Nt. 769). sit thou on the seats of Rç'.

1939-1 (Nt. 769). Purify thy back, even to the vertebrae; let thy hand be upon thine altar,

1939-2 (Nt. 770). thy thousand of bread, thy thousand of beer, thy thousand of cattle, thy thousand of birds,

1939-3 (Nt. 770). thy thousand of all (kinds) of linen, thy thousand of every thing, which the god eats,

1939-4 (Nt. 770). thy thousand of clean (things), also within the dwelling,

1939 (Nt. 771). that thou mayest eat the leg (of meat), that thou mayest pass the cutlet (over thy mouth), that thou mayest devour the double rib,

1939+ 1 (Nt. 771). at the place of slaughter for ever and ever.

1940 (Nt. 771). O N., they defend thy name, with thee.

1940+ 1 (Nt. 771). Thou shalt not speak to them, crying out,

1940+ 2 (Nt. XXX 771). what, say they, is done to thee,

1940+3 (Nt. 772). by "the throne" it was done, sayest thou,

1940+4 (Nt. 772). *S̃s̃s̃*, his grave, ruling his brick, sayest thou.

1940+ 5 (Nt. 772). An offering of his cake (?) in the castle (?).

1940+ 6 (Nt. 772). Hail, he himself (i.e. she herself, the queen)!

1941a (Nt. 772). O N., eat this for thyself alone;

1941b (Nt. 773). thou shalt not give (it) to those people; these by thy side.

1946 + 1 (Nt. 773). O N., this hour of the morning, of this third day, is come,

1941b + 2 (Nt. 773). when thou surely passest on to heaven, together with the stars, the imperishable stars.

1941b + 3 (Nt. 774). O N., be it said to thee: "in peace;

1942a (Nt. 774), thou art beautiful; great is that which thy position does for thee as First of the Westerners."

1942b (Nt. 774). The seated one is put near the king.

1942b + 1 (Nt. 774-775). Thou choosest among (?) the first of thy land those who will make thy halls.

Utterance 667 A.

1943a-1 (Nt. 775). To say: It is beautiful to see, it is peaceful to hear that Osiris stands at the door of the gods.

1943a-2 (Nt. 775). Thy sanctuary, N.,

1943a-3 (Nt. 775). is to thee as (?) a heart of secret places;

1943a (Nt. 775-776). it opens for thee the double doors of heaven, it opens for thee the double doors of the way;

1943b (Nt. 776). it makes for thee a way, that thou mayest enter there among the gods,

1943b + 1 (Nt. 776). that thou mayest live as thy soul.

1944a (Nt. 776). O N., thou art not like the dead, who art dead,

1944a + 1 (Nt. 776-777). thou art living, thou art alive, together with them, the spirits, the imperishable stars.

1944a. + 2 (Nt. 777). The time of inundation comes, the *w3g*-festival comes, to the uplands, it comes as Osiris.

1944a + 3 (Nt. 777). Horus is purified with the eye of his brother Set;

1944a + 4 (Nt. 777-778). Set is purified with the eye of his brother Horus;

1945b (Nt. 778). N. is purified from every evil thing;

1945c (N. X 736). the Watchers of Horus are purified in his reed-float.

1945c + 1 (Nt. XVII 487). Father Osiris dawned over the sea, upon his throne, named "brilliant" for him, like his spirit;

1946a-1 (Nt. XXX 779). he was warned against *Hr.ti* lest he be not given to Osiris, (so)

1946a-2 (Nt. 779). there was opened for him the opposing door;

1946a-3 (Nt. 779). there was done for him that which was done (for him) as an only (unique) star without its equal

1946a (Nt. 779). among them, the gods, thou who sittest upon thy great seat.

1946b (N. X 737). Thy bread is *t-wr* (bread); thy bread is in the broad-hall (temple hall).

1947a (N. X 737). The Watchers dance for thee,

1947b (Nt. XXX 780). as the mourning-women of Osiris call for thee.

1947b + 1 (Nt. 780). Raise thyself up, N.;

11947b + 2 (Nt. XVII 489). collect to thee thy bones;

1947b + 3 (Nt. XXX 781). take to thee thy head————a command of the Ennead,

1947b + 4 (Nt. XVII 490). sit thou for thy great bread;

1947b + 5 (Nt. XXX 781). choose thou the leg of meat on the great place of slaughter;

1947b + 6 (N. X 738). let there be given to thee the double-rib piece on the place of slaughter of Osiris.

1948a (Nt. XVII 490). O N., raise thyself up like Min.

1948b (N. X 738). Thou fliest up to heaven; thou livest with them;

1948c (N. X 738). thou causest thy wings to grow;

1948c + 1 (Nt. XVII 491). thy feathers on thy head; thy feathers on thy two arms.

1948c + 2 (Nt. XXX 782). Thou hast made the sky clear; thou givest light to them, like a god;

1948c + 3 (Nt. XVII 491). thou remainest chief of heaven like Horus of the *Dꜣ.t.*

Utterance 667 B.

1948c + 4 (Nt. XVII 491-492). Vigilant (?) is this eye of Horus, which he gave to Osiris;

1948c + 5 (Nt. 492). he gave (it) to thee, that it may destroy thy face.

1948c + 6 (Nt. 492)————smell

1948c + 7 (Nt. 492). this word of Horus is, for it, says Geb.

Utterance 667 C.

1949-1 (Nt. XXX 783). To say: I am N. of secret places;

1949 (Nt. 783). I ascend (as) thy good messenger from *ḳbḥ.w;*

1950a (N. X 739). I have threshed the barley, I have reaped the spelt,

1950b (N. 739). that thy livelihood may be secured thereby.

1950c (Nt. 783). Thou ascendest; thou art complete, N.

1950c + 1 (Nt. 784). Thou art powerful in————

1950c + 2 (Nt. 784). I did not see thee, (it is) thou who seest me.

1951-1 (Nt. 784). This Great One has seen the face of that Great One-the seeing of two eyes.

1951-2 (Nt. 784). *Iw* who binds hair is his avenger;

1951a (Nt. 785). he stands, like Horus, who is on the shores,

1951b (N. X 740). his two sisters, at his side————Isis and Nephthys.

1952 (Nt. XXX 785). Raise thyself up, N.,

1952 + 1 (Nt. 785). unite thy bones, collect thy limbs.

1952 + 2 (Nt. 785-786). Raise thyself up, N.,

1952 + 3 (Nt. 786). receive thy head————

1952 +4 (Nt. 786)————thy face————born of *Nwn.t,*

414

1952 + 5 (Nt. 786). thy mother, who makes thee glad.

1952 + 6 (Nt. 786). She cleanses thee like a papyrus roll of the flesh (skin?) of *Mrw*.

1953a (N. X MI). Shu, Shu, he passes by the walls,

1953b (N. 741). he outdistances the walls,

1953c (Nt. 787). N. is enclosed in secret places.

1954.————

1955a-1 (Nt. 787). when she does not pass you by, (when) she does not outdistance you.

1955a-2 (N. 742)————

1955a-3 (N. 742)————*ḥmwś.t*

1955a (N. 742). four————

1955b (N. 742). they pass by the walls; they outdistance the walls;

1955c (N. 742). thou, N., art enclosed in secret places.

1956 (N. 742)————

1956 + 1 (N. 742)————

1956 + 2 (N. 742)————*nn.wt*

1957a (N. 742). thy thousand of————of stone vessels,

1957b (N. 743). thy thousand of all (kinds) of linen,

1957c (N. 743). thy thousand of cattle, thy thousand of birds, thy thousand of all sweet things,

1958a (N. 743). that thou mayest carry thyself in a festive manner as a god————

1958b (N. 744)————by thee, *ḥw*————

1958b + 1 (N. 744)————to *Pdw-ś*.

Utterance 668.

1959a (N. X 749). To say: N. is the crying falcon, encircling the eye of Horus in the *Dȝ.t*.

1959b (N. 750)————

1959b + 1 (N. 750)————N.————

1960a-1 (N. 750). N. is a sacrificing falcon;

1960a-2 (N. 750). N. has put you there.

1960a (N. 750). N. goes to the eastern side of the sky,

1960b (N. 750). where N. was conceived, where N. was born.

Utterance 669.

1961a. To say: A prince ascends———a great burnt-offering on the interior of the horizon;

1961b. he has seen the preparation of the feast, and the preparation of the fire-pan,

1961c. at the birth of the gods, on the five epagomenal days, who are before thee,

1961d. "Great-his-breast," thou who art before the *Bstw.w.*

1962a.———

1962a + 1 (N. X 755)———N. of his mother; *Twt,*

1962a + 2 (N. 755). he who was born, a double, in the nest———Thot

1962b. in the interior of the field of the tamarisk, at the source of the gods,

1963a. for N. is my brother, proceeding from the thigh,

1963b. who separated the two brothers, put apart the two fighters, who split your heads, O gods.

1964a.———of———

1964b (N. 756)———her fillet, N.,

1964c (N. 756). as Nwrw, who is great among you, O gods, you who come to him, O gods;

1964d. as Isis said to Nun:

1965a. "I have given birth to him for thee; I have deposited him for thee; 1 have certainly spit him out for thee."

1965b. He has no feet; he has no arms,

1965c. and how shall he be assembled?

1966a. Then let this copper be brought———the *ḥnw*-boat———with it.

1966b (N. 756). [Come ye] with him, nourished, with him in your arms, say they, the gods.

1966c (N. 756). Behold, he is born.

1966d. Behold, he is assembled; behold he exists.

1967. Wherewith shall we break that which appertains to his egg, say they, the gods.

1968a. Let then Seker of *pdw* come,

1968b. that he may mould (smelt) his bones, that he may construct his skeleton

1968c.———

1968d. It is he who shall break the e[gg], and [loose] the copper,

1969a (N. 758). so that the two followers of the gods, with sharp teeth and long claws, may bring the god forth by his hands.

1969b. Behold, N. exists; behold, N. is assembled;

1969c. behold N. has broken (his) egg.

1970a. Wherewith shall N. be caused to fly?

1970b (N. 758-759). Then let there be brought to thee———*ḥnw*-boat, built by *Mw-ḥn*,

1970c. that thou mayest fly therewith, that thou mayest fly therewith,

1970d (N. 759). the south-wind for thy foster-mother, the north-wind for thy nurse.

1971. N. flies; N. alights on the two wings (lit. feathers) of his father, Geb.

51.

THE DEATH, RESURRECTION, AND SPIRITUALIZATION OF THE KING, UTTERANCE 670.

Utterance 670.

1972. To say: The double doors of heaven are open; the double doors of the bows are open.

1973a. The gods in Buto were filled with compassion, when they came to Osiris N.,

1973b. [at the voice of we]eping of Isis and at the lamentation of Nephthys,

1973c. at the wailing of these two spirits

1973d. [for this Great One who comes forth] from the *D3.t.*

1974a. The Souls of Buto dance for thee;

1974b. they beat their flesh for thee; they hit their arms for thee;

1974c. they dishevel their hair for thee;

1974d. they smite their legs for thee.

1975a. They say to thee, Osiris N., "thou art gone, thou art come;

1975b. thou art asleep, [thou art awake]; thou art [dead (lit. thou landest)], thou art alive.

1976a. Stand up, see that which thy son has done for thee;

1976b. awake, hear [that which] Horus [has done for] thee.

1977a. He has beaten for thee him who beats thee, li[ke an ox];

1977b. he has killed for thee him who kills thee, like a wild-bull;

1977c. he has bound for thee him who binds thee;

1977d. he has put him under thy great daughter who is in *Ḳdm*,

1978a. so that mourning ceased in the two *'iṭr.t*-palaces of the gods."

1978b. Osiris speaks to Horus:

1978c. After he had exterminated the evil [which was in N. on] his fourth day,

1978d. after he had annulled that which he did against him on his eighth [day].

1979a. [Thou hast come forth] from the lake of life; [thou art] purified [in the lake of] *ḳbḥ.w*,

1979b. and art become Wepwawet; and thy son Horus conducts thee,

1979c. when he has given to thee the gods, thine enemies, and Thot has brought them to thee.

1980a. How beautiful indeed is the sight, how agreeable is the view, the sight of Horus,

1980b. in that he gave life to his father, [in that he offered] satisfaction to Osiris,

1980c. before the gods of the west!

1981a. Thy libation is poured by Isis, [Nephthys has purified thee]————

1981b. [thy two sisters] great and powerful, who collected thy flesh,

1981c. who bound together thy limbs, who made thy two eyes to appear in thy face————

11982a. the boat of the evening and the boat of the morning,

1982b. Atum has given to thee, and the Two Enneads have made for thee.

1983a. The children of thy child have raised thee up, perfect————

1983b. *Ḥȝpi, 'Imś.ti, Dwȝ-mu.t-f, Ḳbḥ-śn.w.f,*

1983c. who made for thee [their] names [into *tt.wi*],

1983d. [who washed thy face], [who dried] thy tears,

1983e. who opened thy mouth with their copper (or, iron) fingers.

1984a. Thou mountest, thou mountest towards the broad-hall of Atum;

1984b. thou marchest towards the Marsh of Reeds;

1984c. thou voyagest over the places of the great god.

1985a. To thee heaven is given, to thee the earth is given, to thee the Marsh of Reeds is given,

1985b. [by] the two great gods who row thee over-

1985c. Shu and Tefnut, the two great gods of Heliopolis.

1986a. The awakening [of the god], [the rising of the god],

1986b. [for this spirit, who ascends from] the $D\mathfrak{z}.t$, (even) Osiris N. who ascends from Geb.

52.
TEXTS OF MISCELLANEOUS CONTENTS, UTTERANCES 671-675.

Utterance 671.

1987a. To say: O N., thou art the son of a Great One;
1987b. thou art purified in the lake, *D3.tì*;
1987c. thou takest thy throne in the Marsh of Reeds.

Utterance 672.

1988a. To say: The truth of Horus is the truth of this N., O N.
1988b. Thou art come, N., clothed; thou comest vested.
1989a. N. has inherited him who is not mourned any more, him who comes into being smiling.
1989b. Greetings to thee N.; thou comest in peace.

Utterance 673.

1990a. To say: O father N.,
1990b. thou comest, that is, thou hast come like a god, thou who art come (in boat) like *ḳbḥ.w*.
1991a. Thy messengers hasten; thy runners run;
1991b. they ascend to heaven; they announce to Rç'
1992a. that thou standest in the double *'itr.t*-palace of the horizon, upon Shu of Nut;

1992b. that thou art seated upon the throne of thy father, Geb, as chief of the *'itr.t*-palace,

1992c. upon this throne of copper (or, iron), the wonder of the gods.

1993a. The Two Enneads come to thee with salutations;

1993b. thou commandest men

1993c. like Min, who is in his house, and like Horus of *Db'.wt*.

1993d. And Set was not free from bearing thy weight.

Utterance 674.

1994a. To say: I have come to thee, I am thy son; I have come to thee, I am Horus;

1994b. I give to thee thy mdw-staff before the spirits and thy *nḥb.t*-sceptre before the imperishable stars.

1995a. [I have found thee assembled], [thy (lit. his) face] like (that of) a jackal, thy (lit. his) seat like (that of) *ḳbḥ.wt*;

1995b. she refreshes thy heart in thy body, in the house of her (lit. thy) father Anubis.

1996a. Be pure and sit at the head of those greater than thou.

1996b. Thou art seated on thy firm throne, on the throne of the First of the Westerners;

1996c. thy *śtiś.w*, they are young.

1997. *Śmnt.t* salutes thee, like Isis; *Hn.t* acclaims thee like Nephthys.

1998a. Thou standest at the head of the *śn.wt*, of the double palace, like Min;

1998b. thou standest at the head of Egyptians (*km.tiw*), like Ḥapi;

1998c. thou standest at *Pdw-ś*, like Seker.

1999a. Thou standest before the *Rd-wr*-lake.

1999b. Thou hast thy *'b3*-sceptre, thy wire, thy fingernails; which are at hand (lit. "at thy fingers");

1999c. those who are before Thot are slain with the knife, coming from Set.

1999d. Thou givest thine arm to the dead, to the spirits, who will take thine arm to the First of the Westerners.

Utterance 675.

2000a. To say: O N., "come in peace," says Osiris to thee;

2000b. messenger of the Great God, "come in peace," says the Great God to thee.

2001a. The double doors of heaven are open for thee; the (double doors of the) *šḥd.w*-stars are open for thee,

2001b. after thou art descended (into the grave) as the jackal of Upper Egypt,

2001c. as Anubis on his belly (side), as *Ḥpi.w* who resides in Heliopolis.

2002a. The great damsel who lives in Heliopolis has given her arm to thee.

2002b. O N., thou hast [no] father, among men, who conceived thee;

2002c. thou hast no mother, among mankind, who bore thee.

2003a. Thy mother is the great wild-cow who lives in el-Kâb,

2003b. the white crown, the royal head-dress, she with the long feathers (hair?), she with the two hanging breasts,

2003c. she will nurse thee; she will not wean thee.

2004a. Raise thyself up, N., dress thyself in thy fringed-vestment, the first (best) in the house,

2004b. thy *ḥd*-mace on thine arm, thy Horus-weapon (*ʒmš*) in thy hand, thine *ʒmš*-sceptre on thine arm, thy *ḥd*-mace in thy hand.

2005a. Thou standest as he who is chief of the double *'itr.t*-palace, who, judges the words of the gods.

2005b. O N., thou belongest to the *nḥḥ.w* (-stars), when Rç' shines behind the morning star.

2006a. Lo, no god escapes from what he has said;

2006b. he will offer thee thy thousand (loaves) of bread, thy thou sand (mugs) of beer, thy thousand of oxen, thy thousand of geese,

2006c. thy thousand of everything on which a god lives.

53.

RESURRECTION, TRANSFIGURATION, AND LIFE OF THE KING IN HEAVEN, UTTERANCE 676.

Utterance 676.

2007a. To say: Thy water belongs to thee, thine abundance belongs to thee, thine efflux belongs to thee,

2007b. which issues from Osiris.

2008a. Collect thy bones; arrange thy limbs;

2008b. shake off thy dust; untie thy bandages.

2009a. The tomb is open for thee; the double doors of the coffin are undone for thee;

2009b. the double doors of heaven are open for thee.

2009c. "Hail," says Isis; "(come) in peace," says Nephthys,

2009d. when they see their brother at the feast of Atum.

2010a. These thy libations, Osiris, are in Busiris, in *Grg.w-b3(.f)*;

2010b. thy soul is in thy body; thy might is behind thee; remain chief of (or, master of) thy powers.

2011a. Raise thyself up, N.,

2011b. travel over the southern regions; travel over the northern regions;

2011c. be thou powerful over the powers that are in thee.

2011d. Thy spirits, the jackals, are given thee which Horus of Hierakonpolis has given to thee.

2012a. Raise thyself up, N., be seated on thy firm (or, copper) throne.

2012b. Anubis, who is chief of the divine pavillion (*s̲ḥ-ntr*), has commanded

2012c. thy purification with thy eight *nmś.t*-jars and (thy) eight *ꜣb.t*-jars, which come from the *s̲ḥ-ntr*.

2013a. Thou art a god who supports the sky, who beautifies the earth.

2013b. The *śmnt.t*-woman laments for thee; the great *min.t* mourns for thee;

2014a. arms agitate for thee; feet tremble for thee,

2014b. when thou ascendest as a star, as the morning star.

2014c. He comes to thee, his father; he comes to thee, Geb;

2015a. take his hand, let him sit upon the great seat;

2015b. let him unite with the two *mt*-lakes of *ḳbḥ.w*;

2015c. purify his mouth with natron on the lap of *Mḫnti-'irti*;

2015d. purify his nails, upper and lower.

2016a. Let one do for him what thou didst do for his brother, Osiris, . on the day of counting the bones,

2016b. of making firm the sandals, of ferrying over the lake *Rd-wr*.

2017a. To thee come the wise and the understanding;

2017b. thou art called to the southern *'itr.t*-palace;

2017c. to thee come (the gods of) the full northern *'itr.t*-palace, with a salutation.

54.

TEXTS OF MISCELLANEOUS CONTENTS, UTTERANCES 677-683.

Utterance 677.

2018a. To say: A Great One is fallen on his side; he is up like a god;

2018b. his *šhm*-sceptre is with him; his white crown is upon him.

2019a. N. is fallen on his side; N. is up like a god;

2019b. his *šhm*-sceptre is with him; his white crown is upon him, like the white crown of Rç',

2019c. when he ascends in the horizon, and when he is greeted by Horus in the horizon.

2020a. O N., raise thyself up;

2020b. receive thy dignity, which the Two Enneads made for thee (e.g. "conferred upon thee").

2021a. Thou art on the throne of Osiris, in the place of the First of the Westerners.

2021b. Thou hast taken his *šhm*-sceptre; thou hast carried off his great white crown.

2022a. O N., how beautiful is this, how great is this which thy father, Osiris, has, done for thee!

2022b. He gave thee his throne,

2023a. that thou mayest rule those of secret places, that thou mayest lead their venerable ones,

2023b. and that all the glorified ones may follow thee in this their name of "Secret places."

2024a. O N., thou art happy; thou art proud;

2024b. thou art an Atum; thou wilt not depart from his destiny.

2025a. Rç' calls thee, in thy name of "Him whom all the glorified ones fear."

2025b. Thy dread is in the hearts of the gods, like the dread of Rç' of the horizon.

2026a. O N., who keeps secret his form, like Anubis on his belly,

2026b. receive thy face of a jackal; raise thyself up; stand up.

2027a. Sit down to thy thousand (loaves) of bread, thy thousand (mugs) of beer, thy thousand of oxen, thy thousand of geese,

2027b. thy thousand of every good thing whereon a god lives.

2028a. O N., pure one, Rç' finds thee standing with thy mother Nut;

2028b. she leads thee on the ways of the horizon,

2028c. where thou makest thine abode. How beautiful it is (to be) with thy *ka*, for ever and ever.

Utterance 678.

2029a. To say: *Ih̭mti, Śdmti,*

2029b. do not hearken to N.; do not listen to N.;

2029c. do not demand the magic of N.;

2029d. do not ask for the magic of N. from N.

2030a. Thou hast thy magic; N. has his magic.

2030b. May N. not break thy pen; may he not crack thy palette!

2030c. May N. have (his) offering!

Utterance 679.

2031a. To say: Thy water belongs to thee; thine efflux belongs, to thee; thine inundation belongs to thee,

2031b. issuing from Osiris.

2032a. Thou makest them *ḥśd* like Horus; thou openest them like Wepwawet,

2032b. for thou art the Wr, the Eldest Son.

Utterance 680.

2033. To say: Osiris N., take to thee the eye of Horus; it is thine.

Utterance 681.

2034a. To say: Great heaven, give thy hand to N.;

2034b. great Nut, give thy hand to N.;

2034c. it is N. thy divine falcon.

2035a. N. is come; he ascends to heaven; N. opens *ḳbḥ.w*;

2035b. N. greets his father, Rç'.

2036a. He crowned him as a Horus, in which (form) N. comes;

2036b. he gives to N. two real crowns;

2036c. (and) he establishes for N. his two divine eyes.

2037a. N. ascends to him, great, as Horus of the sky, at the zenith of heaven;

2037b. he who smites the crowns of the North, who gives commands to the *Wtn.w*.

2038a. N. is followed by the *'fti.w*.

2038b. Those in heaven and on earth come to him with salutations,

2038c. as well as jackals, as (lit. (in) place of) Setite spirits,

2038d. superiors and inferiors.

2039. He is anointed with perfume, clothed with *p3-t*, living on offerings.

2040a. N. commands; N. confers distinctions;

2040b. N. awards places;

2040c. N. makes offerings; N. conducts the presentations.

2041. It is N.; N., is the one of heaven; he exercises power before Nut.

Utterance 682.

2042a. To say: Greetings to thee from Seker, N.

2042b. Thy face is washed by *Dw3-wr.*

2042c. N. flies as a cloud (or, high) like a divine falcon;

2042d. N. is cool like the heron; N. flies low (?) like a *śmn*-goose.

2043a. The wings of N. are like (those of) a divine falcon;

2043b. the tips of the wings of N. are like (those of) a divine falcon.

2043c. The bones of N. are fastened together; N. is purified.

2044a. The fillet of N. is at his back; the bodice of N. is upon him;

2044b. his girdle is of *śnp.*

2045a. N. descends with Rç' into his great boat,

2045b. in which he transports him to the horizon to judge the gods with him.

2046a. Horus voyages in it with him to the horizon;

2046b. N. judges the gods with him in the horizon,

2046c. for N. is one of them.

Utterance 683.

2047a. To say: Behold, this, is what they said to N., what the gods said to N.

2047b. The word of the gods is fallen upon N.:

2047c. "It is Horus, who comes forth from the Nile; it is the bull, which comes forth from the fortress;

2047d. it is the *d.t*-serpent which comes forth from Rç'; it is the *'i'r.t*-serpent which comes forth from Set.

2048a. Everything which will happen to N. happens likewise to *Mdd.t-'it,*

2048b. daughter of Rç', who is on his two legs;

2048c. everything which happens to N. happens likewise to *Md3,*

2048d. daughter of Rç', who is on his two legs,

2049. for N. is *Wdȝ*, son of *Wdȝ*, who comes forth from *Wdȝ-t*.

2050a. N. is intact; N. is intact; (as true as) the eye of Horus is intact in Heliopolis;

2050b. N. lives; N. lives; (as true as) the eye of Horus lives in Heliopolis."

55.
THE DECEASED KING ASCENDS TO HEAVEN, UTTERANCE 684.

Utterance 684.

2051a. To say: N. ascended at thy ascension, Osiris;

2051b. N. has spoken (with) his *ka* in heaven.

2051c. The bones of N. are firm (or, copper), and the limbs of N.

2051d. are like the stars, the imperishable stars.

2052a. Given that N. be encompassed, then a great one falls into the hands of N.

2052b. The mother of N. is Nut;

2053a. the father of N. is Shu; the mother of N. is Tefnut.

2053b. They take N. to heaven, to heaven-on the smoke of incense.

2054. N. is purified; N. lives; N. makes his seat like Osiris;

2055a. N. sits at thy side (lit. shoulder), Osiris; N. spits on thy hair, Osiris;

2055b. he will not let him become diseased; N. will not permit him to be bald,

2055c. at the mouth of N. daily, at the beginnings (of the feast) of the half months, at the beginnings (of the feast) of the months.

2056a. N. sits at thy side (lit. shoulder), Horus; N. spits on thy hair, Horus;

2056b. he will not let it become diseased; N. will not permit himself to be bald,

2056c. at the mouth of N. daily, at the beginnings (of the feast) of the half months, at the beginnings (or the feast) of the months.

2057. N. is one of these four beings, sons of Atum, sons of Nut,

2058a. who do not rot; N. does not rot;

2058b. who do not decay; N. does not decay;

2058c. who do not fall upon earth from heaven;

2058d. N. does not fall upon the earth from heaven.

2059a. N. was sought; N. is found with them;

2059b. N. is one of them, praised by the bull of heaven.

2060. N. makes his *ka* arise; N. returns (?); N. strides————

2061a. the good companion makes his *ka* arise, returns (?), strides.

2061b. N. rests at home, on the under (side) of the body of the sky, like a *nfr.t*-star,

2061c. at the meanderings of the Winding Watercourse.

2062a. When N. ascends to heaven, give him this formula: "Rç' is good each day."

2062b. N. put himself on thy way, Horus of *Šsm.t*, on which thou leadest the gods

2062c. to the beautiful ways of heaven and of the Marsh of Offerings.

56.
TEXTS OF MISCELLANEOUS CONTENTS, UTTERANCES 685-689.

Utterance 685.

2063a. To say: The waters of life which are in the sky, the waters of life which are in the earth come.

2063b. The sky burns for thee, the earth trembles for thee, before the birth of the god.

2064a. The two mountains divide, a god comes into being, the god has power over his body.

2064b. The two mountains divide, N. comes into being, N. has power over his body.

2065a. Behold N., his feet shall be kissed by the pure waters,

2065b. which come into being through Atum, which the phallus of Shu makes, which the vulva of Tefnut brings into being.

2066a. They have come to thee, they have brought to thee the pure waters which issue from their father;

2066b. they purify thee, they fumigate thee, N., with incense.

2067a. Thou liftest up the sky with thy hand; thou treadest (lit. layest) down the earth with thy foot.

2067b. A libation is poured out at the gate of N.; the face of every god is washed.

2068a. Thou washest thine arms, Osiris; thou washest thine arms N.

2068b. Thy rejuvenescence is a god. Your third is a *wd*-offering.

2068c. The perfume of an *Ỉḥ.t-wt.t*-serpent is on N.

2069a. A *bnbn*-bread is in the house of Seker; a leg of meat is in the house of Anubis.

2069b. N. is intact; the '*itr.t*-palace is standing; the month (i.e. the moon) is born; the nome lives,

2070a. which measurements have traced. Thou tillest the barley; thou tillest the spelt,

2070b. with which N. will be presented for ever.

Utterance 686.

2071a. To say: Horus has ointment; Set has ointment.

2071b. Horus has taken his eye; he has taken it away from his enemies,

2071c. without Set being a gainer thereby.

2072a. Horus fills himself with ointment;

2072b. Horus is satisfied with his eye; Horus is furnished with his *św.t*-plant (?).

2072c. The eye of Horus is united with him; its perfume belongs to him.

2072d. Its anger falls upon his enemies.

2073a. N. has ointment; N. fills himself with it;

2073b. its perfume unites with him;

2073c. its anger falls upon his enemies.

Utterance 687.

2074a. To say: O N., I have come; I have brought the eye of Horus which is in its heat;

2074b. its perfume belongs to thee, N.;

2075a. its perfume belongs to thee; the perfume of the eye of Horus belongs to thee, N.

2075b. Thou art a *ba* thereby; thou art a *śḥm* thereby; thou art honoured thereby.

2075c. Thou conquerest the *wrr.t*-crown thereby, among the gods.

2076a. Horus comes rejoicing at thy approach,

2076b. as he rejoices at the approach of his eye which is upon thee.

2076c. Behold N., who is before the gods, equipped as a god, his bones assembled, is like Osiris.

2077a. The gods do homage at the approach of N.,

2077b. as the gods do homage at the approach of the dawning of Rç' when he ascends in the horizon.

Utterance 688.

2078a. To say: These four grandsons stand up for N.,

2078b. 'Ims.ti, Ḥ3pi, Dw3-mu.t.f, Ḳbḥ-śn.w.f,

2078c. the offspring of Horus of Letopolis.

2079a. They bind a ladder for N.;

2079b. they make firm a ladder for N.

2079c. They cause N. to ascend to Khepri,

2079d. he who exists on the eastern side of the sky.

2080a. Its rungs are hewn by *Šś3*;

2080b. the ropes which are on it are made solid

2080c. by means of sinews of *G3św.ti*, the bull of heaven;

2080d. the uprights at its sides are fastened,

2080e. like the skin of 'Imi-wt, son of *Ḥś3.t*;

2080f. the "supporter of the Great One" is set under it by *Śpḥ-wr.t.*

2081a. Cause ye the *ka* of N. to ascend to the god;

2081b. lead ye him to the two lions; cause him to ascend to Atum.

2082a. Atum has done that which he said he would do for N.,

2082b. (for) he binds the ladder for him, he makes the ladder firm for N.

2082c. (Thus) N. is removed from the horror of mankind;

2082d. the arms of N. are not a horror to the gods.

2083a. N. has not eaten the *d3ś*-plant;

2083b. N. has not chewed *bd3*-goose on the first of the month;

2083c. he has not slept during the night, (though) he did not keep watch;

2083d. he ignores his body in one of these two seasons of Khepri.

2084a. The inhabitants of the *D3.t* have counted their bodies;

2084b. they opened their ears, to the voice of N.,

2084c. when he descends among them.

2085a. "Heavy-is-his-sceptre" has said to them

2085b. that N. is one of them.

2085c. The might of N. is among them like "Great mighty one," who will lead to the Great West.

2086a. The dignity of N. is great in the house of the two lions,

2086b. for the wrong which appertains to N. is driven off by him who drives off evil (*'Idr-isf.t*)

2086c. from before *Mḫnti-'irti* in Letopolis.

Utterance 689.

2087a. To say: Geb has raised the eye of Horus, which is *K33* (or, *K33.t*),

2087b. which is over his great *kas*, which is first of his ordinary *kas*.

2088a. Thy head (O Eye of Horus) is given (to thee), that thou mayest see Horus who has caused to sit———

2088b. so that the judgment may take place.

2089a. Isis comes; she has laid hold of her breasts for her son Horus, justified.

2089b. N. has found the eye of Horus.

2090a. (Thou), who has found that eye of Horus,

2090b. to which its head is given, for which a front is made, like the forehead of Rç', furious like a crocodile,

2090c. thou hast followed the eye of Horus to heaven, to the *šḥd.w*-stars of the sky,

2090d. go thou, as one who shall row Horus, with his eye.

2091a. O Shu, thou who bearest up Nut,

2091b. thou hast borne up the eye of Horus to heaven, to the *šḥd.w*-stars of the sky,

2091c. because Horus sits upon his firm (or, copper; or, brilliant) throne.

2091d. Go thou, as one who shall row Horus, with his eye.

57.
A SERIES OF ADDRESSES TO THE DECEASED KING AS A GOD, UTTERANCE 690.

Utterance 690.

2092a. To say: Wake up, Osiris; let the weary god awake.

2092b. The god stands up; the god is powerful over his body.

2093a. Wake up, N.; let the weary god awake.

2093b. The god stands up; the god is powerful over his body.

2094a. Horus stands up; he clothes N. with linen————him who came forth from him.

2094b. N. is equipped as a god, standing in the *pr.wr*-palace, sitting with the Two Enneads.

2095a. "O N., stand up, come in peace," says Rꜥ' to thee; "messenger of the great god,

2095b. thou goest to heaven; thou goest forth through the doors of the horizon;

2096a. Geb sends thee; thou art a soul like a [god, respected like a god];

2096b. [thou art powerful] over thy body, like a god,

2096c. like *Ba*, chief of the living,

2096d. like *Śḥm*, chief of spirits."

2097a. N. comes; he is equipped like a god; his bones are assembled like [Osiris];

2097b. [he comes behind his uraeus].

2097c. Thou hast come, O N., out of Heliopolis; thou art avenged; thy heart is placed in thy body;

2098a. Thy face is like that of a jackal; thy flesh is like that of Atum;

2098b. thy *b3* is in thy body; thy *šhm* is behind thee; Isis is before thee; Nephthys is behind thee.

2099a. Thou journeyest through the regions of Horus; thou travelest through the regions of Set.

2099b. It is Shu and Tefnut who lead thee, when thou ascendest from Heliopolis.

2100a. O N., Horus has woven his tent over thy head;

2100b. Set has stretched out thy canopy;

2100c. be enclosed, O father, by the divine tent; thou art brought there in thy beloved places.

2101a. O N., Horus comes to thee provided with his souls,

2101b. *H3pi, Dw3-mw.t.f, 'Imš.ti, Kbh-śn.w.f.*

2102 a. They bring to thee thy name of "Imperishable";

2102b. thou perishest not; thou diest not.

2103a. O N., thy sister *Kbh.wt* has purified [thee]

2103b. in *Rd-wr* chief of the lakes.

2103c. Thou appearest to them like a jackal, like Horus chief of the living,

2103d. like Geb chief of the Ennead, like Osiris chief of spirits.

2104. Thou commandest spirits; thou leadest the [imperishable stars].

2105a. The evil of Osiris————the evil of N.————the evil of the bull of the Two Enneads————

2105b. the god is loosed (from it), N. has power over his body.

2105c. N. is loosed (from it); N. has power over his body.

2106a. O N., Horus, is standing, he glorifies thee;

2106b. he conducts thee, when thou ascendest to heaven.

2107a. Thy mother Nut receives thee; she lays hold of thine arm,

2107b. that thou mayest not be in need, that thou mayest not moan (like a cedar),

2107c. (but) that thou mayest live like the coleoptera (lives) and endure in [Mendes].

2108a. O N., thou art adorned like a god; thy face is like (that of) a jackal, as Osiris,

2108b. that soul in *Ndi.t*, that mighty one in the great city.

2109. The sky trembles, the earth quakes before the god, before N.

2110a. N. [is not enveloped] by the earth;

2110b. *Iḥ.t-wt.t*, thou art not enveloped by the earth.

2110c. Thy fame is by day; thy fear is by night, as a god, lord of f ear.

2110d. Thou commandest the gods like the mighty one, chief of the mighty.

2111. [O] Osiris, the overflow comes, the inundation hastens, Geb groans.

2112a. I have pitied thee with pity; I have smitten him who acted with evil (intent) against thee;

2112b. that thou mayest live, that thou mayest raise thyself up because of thy strength.

2113. O N., [the inundation comes 1, [the overflow hastens], Geb [groans].

2114a. Exult in the divine efflux which is in thee; let thy heart live;

214b. thy divine limbs are in good condition; loosen thy bindings.

2115a. Horus comes to thee, N.; he does for thee that which he did for his father Osiris,

2115b. that thou mayest live like unto the life of those in heaven, and [that thou mayest come into being] more (truly) than those who are on earth.

2116a. Raise thyself up because of thy strength; ascend thou to heaven.

2116b. The sky bears thee like *S3ḥ*; thou hast power over thy body;

2116c. thou defendest thyself against thine enemy.

2117. [O N.] [I have wept for thee], I have mourned for thee;

2118a. I shall not forget thee; my heart will not weary to give thee offerings every day,

2118b. at the (feast of the) month, at the (feast of the) half month, at the (feast of) covering the fire-pan, at the (feast of) Thot, at the *w3g*-feast,

2118c. at the (feast of) slaughtering, (at) the (feast of) thy years, (at) (the feast of) thy birth, at the beginnings of thy months, during which thou livest as a god.

2119. O N., may thy body be clothed, that thou mayest come to me.

58.

TEXTS OF MISCELLANEOUS CONTENTS, UTTERANCES 691-704.

Utterance 691.

2120a (Nt. XXXII 819). To say: O my father, O Rç', concerning these things which thou hast said:

2120b (Nt. 819). "O that I had a son who is glorified, who dawns, who is a soul, is honoured, is mighty,

2120c (Nt. 820). whose arm is stretched out, whose stride is wide."

2121a (Nt. 820). Behold me, I am thy son, behold I am N.;

2121b (Nt. 820-821). I am glorified, I dawn (or, am crowned), I am a soul, I am honoured, I am mighty;

2121c (Nt. 821). mine arm is stretched out, my stride is wide.

2122a. O N., he is purified;

2122b (Nt. 821-822). I take the rudder, I am glad of my seat on the shoulder of the sky;

2122c. N. voyages on the shoulder of the sky;

2122d. N. directs his rudder on the shoulder of the sky.

2123a. O my father, O Rç', concerning these things which thou hast said:

2123b. "O that I had a son who is glorified, who dawns, who is a soul, is honoured, is mighty,

2123c. whose arm is stretched out, whose stride is wide."

2124a. Behold me, I am thy son, behold I am N.

2124b. I am glorified, I dawn (or, am crowned), I am a soul, I am honoured, I am mighty;

2125a. I am purified;

2125b (Nt. 825). I take my rudder, I am glad of my seat in company with the Ennead;

2125c (Nt. 826). I voyage with the Ennead;

2125d (Nt. 826). I direct my rudder in company with the Ennead.

Utterance 691 A.

2126a-1 (Nt. Jéquier, XXXII 826). To say: The two reed-floats of heaven are placed for Rç';

2126a-2 (Nt. 826-827). the two reed-floats of heaven are placed for Rç',

212 6a-3 (Nt. 827). that he may be high from east to west at the side of his brothers, the gods.

212 6a-4 (Nt. 827-828). His, brother is *S̀ȝḥ*, his sister is Sothis;

2126a-5 (Nt. 828). he is seated between them above (lit. in) this earth for ever.

212 6a-6 (Nt. 828). The two reed-floats of heaven are placed for this N.;

2126a (Nt. 828-829). the two reed-floats of heaven are placed for this N.;

212 6b (Nt. 829). that she (lit. he) may be high from east to west at the side of her (lit. his) brothers, the gods.

2126b + 1 (Nt. 829). Her (lit. his) brother is *S̀ȝḥ* her (lit. his) sister is Sothis;

212 6b + 2 (Nt. 830). she (lit. he) is seated between them above (lit. in) this earth for ever.

Utterance 691 B.

2127a-1 (Nt. Jéquier, XXXII 830). Awake, awake, father Osiris,

2127a-2 (Nt. 83 0). I am thy son, who loves thee, I am thy son, who loves thee.

2127a (Nt. 831). Behold me, enter, I am come, I have brought to thee that which he carried off belonging to thee.

2127b (Nt. SP). He rejoiced over thee; he exulted (?) over thee.

2127b + 1 (Nt. 832). Set exulted over thee, at the side of thy two mourning sisters,

2127b + 2 (Nt. 83 2). the two sisters who love thee, Isis and Nephthys; they are pleasing to thee.

2127b + 3 (Nt. 883). Thou shalt not pass me by, for I am entrusting myself to thee;

2127b + 4 (Nt. 833). thou shalt not pass by the bread of judgment; thou shalt be satisfied with *Ḥr-'imi-pr.f.*

2128a-1 (Nt. 833-834). I have rowed (thee) as Set, like Geb;

212 8a, (Nt. 834). like the remains (of a corpse) (in) jars of viscera;

2128b (Nt. 834). thy forepart being like that of a jackal, thy hinderpart like *Ḳbḥ.wt.*

2128b + 1 (Nt. 834). It is clear that thou receivest a man of god.

212 8b + 2 (Nt. 83 5). 1 have ploughed barley; I have reaped the spelt,

2128b + 3 (Nt. 835). which I have done (given) for thy years (festivals?).

212 8b + 4 (Nt. 83 5). Awake, awake, father, for this thy bread.

Utterance 691 C.

2129-1 (N. Jéquier, XI 1011)————N. he

2129-2 (N. 1011)———— *ȝm*———— ḥ————

2129 (N. 1011-1012)————the might of N.————

2129 + 1 (N. 1012)————they see (?)————

2129 + 2 (N. 1012)————

2129 + 3 (N. 1012). the throne of N. *m*————

2129 + 4 (N. 1012).————this N. on the head of Rꜥ' *dm*————

2129 + 5 (N. 1012)———— *m* (?)————

2130 (N. 1012-1013)————in heaven strong————

2130+ 1 (N. 1013)———— *m(?)ś*

444

2130 + 2 (N. 1013). N———

2130 + 3 (N. 1013). he smote (?) with the '*ḫȝ*-sceptre; he led with the '*iȝȝ. t*-sceptre

2130+4 (N. 1013). this N————with (?) a voice

2130+ 5 (N. 1013). not———

2131 (N. 1013-1014).————his? names

2131 + 1 (N. 1014).———

2131 + 2 (N. 1014).————*ȝȝ rw*———

2131 + 3 (N. 1014).————with braids of hair

2131 +4 (N. 1014).———

2131 + 5 (N. 1014). praise was given, rejoicing———

2132 (N. 1014-1015). *ȝḫ*————Geb———

2132 + 1 (N. Jéquier, XI 1015).———

2132 + 2 (N. 1015).————his two arms guarded before N.

2132 + 3 (N. 1015).———

2132 + 4 (N. 1015).————*śr*

2132 + 5 (N. 1015). N. shines———

2133 (N. 1015-1016).———

2133 + 1 (N. 1016).———

2133 + 2 (N. 1016). N. purified———*'in*———

2133 + 3 (N. 1016). comes as his soul '*inw*———

2133 + 4 (N. 1016)————N., he withdraws by it

2134 (N. 1016). the hand of N. took———

2135 (N. 1016 + 1).———

2136 (N. 1016 + 1).————N. the northern way of the boat of the morning sun———

2136 + 1 (N. 1016 + 1). Harachte commanded thee, N————*pȝw.t ntr*

2136 + 2 (N. 1016 + 1). Khepri————gods, clothes laid aside

2136+ 3 (N. 1016 + 2).———

2136+4 (N. 1016 + 2)————lake of the jackals

2136 + 5 (N. Jéquier, XI 1016 + 2). N. sat————[*Dwȝ*]-*mw.tf*.

2136+ 6 (N. 1016 + 2). *Dwȝ-mw.tf*———

2137———

2138. '*i*——— '*in*———

2139a. (N. Jéquier, XII 1021). To say: Awa[ke]———*ḫnti n.k[m?]*———
—

2139b (N. 1021).———

2140a (N. 1022). the bows bend their head to thee, go[ing] from thee
between (?)———

2140b (N. 1022)———

2141a (N. 1023). the gods rejoiced; exult———

2141a + 1 (N. 1923).———[he?] sees———

2141b (N. 1023-1024).———[Geb], prince of the gods

2142a (N. 1024). he has taken the heritage; [he has] carried off

2142b (N. 1024).———N———

2143a. (N. 1025). Equip thyself with his white crown; eat bread

2143b (N. Jéquier, XII 1025).———[wi]th a presentation

2144a (N. Jéquier, XII 1028-1029).———says Isis; "I have found (him),"
says Nephthys,

2144b (N. 1029). when they saw Osiris on his side on the shore [of *Ndi*.
ł]

2145a (N. 1029).———rise up———

2145b (N. 1029-1030).———my brother, I sought thee;

2145c (N. 1030). raise thyself up, spirit." Geb said:

2145d (N. 1030). "I have smitten———the [Enn]ead

2146a.———for thy father Atum,

2146b. that he may cause thee to be (on) the ḥnti-ocean among the gods,

2146c. as the Great One who is before————

2146d.————

2147a. Those who are in Nun come to thee; mankind (the blessed dead (?)) circulate for thee;

2147b. thou art like Horus————

2148a————with him, in thy time.

2148b. Thine annual (offerings) are made with him, in his hour,

2148c. by order of————

2149a.————

2149b. The way of N. is open for N.; the way of N. is made (prepared?).

2150a. N————

2150b————chief of the two lands.

2150c. N. is Thot chief of heaven; N. is Anubis chief of the house.

2151a. It was brought, open————

2151b.————to N., before N.

2152 a. He is the bittern (šdȝ-bird), which comes from the marsh

2152b.————

2153a.————

2153b. who is in tnw of the four tnw, depart from N.

2154a. N————

2154b. N————

2154c. pure is the tongue which is in the mouth of N.

2155a. Protect N————

2155a + 1 (N. Jéquier, XII 1038).————N————

2155b.————that N. may not be upside down.

2156a. N. is the bull————

2156b. N. is the bull————

2156c. three in heaven; two on earth.

2157a. To say: The diadem comes into being; inundated————*ti*

2157b. *tm*————

2158a. Seat thyself on the throne of Rç', which Horus, removed to the south of the sky.

2158b. removed————*ḫ* (?)————

2158c.————he removed the secret (places) of the Nine (Bows?).

2159a. N. is seated————

2159a + 1 (N. Jéquier, XII 1042).————*n.f nb*————

2159b.————N. upon the sky.

2159c. The two hands of N. are on Heliopolis.

2160a.————*rd.wi* [N.]————

2160b.———— *'ir.ś*

2160b + 1 (N. 1044). the head of N. is above; the legs of N. [are below].

2161a. [N.]————

2161b.————more long than wide;

2161b + 1 (N. 1045). behold N. *św t*[ʒ?]————

2162a.————*śśm*————

2162b. like to her following of Set; like to her foll[owing]————

2162c.————*m*———— *'i*————

2163a (N. Jéquier, XII 1047). O, strong one, jackal, *Dḳḳ*, bring these to [this] N.;

2163b. bring with these to N————

2163c (N. 1048). messenger of Atum, O N., with linen of *Tʒ(?)i.t*

2164a.————

2164b (N. 1049). O! O! come; O! O! come; bring these to N.;

2165a. bring with (these) to N————

2165b. lift him up————
2165b + 1 (N. 1050). messenger of Atum, O N., with linen of *T3(?)i.t*
2166a.————the eye of Horus there
2166b (N. 10511). hurry against the fingers of Set
2166b + 1 (N. 1951). *d3* (or, *wd3*)————*'in(f) m*————*š*————
21607a. (N. 1051-1052)————N. earth in peace
2167b (N. 1052). the two hands of N.————to the heart
2168 (N. 1053). Raise thyself up N., *tsi*————
2168 + 1 (N. 1054). N. raised himself up in this night————
2168 + 2 (N. 1055). *n* these of N————
2168 + 3 (N. 1055 + 1 to 1055 + 2). *ḥtm* (?)————*Šš3*————belonging
   to the god
2168 + 4 (N. 1055 + 2). O N.————
2168 + 5 (N. 1055 + 3). 63————*'im-n.n*————
2168 + 6 (N. 1055 + 5)————he[aven]————
(Following 2168 + 6, there are in N. Jéquier, XII, eight additional columns,
   1055 + 5 to 1055 + 12, the text of which is entirely destroyed).

Utterance 697.

2169a. To say: O N., the mouth of the earth opens for thee; Geb speaks
   to thee:
2169b. "Thou art great like a king; thou art mighty like Rç'.
2170a. Thou purifiest thyself in the lake of the jackal; thou cleansest
   thyself in the lake of the *D3t*."
2170b. "Come in peace," say the Two Enneads to thee.
2170c. The eastern door of heaven is open for thee by *'Imn-k3m*.
2171a. Nut has given her arms to thee, N., she of the long hair, she of
   the hanging breasts;
2171b. she lifts thee high to herself to heaven; she did not cast N. down
   to the earth.
2172a. She gives thee birth, N., like *S'3ḥ*;

2172b. she makes thee remain as chief of the two *'itr.t*-palaces."

21 72c. N. descends into the boat like Rç', on the shores, of the Winding Watercourse.

2173a. N. is transported by the indefatigables;

2173b. N. commands the imperishable stars;

2173c. N. is transported on the *ḥnti*-ocean;

2173d. N. takes the helm to the fields of *ḥзḥз*.

2174a. Thy messengers go; thy runners hasten.

2174b. They say to Rç': "Behold, N. is come; behold, N. is come in peace."

2175a. Do not go by these water-courses of the west;

2175b. those who go there, they do not come back.

2175c. Go thou, N., by these water-courses of the east,

2175d. among the Followers of [Rç']

2175e.————him who lifts up the arm in the east.

2175f.————

Utterance 698.

(This cannot be the beginning of this utterance)

21 76a + 1 (N. 1300). N————N. *pw*————

217 6a + 2 (N. 1309). *mdś ntr.w m*————

2177a (N. 1309).————*śki*

2177b (N. 1309-1310). flesh; protect thyself; give way from behind N.

Utterance 699.

2178a.————

2178b.————Anubis, he lays hold of thine arm; Nut, she gives to thee thy heart.

2179a. Thou fleest cloudlike as a falcon; thou drawest thyself out of the water like a *nwr*-bird;

2179b. thou goest towards the west————

2180a.————

2180b.————[thou livest], thou livest; thou art young, thou art young;

2180c. to the side of thy father, to the side of *S͗h*, to heaven.

2181a. Thou livest————

2181b.————

2181c.————

Utterance 700.

2182a. To say: Father N.,

2182b. raise thyself up on thy right side; support thyself on thy left side.

2182c. Thy flesh has been collected for thee————

2182d.————

2183a.————with which thou art pure as a god.

2183b. The messengers of Rç' come forth for thee; the imperishable stars take thine arm.

2183c. [Thou] diest not————

2184a.————

2184b. [like Anubis] who is in *T͗ḥb.t*.

2185a. Thy *w͗g* (offering) is of bread; *w͗g* is like the eye of Horus,

2185b. in (his) name of "*W͗g*-(offering)."

2185c. Thy presentation————

2185d.————

2186a.————thine enemies are destroyed; they perish;

2186b. they foam in opposing thee; throw them in the lake; throw them in the sea.

2187a. Men come to thee————

2187b.————

2187c.————

2188a. To say: The Great One is fallen in N*di.t*; Isis is loosed from her burden (*tn*).

2188b. Raise thyself up, thou who art in N*trw*; raise thyself up

2189a.————

2189b.————the god is loosed.

2190a. Horus comes forth from Chemmis;

2190b. Buto arises for Horus; he purifies himself there.

2191a. Horus comes purified, that he may avenge [his father]

2191b.————

2192a. [I am thy sister], who loves thee, says Isis, says Nephthys.

2192b. They weep for thee; they awake for thee.

2193a. O N., raise [thyself] up————

2193b.————

2 194a.————

2194b. [(receive) thy thousand (loaves) of bread], [thy thousand (mugs) of beer], thy thousand cattle, thy thousand geese,

2194c. a roast, a double-rib piece from the slaughtering-bench of the god; the great bread and the *rṭḥ*-bread from the broad-hall.

2195a. Provide thyself, N., with————

2195b.————

2196a. Thou hast thy *wrr.t*-crown; the *wrr.t*-crown is on thy head;

2196b. thou hast taken the *wrr.t*-crown before the Two Enneads

2196c. Thou art a spirit among [thy] brothers————

2197a.————

2197b.————spirits.

2198a. O N., stand up;

2198b. sit thou before thy heart like Anubis First of the Westerners.

2199a. Thou art come (again) to [thy] (right) state————

2199b.————

2199c.————

Utterance 702.

2200a. To say: N. is come to you,

2200b. ye great and powerful pair of goddesses, who are on the eastern side of heaven,

2200c. that you both may carry N. and set him on the eastern side of heaven.

Utterance 703.

2201a. To say: O. N., thy soul is with thee

2201b.————as Osiris.

2201c. O N., live, thou shalt not die.

2202a. Horus comes to thee; he separates thy bandages; he casts off thy bonds.

2202b. Horus has expelled thy rivals,

2202c. the earth-gods seize thee not.

2203a. O N., [thy] *ka* is mighty————

2203b. Thy father is not among men; thy mother is not among mankind.

2204a. Thy mother is the great *ḥwr.t*-uraeus, the white (crown), the royal head-dress, resident in el-Kâb,

2204b. she with variegated feather, she with the two hanging (and shaking) breasts.

2205. N. is not seized by————

Utterance 704.

2206a. To say: N. [is a male], coming forth from Rç';

2206b. N. has come forth from between the thighs of the Ennead;

2206c. *Šsm.t.t* conceived him; *Šsm.t.t* gave him birth;

2206d. N. is a falcon coming forth from Rç';

2206e. [N. is the living *'iʾr.t*-serpent], which came forth from the eye of Rç';

2206f. he flies, he hovers over the throne of Khepri, in the bow of his boat in the sky.

59.

A SERIES OF UNCLASSIFIABLE FRAGMENTS, UTTERANCES 705-714.

705.

2207. thy father————

706.

2208a.————[in his name] of Rç'.
2208b. N. was nursed on the milk (of)————
2208c.————your arm.

707.

2209a.————his mother;
2209b. his mother is *Šś3.t-Śti.t* (Satis); guide————
2209c.————

708.

2210a.————one————
2210b.————N————
2210c.————with the '*b3*-sceptre————

2211a.————the Name of N————
2211b.————his beloved son, coming forth from————
2211c.————N. being————
2211d.————to exist————

2212a.————these gods————
2212b.————says the priest of Rç' to [N.]
2212c.————of the gods, he satisfies the spirits.
2212d.————N. the sky with————
2212e————his pellet of incense is broken————
2213a. Horus has put his arm around [N.]————
2213b.————before N. N————
2213c.————N. with natron————
2213d. Thou art Thot who avenges it; thou art not [like Set who took it].
2213e.————

2214a.————
2214b. Thou has seen the Delta————
2214c. N. voyages there to the shore (of)————
2214d.————N. separates————
2214e.————

2215a.————behind N————
2215b.————

713.

2216a.————to attack————
2216b.————N————
2216c.————N————

714.

2217a————
2217b————N————

Ingram Content Group UK Ltd.
Milton Keynes UK
UKHW020750270323
419227UK00007B/508